FEMINISMS AND DEVELOPMENT

Disrupting taken-for-granted assumptions, this expert series redefines issues at the heart of today's feminist contestations in a development context. Bringing together a formidable collective of thinkers from the global South and the North, it explores what it is that can bring about positive changes in women's rights and realities.

These timely and topical collections reposition feminism within development studies, bringing into view substantial commonalities across the countries of the global South that have so far gone unrecognized.

Series editor
Andrea Cornwall

Forthcoming title

Feminisms, Empowerment and Development:
Changing Women's Lives
Andrea Cornwall and Jenny Edwards

About the Editors

Andrea Cornwall is professor in anthropology and development at the University of Sussex, where she is an affiliate of the Centre for the Study of Sexual Dissidence and director of the Pathways of Women's Empowerment programme. As a teenager, she harboured a secret desire to be an agony aunt when she grew up, inspired by clandestine readings of her mother's *Cosmopolitan*, but became an anthropologist instead, focusing much of her research on gender, sexuality, sex and relationships. Joining the Institute of Development Studies (IDS) as a fellow in 1998, she supported the emergence of work on sexuality and helped establish the Sexuality and Development Programme. She has published widely on gender and sexuality in development and is executive producer of *Save us from Saviours*, a short film on Indian sex workers' challenge of the rescue industry.

Kate Hawkins is director of Pamoja Communications and a visiting fellow at the Institute of Development Studies (IDS). She has worked as a policy analyst and advocate on sexual and reproductive health and rights. With Susie Jolly, Andrea Cornwall and others, Kate has contributed to the Sexuality and Development Programme at IDS with a particular focus on how research influences policy and practice and the improvement of communication and knowledge exchange. Kate is on the Steering Committee of The Pleasure Project, an initiative which aims to make sex safer by addressing one of the major reasons people have sex: the pursuit of pleasure.

Susie Jolly is a hybrid activist/researcher/communicator/trainer and is currently also a donor. From her different positions she consistently seeks to challenge the 'straitjacket' of gender and sexuality norms that disempower so many people. She currently leads the Ford Foundation sexuality and reproductive health and rights grant-making programme in China. Previously, she founded and led the Sexuality and Development Programme at the Institute of Development Studies (IDS). She has had extensive engagement with gender and development issues internationally, with six years' experience at the BRIDGE gender information unit, IDS, as well as a lifetime of feminist activism.

Women, Sexuality and the Political Power of Pleasure

edited by
Susie Jolly, Andrea Cornwall and Kate Hawkins

Zed Books
LONDON & NEW YORK

*This book is dedicated to Susie Jolly's mum Alison Jolly,
to Andrea Cornwall's daughter Kate Cornwall Scoones,
and to Kate Hawkins' friend Heather White.*

Women, Sexuality and the Political Power of Pleasure was first published in 2013
by Zed Books Ltd, 7 Cynthia Street, London N1 9JF, UK and
Room 400, 175 Fifth Avenue, New York, NY 10010, USA

www.zedbooks.co.uk

Designed and typeset in Bembo with Good display by Kate Kirkwood
Index by John Barker
Cover design: www.alice-marwick.co.uk
Printed and bound by TJ International Ltd, Padstow, Cornwall

Distributed in the USA exclusively by Palgrave Macmillan, a division of
St Martin's Press, LLC, 175 Fifth Avenue, New York, NY 10010, USA

A catalogue record for this book is available from the British Library
Library of Congress Cataloging in Publication Data available

ISBN 978 1 78032 572 9 hb
ISBN 978 1 78032 571 2 pb

Contents

Abbreviations

· ·

FBO	faith-based organization
FGM/C	female genital mutilation/cutting
HIV/AIDS	human immunodeficiency virus/acquired immunodeficiency syndrome
HREP	Human Rights Education Programme for Women
INCRESE	International Centre for Reproductive Health and Rights
LGBTQ	lesbian, gay, bisexual, transgender, queer
LS	life skills
LSE	life skills education
NGO	non-governmental organization
NHS	National Health Service (UK)
SH&DA	Sexual Health and Disability Alliance
SPOD	Sexual Problems of the Disabled
SRH	sexual and reproductive health
SSA	sub-Saharan Africa
STD	sexually transmitted disease
STI	sexually transmitted infection
WHO	World Health Organization
WWHR	Women for Women's Human Rights – New Ways

Acknowledgements

●●●

We would like to gratefully acknowledge the financial support of the UK government's Department for International Development and the Swedish International Development Cooperation Agency (Sida) for the Institute of Development Studies Sexuality and Development Programme and the Pathways of Women's Empowerment Research Programme Consortium (www. pathways-of-empowerment.org), which made this publication possible. We are also very grateful to Jenny Edwards and Kirsty Milward for editorial support.

Preface

Andrea Cornwall

This book brings together contributions that explore, debate and demonstrate the power of pleasure as an entry point for work that seeks positive change in women's lives. It forms part of a new series dedicated to feminist engagements with development associated with the Pathways of Women's Empowerment programme (www.pathways-of-empowerment.org), and is the fruit of collaboration between Pathways and the pioneering Sexuality and Development Programme of the Institute of Development Studies.

Pathways set out to understand women's pathways of empowerment in diverse settings, sectors and contexts. Focusing on work, body and voice as arenas for feminist engagement with development, Pathways sought to map women's experiences of empowerment and to seek out 'hidden pathways', beyond the gaze of conventional development strategies, through which significant changes might be taking place.

Sexuality is one such hidden pathway. International development has paid little attention to the part that pleasure plays in women's experiences of empowerment. When it comes to women's bodies and sexualities, the focus all too often is on disempowerment: on violence and violation, harm, risk and hazard. Even to speak of pleasure in the same breath as development causes a stir. One development bureaucrat admitted that she simply could not countenance holding the words 'pleasure' and 'poverty' together in her mind; others have said or implied that sexuality and pleasure are too 'frivolous' for development to deal with, too far down the list of urgent priorities. And yet, as the contributors to this book demonstrate, a positive, pleasure-focused approach to sexuality can be a way to address a host of issues that affect women's well-being, including violence against women.

For too long, we've seen international development favour functional, instrumental approaches that lack much of a connection with what moves and motivates us. We've gone from 'community-based' to 'rights-based' to 'results-based' and 'evidence-based' and back again. What this book shows so powerfully is that what is needed to really connect with women's lives is a 'pleasure-based approach' to women's sexuality, one that celebrates and affirms women's rights to an enjoyable sexuality of their own choosing. Read – and enjoy!

INTRODUCTION
Women, Sexuality and the Political Power of Pleasure

● ●

Susie Jolly, Andrea Cornwall and Kate Hawkins

> People thought we were wasting time talking about sex and pleasure, when maternal mortality is so high … but I was convinced that if this delicate taboo thing – sexual pleasure – could be negotiated by women, then almost anything can be negotiated … and that idea gave me multiple orgasms! (Dorothy Akenova, INCRESE, Nigeria, cited in The Pleasure Project 2008: 52)

Images of women as victims are rampant in gender and development. This is particularly the case in discussions of sexuality, where the world is portrayed as so fraught with dangers it seems almost impossible to imagine women enjoying themselves. This focus on the negative can be paralysing – both in terms of ease with one's own body, and in terms of mobilizing around women's wants and desires. Such narratives dovetail with religious right agendas to protect women's chastity. Yet, at the same time, sexual pleasure is an obsession in women's magazines, pornography and a whole variety of other media. Contemporary pressures – fuelled by these media, as well as the pharmaceutical industry and the market more broadly – set up new imperatives as to what counts as good sex and how this should be performed. These suggest that only particular kinds of people are eligible for sexual pleasure (like young, able-bodied, HIV-negative) and that particular kinds of sex are superior (like heterosexual, Viagra-style sex where men get and maintain an erection easily, vaginal intercourse, g-spot

1

and clitoral stimulation, and simultaneous orgasms). These kinds of sex may be far from most people's experience; they set up an unrealistic model that hinders an exploration of what they themselves can and wish to enjoy (Boynton 2001; Tepper 2000).

So, how to react to the suppression of pleasure in some domains, and its commodification in others? These were issues hotly debated in the feminist 'sex wars' of the late 1970s and 1980s, mostly in the US and in Europe (Duggan and Hunter 1995; Ferguson 1984; Vance and Snitow 1984; Wilson 1983). 'Anti-pornography feminists' called for an abolition of pornography, which they saw as a key facet of male violence against women (Dworkin 1979). 'Pro-sex feminists' saw censorship of pornography as part of a broader censorship of sexual expression, of both women and men and in particular of people with non-normative sexual desires (Rubin 1998). Charges were levelled at anti-pornography feminists of subscribing to essentialist stereotypes of women's sexuality as only about intimacy and bonding, thus reinforcing conventional moral condemnation of promiscuous women (Ferguson 1984). In turn, pro-sex or sex-positive activists were accused of setting up a new normative standard where 'liberatory, depersonalized' sex was posited as superior and intimacy as 'aberrant' (Philipson 1984: 117).

More recently, in Australia, Europe and North America, some of these debates have been reinvigorated and revived under the banner of a concern over the 'sexualization' or 'pornification' of popular culture, sometimes referred to as 'raunch culture', through the mainstreaming of 'sexy' and 'sexually explicit' imagery in marketing, popular music, fiction, television, film and computer games, etc. (Bailey 2011; Levy 2005; Walter 2011). There are fears that the objectification of women and unrealistic and harmful norms around sexuality and gender being posited as the mainstream may lead to psychological harm, particularly amongst girls and young women. Critics of this position argue that much research and analysis on the effects of sexualization fails to take the views of young people into account; underestimates young people's critical abilities to assess the veracity of the images and messages aimed at them; underestimates the power of sexuality as a potentially positive force as well as the potential of the creation of spaces for the discussion of sex and identity; and that it conflates a number of disparate social phenomena (Bragg *et al.* 2011; Smith 2010a, 2010b).

While in the global North debates about women's sexualities continue to be bifurcated along the lines inherited from the era of the 'sex wars', debates in the global South offer another set of lenses through which to view questions of sexuality and pleasure. African feminists Patricia McFadden (2003), Charmaine Pereira (2003) and others have been part of vibrant debates in the journal *Feminist Africa* about how and if sexual pleasure as a feminist choice can be part of reclaiming women's agency. *Sexuality in Africa* magazine ran a special issue on pleasure in 2007, critiquing the emphasis on disease and pain in research and programmatic approaches to African sexuality, and calling for an inclusion of pleasure in the frame. In the same year, the Malaysia-based *Journal of the Asian-Pacific Resource and Research Centre for Women* ran an issue entitled 'Why Affirm Sexuality?' that featured an article by a leading Chinese sexuality researcher calling for an exploration of Chinese terms and sayings that suggest women's sexual strength and agency such as: 'Women in their 30s are wolves, in their 40s are tigers, and in their 50s could even absorb the dust' (Huang 2007: 4). Such discussions consider how sexual pleasure can be affirming and empowering for people not seen by their societies as deserving of this kind of enjoyment, and how pleasure can also provide energy to fuel political mobilization.

Much as the discussion on pleasure has begun to break the silence on the positive and empowering dimensions of women's sexualities, there has been relatively little analysis of the policy implications of these connections, or documentation of practical initiatives that seek to empower women and others through positive approaches to sexuality. This is what this book seeks to do. Most contributors to this book do not take up the arguments of the sex wars in very direct ways. Instead they tend to provide practical examples of how negative approaches to sexuality play out in their communities and contexts, and of how people create spaces for pleasure by reworking negative aspects of traditions, as in women's new formulations of the *Ssenga* tradition in Uganda or Christian sexuality education for young people in Malawi. Several contributors describe interventions that take pleasure as an explicit approach, in order to empower women, or marginalized groups, and there are also examples of men being empowered or benefiting from work on pleasure. This is what is new about this book: the contextual descriptions and the descriptions of interventions and proposals of frameworks for action, such as a model for service providers to recognize the sexualities of people with disabilities or recommendations on how to make porn empowering and how to increase possibilities for sex workers to enjoy their jobs. At the same time, some practical examples serve as evidence to document and explain the relationship between sexuality and empowerment on a conceptual level.

The book had its genesis in a workshop held in the Institute of Development Studies in 2009, a joint initiative of the IDS Sexuality and Development Programme and the Pathways of Women's Empowerment research consortium. The workshop brought together activists, practitioners and academics from around the world to explore what a positive, pleasure-focused approach to sexuality might offer development. Our subsequent work on this topic has convinced us that there is an appetite amongst women for more opportunities to speak openly about pleasure and to better understand the potential of a pleasure-focused approach. For example, a session that we ran with some of the authors from this book at the global Forum of the Association of Women's Rights in Development (AWID) in Turkey in 2012 was voted one of the ten most popular sessions, and led participants to call for a 'Pleasure Plenary' at the next forum.

Why we need to talk about pleasure

Sexuality is generally represented in development discourses as a source of hazard and harm; sex is reduced to a risk-laden practice that is a cause of disease, overpopulation and untimely death. Sexual rights activism has focused on the harms of discrimination, exclusion and violence, and sexuality educators on preventing adolescent pregnancies and mitigating the harms of the HIV epidemic. Gender and Development practitioners and feminist activists have made important strides in bringing sexual violence – in intimate partnerships as well as in war – into the public eye, making sexual violation a matter of public policy concern. Family planning is back on the international development agenda, driven by renewed concerns about unmet need for contraception, and unwanted pregnancy. And yet, in the midst of all this noise, there is a silence over what might be positive, pleasurable and empowering about sex and sexuality.

In many countries, feminists have largely been either silent on sexuality or focused on 'subordination and oppression of women's bodies', as Huang *et al.* (2009: 284) observe for China. Their silence can reinforce societal silences about women's sexuality, just as their focus on the violation of women's bodies chimes with societal impulses to contain women's sexuality. This focus on the negative subsumes women's sexuality under violence and fear in a way that compresses space to explore their own desires. The effect can be benumbing, especially, as Bibi Bakare-Yusuf points out in her contribution to this book, for younger women just coming into sexual consciousness. Victim discourses are not just disempowering, they also lead to wrong solutions such as criminalization of transmission of HIV. And dangerous conversions also take place between certain feminist positions aiming to protect women from sexual violence, and conservative forces concerned with women's chastity. This has already been observed in several instances: feminist anti-pornography activists making alliances with right-wing groups in the US in the 1980s; some Indian feminists' images of Indian women as chaste and vulnerable to sexual exploitation echoing the Hindu right's portrayal of virtuous Indian womanhood; and the collaborations between some feminist groups and the Bush administration's mobilization against prostitution. Such discourses around protecting women from exploitation – sexual and otherwise – have also been drawn upon by US neo-conservatives to justify the invasions of Afghanistan and Iraq (Petchesky 2005).

Bakare-Yusuf argues that negative representations of women's sexuality collude with patriarchal framings that support the policing of women. The desiring woman becomes transgressive; her sexual agency makes her a potentially disruptive threat to the containment of women, and to family structures built on meeting the desires of men. She contends, 'Thinking through and about sexual pleasure is in fact potentially more dangerous, transformative and contestive of hetero-patriarchal logic than merely focusing on danger and violation.' Focusing on pleasure, as several of the contributors to this book suggest, can be a way of better understanding women's experiences of violence and violation. In her exploration in this book of pleasure and violence in sub-Saharan Africa, Chi-Chi Undie argues that it is important to acknowledge and talk about sexual well-being and pleasure with the victims and perpetrators of violence. Otherwise, survivors remain forever defined by their negative experiences, unable to move beyond these to enjoy sexual relationships again. And if perpetrators only hear stories of sexual violence then they are given the impression that sexual violence is normal, and that no alternative is possible.

In her chapter, Jaya Sharma notes that interventions to end violence against women that do not acknowledge the power of pleasure may misrecognize what it is that women gain from continuing to be part of abusive relationships. Based on testimonies from trainings for both rural Dalit women and NGO activists in India, she argues that some women privilege being in a relationship where they can get sexual pleasure over the safety of leaving a violent relationship – as they'd be leaving sex as well as their partner. Violence against women is also often a response to women expressing desires which are not socially approved – such as wanting to marry a man of another caste or ethnic group, or sexual attraction outside marriage, or for someone of the same sex. Thus understanding the diversity of women's desires, and seeking more possibilities for their expression, is part of what is needed to tackle violence against women. Writing as a woman living with HIV, Alice Welbourn focuses on the forced asexuality that is often foisted on women when they are diagnosed with HIV. She argues that a focus on sexual rights and pleasure can enhance our analysis of the ways in which legal, religious and medical discourses can reinforce fear of women's unfettered sexuality:

> This is not just about invasion, violation and rage. It is also about survival, resistance and agency. There are many of us women with HIV who have managed to restore our self-esteem, our deep belief in our fundamental rights to our sexuality and the sexual pleasure and well-being that go with those rights, as there are also many women who have become rape survivors.

How to talk about pleasure

Whether pleasure is denied or appropriated varies with time and context. Contradictions abound in every culture. In practice, an uncritical celebration of pleasure can be just as damaging as a suppression of the possibilities for pleasure. It can dovetail with market manipulation of pleasure for profit. And it can create new expectations and standards that put pressure on people, rather than enabling them to explore the pleasures they desire, or choose. If sexual pleasure is to be talked about productively, we need first to recognize that, in the realm of sexuality, people's experiences of pleasure come as part of a complex and nebulous mix of different feelings and emotions.

Pleasure and danger are often entwined – not least because, for many, seeking pleasure entails breaking social rules. However, the oppressive frameworks that forbid pursuit of pleasure are not the only dangers associated with sexuality. There may be other fears such as anxieties about loss of control, merging with another, intense sensation, triggering emotions, invoking previous experiences, not being satisfied, fear of losing the object of love or lust, fear of conception, or of catching a sexually transmitted or other infection (Vance 1989). This ambiguity is part of many consensual sexual experiences. One study of young adults' sex and love lives in Nairobi concludes that their 'experiences show that there is a thin line between pleasure and anxiety in sex; and they are not unconnected or mutually exclusive emotions and experiences' (Spronk 2008: 5).

Sharma argues that if pleasure is to be promoted productively, it must be grounded in a political perspective that refuses to set it up as a new norm or standard, and allows for a full diversity of possibilities for pleasure both in terms of who can experience them and how. Xiaopei He, in her account of organizing marginalized women in China, cautions that adequate space must first be provided for tears and for talk of suffering, before people are ready to move on and think about pleasure. Changing narratives of female sexualities calls for the active engagement of women in telling a very different kind of story about women's bodies, desires and pleasures. Bakare-Yusuf asserts:

> Telling stories about female sexual pleasure, agency and power allows us to uncover a tradition and community of powerful, feisty, indomitable women who will not be cowed by oppression or viola-tion. In this way, we begin to show that violation is not the blueprint for women's sexual experience, rather, it is an example of agency gone awry. By telling a different story, still with the understanding that danger is always a potentiality that must be contested, we are providing a different beginning and therefore a different ending to what it means to be a sexual being in the world.

Ana Francis Mor describes how laughter, brought on by cabaret theatre in health workshops in Mexico, was key to changing people – not just their minds, but their hearts and their bodies and what they do with them:

> So we started to work with laughter, to talk loud about our pain, but with the possibility of transforming our identities and our own personal classifications. We wanted to shift from being the ones who moan about pain to being the ones who laugh about it. This is how we built our characters' stories from laughter, from the Mexican tradition of laughing about every solemnity, of laughing even about

death – because at the end of the day, death is the one that has the last laugh.

It may appear that conversations about sexual pleasure are only possible in limited domains. In relation to Islam, writing in the exciting new collection *Sexuality in Muslim Contexts*, Anissa Hélie reflects on how 'the regulation of sexuality has effectively shrunk the public spaces available to women in a variety of contexts' (2012: 10), and describes how:

> The conventional, commonly used construction of 'Muslimness' derives from a conservative political agenda that ... relies heavily on sexual repression, of women and stigmatized sexualities in particular. (Hélie and Hoodfar 2012: 3)

Religious organizations are often the site for some of the most negative prescriptive messages about sexuality and might seem a difficult place to raise such issues. Rubin writes of how Western culture considers sex as 'a dangerous, destructive, negative force' (1984: 278), a legacy of Judaeo-Christian traditions. The spread of Christianity in Africa has contributed to what Signe Arnfred describes for Africa as 'a Christian moral regime' in which 'sexual pleasure for women is defined out of existence, female chastity and passionlessness becoming the model and the norm' (2004: 17). However, there are glimmers within religious institutions of recognition of the power of pleasure, as our chapters by Undie and Anaïs Bertrand-Dansereau suggest. Undie finds justifications in the Bible for sexual pleasure within marriage. Bertrand-Dansereau finds unexpectedly that, in Malawi, church sexuality education was far more open and sex-positive than secular alternatives, which tried to motivate people to safer behaviours through fear of disease. Church education focused on the joys of living, and recognized the power of sexual desire and how difficult it is to abstain from sex – although they still called for 'brave Christians' to take this 'arduous path' until marriage.

Whose pleasure?

Several of the authors in this book explore how particular groups have been denied possibilities to seek pleasure, and how enabling them to do so can be immensely empowering. State-level policies limit women's lives, as Gulsah Seral Aksakal outlines in her piece. Mor describes how women learn gender ideologies from the television soap operas, all-pervasive in Mexico, which take their cue from Catholicism:

> People already know their scripts: woman = virtue = no pleasure = victim = tears = virginity = blackmail = guilt; men = macho or male chauvinist = never cries = alcohol = money = violence = sexual power = success or death.

Sylvia Tamale describes how women have become subject to moralism, shame and sex negativity:

> Colonialists worked hand in hand with African patriarchs to develop inflexible customary laws that evolved into new structures and forms of domination and deployed various legal and policy strategies and discourses in the areas of medical health and hygiene. Traditional customs were reconfigured to introduce new sexual mores, taboos and stigmas. Women's sexuality was medicalized and reduced to reproduction. Through adopting Christianity, Africans were encouraged to reject their previous beliefs and values and to adopt the 'civilized ways' of the whites. A new script, steeped in the Victorian moralistic, anti-sexual and body shame edict, was inscribed on the bodies of African women and with it an elaborate system of control.

Tamale explores how the institution of *Ssenga* among the Baganda in Uganda has endured and changed. Formerly an education by aunts for nieces on how to become good wives and pleasure husbands, it is now as often a commercial service for better sex and relationships. Both earlier and current versions of *Ssenga* largely focus on conformist scripts, privileging men's pleasure over women's. However, some have included elements of subversion, such as one charismatic *Ssenga* of today, who with a similar dynamism to evangelical priests, teaches women clitoral orgasm and ejaculation.

Some contributions to the book focus on the denial of pleasure for particular groups. HIV-positive people are often expected to forgo sex and having children, regardless of their own desires. Welbourn's chapter offers a poignant reminder of the extent to which HIV-positive women experience the pain of forced retirement from sexual pleasure. Welbourn describes how their pleasurable sexual experiences are constrained by the grief of a positive diagnosis; like trauma or rape, she argues, this can lead to forced asexuality. Reclaiming HIV-positive women's rights to pleasure is a vital part of recognizing their rights as humans. She argues that:

> Forced sex and forced asexuality are opposite sides of the same coin: they are both rooted in control over women and over our rights to choose what to do or not do with our bodies. Both forced sex and forced asexuality deny women our rights to our own autonomy with regard to our sexual – and reproductive – pleasure.

In recent years, there has been a wave of new laws criminalizing HIV transmission. These obstruct happy relationships and make it more difficult to support HIV-positive people in deciding whether to have children, and to make it possible to do so without passing on the virus. Efforts are being made to contest these laws, and to affirm the sexual and reproductive desires of people living with HIV. The Salamander Trust has recorded testimonies by women living with HIV about their desires around whether or not to have children. The International Planned Parenthood Foundation has produced a guide for young people living with HIV: 'Happy, Healthy and Hot' (2010) to give information on how to increase sexual pleasure, take care of health, practise safer sex, have children (if they so choose), develop strong intimate relationships and access support.

For people with disabilities in the UK, Lorna Couldrick and Alex Cowan's chapter shows, the situation is in many ways similar to women living with HIV: there is a presumption that people with disabilities are, or ought to be, asexual, and little open recognition of their sexual needs and desires. Couldrick and

Cowan point out that this lack of acknowledgement of the role of sex and sexuality in the lives of people with disabilities can be exacerbated by health and social care practices, arguing that, 'the very delivery of health and social care may undermine the sexual health of disabled people and perpetuate the myth that if you are disabled, intimacy and sex no longer matter'.

Medical professionals often tend to underestimate the importance of sexual pleasure to the people they are supposed to be serving; their own squeamishness about sex prevents them from taking those needs seriously. Years of medical training leave medical professionals with little capacity to have a conversation about sex, let alone about sexual pleasure. And this contributes to an overwhelming silence; the sexualities of disabled people are not only invisible, they are barely even contemplated. Even where sexual needs and desires are acknowledged, Couldrick and Cowan describe how they are regarded as a low priority, an optional extra. Older and severely incapacitated people are assumed to have no sexual needs at all.

While some groups are denied possibilities of seeking pleasure, others may be finding pleasure in unexpected circumstances. The business of sex work involves the provision of pleasure. But it is often assumed that sex workers themselves get no pleasure from their work. Jo Doezema's chapter challenges this assumption, citing research in several locations including India, China, Spain and Finland. She cites one sex worker who reported that if she enjoyed the sex too much, it tired her out and made it more difficult for her to take on more clients. (For the same reason male sex workers may avoid ejaculating at work.) Doezema also cites women for whom pleasure is part of what makes sex work an occupation that they continue to choose to pursue.

Doezema finds that in the research and in sex workers' accounts, several factors affect sex workers' possibilities for pleasure at work such as: levels of choice over clients; the nature of the employment relationship; immigration status; social stigma against sex work; and alternative livelihood possibilities that mean people will not face economic desperation if they leave sex work. She concludes that measures are needed for 'strengthening those elements that give women more control over the sex work encounter'. (Similarly, Seral Aksakal finds more control correlates to more pleasure for women in non-sex work situations.) Doezema also suggests we should see sex workers as a resource for sexuality education in society: 'bringing experience and analysis of positive sexuality beyond youth and beauty'.

How to work with pleasure

Many of the practical approaches described in this book work to uncover norms which restrict pleasure and build new norms which allow for exploration of desires, while trying to avoid setting up new standards of sexual performance. By revealing norms, we can subvert them, as it is precisely because they are often not visible that norms have such a powerful hold on us. By opening up a space to make visible the norms that we have internalized (so much perhaps that we have not even begun to think about the grip they may have on our lives), these interventions offer women opportunities to make their own decisions about whether or not they want to continue to conform or whether they want to explore alternative ways of doing and being (Chambers 2007). Five chapters describe trainings or exchanges that work toward these goals. One chapter looks at how service providers can better support people with disabilities to enjoy their sexuality. And one chapter explores if and how pornography can be part of the solution.

Seral Aksakal details the policing of women's sexualities, which extends from violence by the state through to that of measures taken by family members, especially older women, to constrain and contain younger women. Participants in trainings by Women for Women's Human Rights – New Ways (WWHR) in Turkey, tell of being slapped around the face by older women when their periods started, and being punished for knowing or enquiring about sex. In Turkey, as in so many contexts, women lack information and education about sexuality. This allows myths to thrive, such as the myth that women naturally have lower sex drives, and are sexually passive. Combined with a conservative political context, this further undermines women's capacity to enjoy pleasurable sexual relationships, acting as a quiet form of violence that permeates society and exerts a powerful oppressive influence in women's – and men's – lives.

These negative social messages about sexuality make it difficult for women to have enjoyable sexual relationships. One participant in a WWHR workshop summed up the impact of all of this negativity on people's enjoyment of sexual pleasure even within socially sanctioned relationships:

> For years you're taught that sex and sexuality are the devil to be feared. Then in one night [the wedding night], they're supposed to become an angel to be loved. This is just not possible!

WWHR's four-month training on human rights aims to empower women in a broad sense. It includes two modules on sexuality that talk about 'sexual pleasure as a woman's human right'. These modules include 'the basic rights to know and like one's sexual organs, the right to seek sexual experiences independent of marital status, the right to orgasm, the right to expression and pursuit of sexual needs and desires, and also the right to choose NOT to experience one's sexuality'. These modules come in the ninth and tenth weeks; by then the women have built up mutual trust and had space to discuss sexual and other violence, sexually transmitted infections and reproductive rights. The modules on sexual pleasure are overwhelmingly the most popular. The programme has been running since 1993 and over 10,000 women have been trained to date. Impacts on participants range from reduction in domestic violence to greater participation in the labour market, as well as better sex. Once, a husband of one of the women came to see the course facilitator, and said to her:

> What have you done to my wife to help her relax about sexuality? I used to be driven to despair chasing after her, and she'd always tell me it was shameful and sinful, and that I should stay away from her. Now all that has changed. Please tell me what you told her, so I can

tell my friends who are having the same kind of problem with their wives.

Dorothy Aken'Ova reports in her chapter that within marriage women are expected to pleasure their husbands, and preparation for marriage focuses on teaching the girl how to do this. One married women said that when she had expressed pleasure during sex, her husband accused her of being like a prostitute and beat her. In contrast, non-married women were expected to enjoy sex with their boyfriends. Yet, what emerged from research by Aken'Ova's organization INCRESE (the International Centre for Reproductive Health and Rights) was women's deep lack of sexual pleasure in their relationships, married or not. Some men mistakenly believed they were giving great pleasure to their lovers, and had not discovered the truth due to lack of communication.

After two years of research, INCRESE developed better sex and communication training for couples to address these findings. The training uses 'sexual pleasure as an entry point to promote women's rights and health' and challenges assumptions about men's performance and women's pleasures. In some cases, couples taking the trainings have broken up as they realize they cannot give each other what they want, in bed or in life. However, in other cases the trainings have led to greater equality in relationships, reduced domestic violence, and happier sex lives.

Stereotypes of the 'good' and the 'bad' woman can be just as effective in crushing desires as more overt means of repression. Sharma reflects on how the normative ideal of the 'good woman' acts as a brake on women's realization of their own desires. Constantly held up against this ideal, by ourselves as well as by others, we may find it hard to break with the norms embodied in the image of the 'good' or 'proper woman' (Jassey and Nyanzi 2008). Sharma describes how in the trainings conducted by her organization, Nirantar, women come to name and acknowledge the power of these norms and to reflect on how they conform to as well as challenge norms in their everyday lives. She gives an example from the discussions in one of these trainings:

> If a woman says 'no' to a man who makes a pass at her, it is common for him to dismiss that by saying 'When a woman says no, she actually means yes.' And if a woman says 'yes' to a man who has expressed interest in her, she will immediately be labelled a 'loose' woman. Women don't have the space to say yes, even when they want to. This opens up the space for men who are rebuffed to invalidate women when they say no.

The discussion, Sharma reports, 'concluded with the insight that women will have the right to say "no" only if they have the right to say "yes"'. More broadly, she links the analysis of pleasure in Nirantar's trainings to politicizing women's understandings of sexuality, of marriage and of societal expectations of them.

The Chinese NGO Pink Space organizes exchanges to build solidarity between people marginalized because of their sexuality and challenge the sources of their oppression, as He explains. Pink Space brings together HIV-positive women, lesbians, bisexual women, female sex workers, transgender men, and women married to gay men. Fun, laughter and discussions of sexual pleasure are always part of the agenda. He writes:

> Sharing experiences helps people who are marginalized to realize that social and cultural norms such as marriage normativity and compulsory heterosexuality oppress not only women but also men; not only LGBTQ people but also straight people. With this realization, a united struggle against social norms becomes possible. These exciting stories, erotic desires and colourful lives of our participants from different marginalized communities – and the boundary-breaking good humour with which they are often shared – motivate Pink Space to continue the collective struggle for rights to pleasure.

Mor describes trainings on health run in rural Mexico for women, men and children. The three-year programme trained over 30,000 people in total, in four day-long trainings that included participants first identifying key health issues in small groups, and a cabaret theatre working on these issues in the afternoon, and performing in the evening. Cabaret characters included 'the neighbour' who:

> embodied every possible and imaginable health issue related to or derived from disinformation and embarrassment. Her circumstances were so hilariously ridiculous that no one wanted to be like her. In one scene, this character mentioned that her decency had never allowed her to open her legs to check herself, and she began a detailed, disgusting description of the great variety of fauna and flora living in her genitals. The scene was gross – and very funny.

Another character was a woman who announced that if any members of the audience were to find the father of her child, they should please tell him not to come back, because she had already found love with the child's godmother. Laughter and emotional engagement enabled people to reflect and change, and to really take on board the information instead of just hearing it and not acting upon it.

Putting pleasure into the practice of the health and social care of people with disabilities involves a radical readjustment of the ways in which professionals engage with people with disabilities. In some countries, policies have developed that recognize the impact physical impairment has on the capacity of people with disabilities to seek sexual pleasure. The Netherlands, for example, provides funding for sexual surrogacy for people who are unable to masturbate because of their impairment. Couldrick and Cowan suggest that the Recognition Model can provide a way of opening up a dialogue that can lead to a collaboration which enables people with disabilities to have and enjoy the sexuality they want. This model starts with service providers recognizing that service users are sexual beings, and guides them on how to address this issue. The simple first step of the provider asking their client whether they have any sexual issues which they would like to discuss can lead to a more productive relationship where people's sexual needs and desires are taken into account. Taking sexuality seriously means, they argue, thinking about who might be best placed to provide support, raising the possibility of recruiting sex workers to improve services for people with disabilities, not just for sex but to position people, prepare them for sex and deal with the discomfort of care workers.

The focus shifts from service providers to porn in the chapter by Anne Philpott and Krissy Ferris, which explores how pornography can eroticize safer and less gender normative sex. They point out that pornography is a huge industry, and one of the most important sources of information on sexuality for young people in many countries: 13 per cent of all internet searches are for porn. Even if you think pornography is inherently harmful, a 'harm-reduction' approach could be justified, where, as in providing clean needles to people who inject drugs, the harm is not ended, but its negative effects are mitigated. They advocate such an approach, and cite examples of porn that eroticizes safer sex with actors using female and male condoms. One director sticks to a 'condom optional' approach because some male actors are unable to sustain erections over a whole day of filming if they use condoms. However, for the US gay porn director Chi Chi LaRue, this is no justification for exposing porn actors to HIV, or suggesting to audiences that condoms are optional. Philpott and Ferris cite Sarah Headley, editor of *Scarlet*, a British magazine targeted at women:

> As house policy all erotic fiction stories feature condom use. It's referred to in an evocative language that invites the reader to be aroused when they hear the crisp, enticing tear of the condom packet, the naughty, sharp twang of rubber.... We don't gloss over it – we enjoy it. We indulge in it. By eroticizing condom use, the presence of condoms becomes part of sex play, rather than a problem.

Female directors are introduced who seek to satisfy an audience of women. Some female porn makers say women want more of a story line, character building, humour, and build-up as well as the explicit sex acts. Several aspire to making porn which looks more 'real', avoiding the clichés of perfectly performed gender normative sex between people with 'perfect' bodies.

How not to work on pleasure

Over half the contributions look at how pleasure can be promoted productively. In contrast, Petra Boynton's piece shows that work on pleasure can be subject to the same pitfalls as any other development intervention. Her account relates to the much-debated issue of female genital mutilation (FGM).

FGM has been presented as the extreme of suppression of women's pleasure. It is widely practised in parts of East and West Africa, and has become a cause that has engaged sex-positive sexologists, sexual rights activists and feminists alike. Representations of these practices often tend to classify them as 'traditional', evoking images of 'backward' customs; yet in some parts of Africa female genital mutilation rituals are associated with being and becoming 'modern' (Dallenborg 2004). These practices range from the complete evisceration of the vulva and stitching of the vagina, to the excision of the clitoris, the removal of the clitoral hood, the pricking of the clitoris and to the lengthening of the labia minora – a practice that, as Signe Arnfred (2004) and Tamale in her contribution to this book points out, can enhance women's sexual pleasure, but which is included by the WHO alongside these other genital mutilations as a harmful practice. It has been argued that female genital mutilation, including removal of the clitoris, need not limit women's sexual pleasure, and indeed can be empowering to women. Ahmadu argues, for example, that, 'African women … like Western women who opt for cosmetic genital surgeries, should be free to decide for themselves what to do with their own bodies' (2009: 17). But to many in the West, female genital mutilation, of any kind, including cosmetic surgery, is one of the expressions of patriarchal dominance (Berer 2010).

Boynton tells the fascinating story of 'Clitoraid' an American initiative started by the believers of the Raelian religion that set out to raise funds to build a 'pleasure hospital' in Burkina Faso that would perform operations to 'restore' the capacity of excised women for clitoral orgasm. Boynton raises questions about the project itself – its financial transparency and technical competence. Why haven't women from Burkina Faso themselves been consulted? Why is Clitoraid trying to build their own hospital instead of support the existing hospitals there, which are already providing surgery for women to undo some of the effects of FGM? She critiques the colonial overtones of Western occupation of African bodies, with Westerners being invited to donate by 'adopting' an African woman's clitoris. And she challenges the notion that only women with clitorises can experience pleasure, and that the solution to a lack of pleasure would necessarily be another operation.

Clitoraid has all the hallmarks of the worst kind of development intervention: a limited focus on infrastructure and technical fixes, undertaken by outsiders with a religious agenda, without regard for existing services or consultation with the proposed 'beneficiaries', and with Westerners posited as saving oppressed African women from wounds inflicted upon them by their supposedly barbaric culture. Boynton's story is an important reminder that, along with sex positivity, we need transparency, accountability, anti-colonialism and a democratic approach.

Echoes of this story are found in the medical discourse on an industry around sexual dysfunction, which adopts a limited normative definition of pleasure, produced by outside 'experts' rather than by the people themselves facing 'dysfunction', and proposes technical fixes for people who do not meet the standards. Couldrick and Cowan critique the definitions of sexual dysfunction in the International Classification of Diseases (ICD-10, WHO 1992) and the Diagnostic Statistical Manual (DSM IV), arguing that:

> Firstly … these classifications are phallocentric. They revolve around penis/vagina penetration with orgasm as the goal. Using this criterion, many disabled people may be inappropriately labelled as sexually dysfunctional. The man unable to have an erection or the woman unable to have an orgasm, due to physical impairment, by these classifications have a sexual dysfunction even though they may have rewarding and satisfying sexual lives.

And there is money to be made from this definition of dysfunction by pharmaceutical companies that promote drugs as the solution (Boynton 2004).

Pleasure and/as empowerment

This book shows why we should work with pleasure, and how we can do so in ways that change people's lives, on an individual and collective level. It also shows how pleasure can contribute to empowerment.

Making space for pleasure can contribute to challenging gender and other power relations. Three of the contributors to this book explicitly argue that a pleasure-based approach can radically undermine patriarchal control of women. Bakare-Yusuf declares:

> Positioning women as weak or damaged subjects gives renewed legitimacy to patriarchally motivated discourses of control and protection. What this does is to set artificial limits on how we talk about women's sexual agency ... we lose our capacity to resist and change our situation, and to imagine new horizons of possibilities around sexual safety, choice, autonomy and pleasure.

Aken'Ova concurs that promoting women's pleasure challenges patriarchy, and describes what she observes in her trainings for couples:

> Women move from negotiating for orgasms to demands for a guarantee of other rights ... including ... for further education, acquisition of literacy skills, and jobs ... addressing any of these issues means taking a strong position in challenging patriarchy, and therein lies the strength of this intervention strategy. It provides the space to deconstruct male-dominated value systems and replace them with a system built and driven on feminist principles, a system that upholds the principle of erotic justice; a system where female agency is visible, protected and promoted.

Mor sees gender inequality denying women's pleasure and argues that pleasure and laughter can challenge this inequality. She writes of the trainings she ran:

> How could we shatter monoliths as huge as male chauvinism?... By showing ... how ridiculous they are, so their unfairness is clearly brought to light. The logic is to ridicule tyranny to knock it down; to laugh about our own disgrace to diminish its power ... Laughter generates pleasure; it is felt through the body and leaves traces of the possibility of happiness.

The transformation that is needed, she argues, is both conceptual and physical. Through the bodily experience of laughter, people can reach a conceptual understanding that male chauvinism makes no sense, and transform their own response from victimhood to empowerment:

> How can I transform my own self from feeling sorry to laughing about myself? Laughter gives us a route to this transformation, which is why it is so empowering. By laughing, the body feels able to transform pain into pleasure – and that is such a great power, like turning lead into gold.

Other contributors, including Sharma, Seral Aksakal, He, Undie, Doezema and Tamale, make more specific claims about the power of pleasure. They do not explicitly describe pleasure as controlled by patriarchy, or as posing a threat to the whole system of gender inequality. Instead, they document how trainings and activities that focus on women's pleasure have had immensely empowering effects on participants. Sometimes, this is because the focus on pleasure undoes the effects of inequalities between women and men. Sometimes, the focus on pleasure is empowering for other reasons, for example, by bringing about bodily liberation, shifts in thinking, or building solidarity between women.

Several of these authors provide examples of pleasure empowering women on a personal level. Seral Aksakal writes of how the human rights training programme run by WWHR sought to undo some of the powerful negativity about women's bodies that women grow up with in Turkey. She addresses the custom in rural Turkey of girls being slapped across the face when they first menstruate, and of the lack of information given to girls about menstruation, and quotes one of the participants:

I had to undergo psychiatric treatment after having my first menstrual cycle because I lost the ability to speak as a result of the fear I experienced. The impact of this dreadful experience continues to this date, despite the fact that I am now a mother of two children.

Seral Aksakal describes how the training courses try to undo such effects by opening up possibilities for women to be happy in their bodies.

Sharma also shows that by adopting a positive approach to women's sexuality, Nirantar's training work with women in India gave participants an opportunity to focus on their own happiness. She reflects on how liberating this can be, enabling women to let go of the worries or guilt they felt for violating gender norms. One trainee described her experience: 'After this training I felt freer. I feel lighter. If I have to talk to someone, I feel I can do that.' Both Sharma and He describe how a focus on sexual pleasure promoted solidarity between women. Sharma explains:

Sexuality seemed to reduce power hierarchies, including those between facilitators and participants. Perhaps this is partly because we all have irrational, unresolved issues of sexuality that we are grappling with.

In China, He's organization Pink Space brought together women from different marginalized groups such as lesbians, bisexual women, women living with HIV, sex workers and wives of gay men. By working together, they moved beyond victimhood, with the realization that other groups might face even more obstacles than they did. And through talking about pleasure and sexuality they found common ground on which to build solidarity. For Pink Space pleasure and positive approaches are a means as well as an end: the trainings are intended to be pleasurable in themselves, and also to lead to empowerment that includes more pleasure.

Arguments for the empowering benefits of a positive approach to sexuality are also strengthened by evidence from some of the other contributions to this book that show just how disempowering negative approaches to sexuality can be. Boynton's chapter provides a particularly poignant illustration of this, describing an intervention that is ostensibly pleasure-promoting, but becomes profoundly disempowering as it falls into the trap of the worst kind of development intervention, imposed by outsiders with no consultation with or accountability to the so-called 'beneficiaries'. Couldrick and Cowan discuss how service providers often deny people with disabilities in the UK any expression of sexuality, and give examples of how distressing this can be for people with disabilities. Bertrand-Dansereau describes how secular sexuality education interventions create even less space for discussion of pleasure than religious interventions in Malawi, and how negativity about sex and sexuality limits their effectiveness.

Contributions show that going beyond the negativity of a focus on harm, hazard and disease by taking a positive approach to sexuality can be an empowering way to tackle a host of issues relating to the body, from gender-based violence to sexual rights. Tamale contends that

> when we go beyond the traditional studies on African sexuality (which primarily focus on reproduction, violence and disease) to explore the area of desire and pleasure, we gain deeper insights into this complex subject. Broadening the scope of our research on sexuality in this way offers a fresh perspective on strategic interventions for critical areas such as sexual rights, HIV/AIDS and development.

It is this 'fresh perspective' that the contributors to this book bring, demonstrating in and through their work that pleasure can be empowering not just for women but for young people, people with disabilities, marginalized groups more broadly, and for society as a whole.

References

Ahmadu, F. S. (2009) 'Disputing the Myth of the Sexual Dysfunction of Circumcised Women', *Anthropology Today*, Vol. 25, No. 6, pp. 14–17.

Arnfred, S. (2004) 'Re-thinking Sexualities in Africa: Introduction', *Re-thinking Sexualities in Africa*, Nordiska Afrika Institutet, Uppsala.

Bailey, R. (2011) 'Letting Children be Children: Report of an Independent Review of the Commercialisation and Sexualisation of Childhood', UK Department for Education, https://www. education.gov.uk/publications/eOrderingDownload/Bailey%20 Review.pdf (accessed 20 August 2012).

Berer, M. (2010) 'Labia Reduction for Non-Therapeutic Reasons vs Female Genital Mutilation: Contradictions in Law and Practice in Britain', *Reproductive Health Matters*, Vol. 18, No. 35, pp. 106–10.

Boynton, P. (2001) 'Why Perfect Sex Is Bad for Us', *New Scientist*, No. 2304, p. 18.

—— (2004) 'Better Dicks through Drugs? The Penis as a Pharmaceutical Target' *SCAN Journal of Media and Communication*, Vol. 1, No. 3, http://www.scan.net.au/scan/journal/display.php?journal_id537 (accessed 3 September 2012).

Bragg, S., D. Buckingham, R. Russell and R. Willett (2011) 'Too Much, Too Soon? Children, "Sexualisation" and Consumer Culture', *Sex Education*, Vol. 11, No. 3, pp. 279–92.

Chambers, S. A. (2007) '"An Incalculable Effect": Subversions of Heteronormativity', *Political Studies*, Vol. 55, No. 3, pp. 656–79.

Dallenborg, L. (2004) 'A Reflection on the Cultural Meanings of Female Circumcision: Experiences from Fieldwork in Casamance, Southern Senegal', in S. Arnfred (ed.), *Re-thinking Sexualities in Africa*, Nordiska Afrika Institutet, Uppsala.

Duggan, L. and N. D. Hunter (1995) *Sex Wars: Sexual Dissent and Political Culture*, Routledge, New York.

Dworkin, A. (1979) *Pornography: Men Possessing Women*, E. P. Dutton, New York.

Ferguson, A. (1984) 'Sex War: the Debate between Radical and Libertarian Feminists', *Signs: Journal of Women in Culture and Society*, Vol. 10, No. 1, pp. 106–12.

Hélie, A. and H. Hoodfar (2012) *Sexuality in Muslim Contexts: Restrictions and Resistance*, Zed Books, London.

Huang Yingying (2007) 'Perspective Matters: Moving Towards Affirmative Thinking on "Xing" in Contemporary China', *Why Affirm Sexuality?* Newsletter, Vol. 13, No. 2, Asian Pacific Research and Resource Centre for Women (ARROW), Kuala Lumpur.

Huang Yingying, Pan Suiming, Peng Tao and Gao Yanning (2009) 'Teaching Sexualities at Chinese Universities: Context, Experience, and Challenges', *International Journal of Sexual Health*, Vol. 21, No. 4, pp. 282–95.

International Planned Parenthood Foundation (2010) *Healthy, Happy and Hot: a Young Person's Guide to their Rights, Sexuality, and Living with HIV*, http://www.ippf.org/NR/rdonlyres/B4462DDE-487D-4194-B0E0-193A04095819/0/HappyHealthyHot.pdf (accessed 13 March 2012).

Jassey, K. and S. Nyanzi (2008) *How to Be a 'Proper' Woman in the Time of AIDS*, Nordiska Afrika Institutet, Uppsala.

Levy, A. (2005) *Female Chauvinist Pigs: Women and the Rise of Raunch Culture*, Simon and Schuster, London.

McFadden, P. (2003) 'Sexual Pleasure as Feminist Choice', *Feminist Africa*, No. 2, pp. 50–60.

Pereira, C. (2003) 'Where Angels Fear to Tread? Some Thoughts on Patricia McFadden's "Sexual Pleasure as Feminist Choice"', *Feminist Africa*, No. 2, pp. 61–5.

Petchesky, R. (2005) 'Rights of the Body and Perversions of War: Sexual Rights and Wrongs Ten Years Past Beijing', *UNESCO's International Social Science Journal*, special issue on Beijing Plus Ten, Vol. 57, No. 2, pp. 301–18.

Philipson, I. (1984) 'The Repression of History and Gender: a Critical Perspective on the Feminist Sexuality Debate', *Signs: Journal of Women in Culture and Society*, Vol. 10, No. 1, pp. 113–25.

Rubin, G. S. (1984) 'Thinking Sex: Notes for a Radical Theory of the Politics of Sexuality', in C. S. Vance (ed.), *Pleasure and Danger: Exploring Female Sexuality*, Routledge, London.

—— (1998) 'Thinking Sex: Notes for a Radical Theory of the Politics of Sexuality', in P. M. Nardi and B. E. Schneider (eds), *Social Perspectives in Lesbian and Gay Studies*, Routledge, New York.

Smith, C. (2010a) 'Review: Papadopoulos, Linda: "Sexualisation of Young People Review", London: Home Office Publication, February 2010', *Participations: Journal of Audience and Reception Studies*, Vol. 7, No. 1, pp. 175–9.

—— (2010b) 'Pornographication: a Discourse for All Seasons', *International Journal of Media and Cultural Politics*, Vol. 6, No. 1, pp. 103–8.

Spronk, R. (2008) 'Beyond Pain: Toward Pleasure in the Study of Sexuality in Africa', *Sexuality in Africa Magazine*, Vol. 4, No. 3, pp. 6–14.

Tepper, M. (2000) 'Sexuality and Disability: the Missing Discourse of Pleasure', *Sexuality and Disability*, Vol. 18, No. 4, pp. 283–90.

The Pleasure Project (2008) *The Global Mapping of Pleasure*, The Pleasure

Project and Realizing Rights Research Programme Consortium, Brighton.

Vance, C. (ed.) (1989) *Pleasure and Danger: Exploring Female Sexuality*, Pandora Press, London.

Vance, C. S. and A. Barr Snitow (1984) 'Toward a Conversation about Sex in Feminism: a Modest Proposal', *Signs: Journal of Women in Culture and Society*, Vol. 10, No. 1, pp. 126–35.

Walter, N. (2011) *Living Dolls: the Return of Sexism*, Virago, London.

WHO (1992) 'The ICD-10 Classification of Mental and Behavioural Disorders: Clinical Descriptions and Diagnostic Guidelines', World Health Organization, Geneva.

Wilson, E. (1983) 'The Context of "Between Pleasure and Danger": the Barnard Conference on Sexuality', *Feminist Review*, No. 13, Spring, pp. 35–41.

1
Thinking with Pleasure
Danger, Sexuality and Agency

Bibi Bakare-Yusuf

The dominant narrative circulating in the world today about women's sexuality, especially African women's sexuality, tends to focus on the more problematic and dangerous aspects – violence, sexual epidemics, population explosion, domination, mutilation, repression and lack of choice. In this narrative, to inhabit an African female body is to live under the daily threat of sexual fear, terror, male rage and violence, disease, psychic suffering and hypersexual reductionism by racist imaginings. Discursively, if not experientially, women's sexuality is rarely if ever conceived outside of this framing.

Of course, no one can deny the many dangers women face and the hetero-patriarchal structures of inequality, violence and moral censure within which women's sexuality is embedded and experienced. Neither can we underestimate the ways in which women's embodied sexuality is brought to the service of the state, power regimes and commodification in the media. Nor can we deny that somewhere, today, many women and girls are being violated sexually, let alone play down the hidden, psychic and visible injuries these violations are causing. As Carole Vance reminds us, 'the threat of male violence is [...] not the only source of sexual danger. Sexuality activates a host of intra-psychic anxieties: fear of merging with another, the blurring of body boundaries and the sense of self that occurs in the tangle of parts and sensations, with attendant fears of dissolution and self-annihilation' (1984: 4–5).

However, to have this as the only hermeneutic paradigm in circulation is both dangerous and paralysing, especially to young women coming to sexual consciousness. Whilst it is important to continue to interrogate and draw attention to patriarchal domination of women's sexuality, we need also to provide their obverse, the counter-narratives to this hegemonic discourse of sexual terrorism. Such counter-narratives must include stories of women's quest for erotic fulfilment, agency, pleasure and desire that transcend discourse of sexual danger. For Vance, in any discussion of female sexuality, we need always to bear in mind two aspects of the female sexual universe: on the one hand, that which represents cohesive power, danger and fear; and on the other, the realm of ecstasy, desire, intimacy, mutuality and pleasure.

In this chapter, I argue that this latter aspect of the female erotic universe is often a precursor, and provides a backdrop, to sexual danger and domination. I also argue that the assertion of women's sexual and embodied agency is potentially more threatening and disruptive to a hetero-patriarchal controlling logic than a focus on danger and violation, hence its repression and suppression. While foregrounding issues around sexual danger and domination continues to be important in our demand for social justice, sexual citizenship rights and freedom, it nonetheless allows for the perpetuation of the idea that women are passive recipients of hetero-masculine prerogatives and therefore in need of protection from normative erotic violence.

This chapter is informed by an existential phenomenological perspective, specifically the work of Maurice Merleau-Ponty and feminists such as Patricia McFadden and Carole Vance, and especially by the latter writer's groundbreaking essay, 'Pleasure and Danger: Toward a Politics of Sexuality' (1984). Across his oeuvre from the *Phenomenology of Perception* (1962) to *The Visible and the Invisible* (1968), Merleau-Ponty is concerned to privilege the role of embodied agency over abstract conceptions of subjectivity. For Merleau-Ponty – and contra Michel Foucault – the body is not simply a passive surface, inscribed by socialization and history and guided by a cognitive realm of knowledge and awareness. Rather, the body is the site of a *precognitive* communication between subject and world, such that the embodied subject is both the recipient of social and environmental signals and the active means of response to those messages. Embodied subjectivity has therefore both passive and active aspects, and works through precognitive operations. Merleau-Ponty's phenomenology therefore provides us with theoretical underpinnings in answering the question of how the embodied realm of sexual pleasure can precede the inscriptive forces of history and hetero-patriarchal socialization, and in contesting theoretical paradigms that privilege passivity and threat over agency and opportunity.

From this theoretical perspective, with its stress on the primacy of the embodied agency of the subject, an overemphasis on sexual harm appears not only to malign but even to erase primary aspects of women's sexual experience, centred around a desire for intimacy, love, curiosity, fantasy, mutuality, respect, adventure and joy. In so doing, sexual terror becomes the foundational experience of women's sexuality, rather than being seen as derivative upon an originary pleasure principle to which the body must now strive to reconnect and re-attune. This prevents us from exploring and fully understanding the inherent contradictions in how our sexuality is psychically, historically and socially organized, lived out and enjoyed.

Sexual danger and fear come to be the dominant interpretive schema for understanding women's lived experience of their own sexual agency. This foundational logic has the unwitting effect of repeating the patriarchal script, which attempts to present women as passive victims. Positioning women as weak or damaged subjects gives renewed legitimacy to patriarchally motivated discourses of control and protection. What this does is to set artificial limits on how we talk about women's sexual agency in experiential, political, social and symbolic terms. It thereby circumscribes the production of meaning and the development of alternative narratives that attempt to portray and articulate female lived experience – today and in years to come.

But most debilitating of all, we lose our capacity to resist and change our situation, and to imagine new horizons of possibilities around sexual safety, choice, autonomy and pleasure.

It is within this context of the over-determination of danger in African female sexual discourse that Patricia McFadden's call to privilege sexual pleasure as a tool for political engagement becomes important and powerful. McFadden suggests that we should step back from the deafening noise surrounding the spectre of disease, death and dread in order to reclaim women's 'agency and begin to move beyond the horrifying places to which sexual domination has driven many women' (McFadden 2003: 1). Such a move allows us to begin to explore the complexity and richness of women's sexuality that, on the one hand, already takes into consideration the need to eliminate sexual danger, disease and domination, and, on the other, is first and foremost motivated by intimacy, yearning and the exploration of desire, fantasy, pleasure and power, where human connections are formed, and where bodily encounters give birth to new cultural configurations and empowered femininity.

Of course, we might choose not to explore these complex emotions, but the point is to see that our sexualities ought not to be first experienced as a violation, negation or lack (even though it is often the case for many women), but as joyful, pleasurable modes of agency and being-in-the-world. It is therefore necessary to understand and bring into critical discourse and practice how women's lived experience of their sexualities contains 'elements of pleasure and oppression, happiness and humiliation' (Vance 1984: 6). It is precisely because our sexualities are often experienced and aligned so closely to these complex and contradictory emotions – which are both so intimate and at the same time public in their framing by social rules, values and harm – that we need to highlight the intimate, emotional and pleasurable dimensions of our sexualities. In this way, women do not fall into a sexual paralysis occasioned by the controlling script of danger and oppression.

If women were allowed to express themselves freely, this would mean that they might elude male control. That would confirm that there is an aspect of desire in the world beyond hetero-patriarchal control. And this threatens the foundation of patriarchy itself. You might ask: how does a desiring woman seeking the fulfilment of her own pleasure threaten patriarchal hegemony? For heuristic purposes let's accept that the heterosexual male is the head of the family and he is in charge of his wife, children and sisters, and that the whole of society is built upon this family model. The ideal is that the male householder is in control of all that takes place in his domain, including the bodies and sexualities of those in his household. Now, imagine if the wife of household A is having an affair with the husband (or wife) in household B. In this case, the husband of household A is no longer in control of his own household. It is easy to see the linkages among households and the rapidly ramifying principle of inter-connectedness. It is not as if, when one woman strays, the consequences are confined to one household. It is rather the case that the straying immediately involves multiple emotional stresses for another household, and as soon as there is a relationship with another household, you have a potential domino effect where everything falls apart – the symbolic and existential stability of the household structure is threatened.

To show more concretely how female sexual desire can contest patriarchal control when monogamy is not normative, let us draw on some anecdotal examples from my experience of talking to Yoruba women in south-western Nigeria from across a range of social, age and educational backgrounds. I have noticed that amongst groups of women who do not conform rigidly to evangelical or Pentecostal forms of Christianity, as with their husbands, monogamy is not a lived normativity. For a variety of reasons to do with women's increasing economic vulnerability, the social pressure to marry 'right and up', and women's own desire for emotional reciprocity and erotic fulfilment, we can observe some women having long-term relationships with multiple male partners to address these stresses: the symbolic husband on display for formal events, social legitimacy and inheritance rights for children, but marked by the absence of erotic or emotional connection; the 'man friend' for romantic and erotic ecstasy; and the 'cash daddy' for economic security. This fluid and complex agency in the context of intimate relationships goes hand in hand with traditions of strong expectation for women's economic autonomy in Yorubaland; we can point to the role of women in organizing and controlling the markets of Lagos as an obvious example that frames this horizon of expectation. It is in this socio-economic and cultural context that we see patriarchal conventions eroded in the face of alternative ways of being that privilege the agency and assertiveness of women.

By examining counter-examples such as non-monogamous practices among Yoruba women, we can see that the traditional patriarchal family unit is structured in part by desire: the desire of the male head of household, who gives directives and tries to control other desires in the household and society. However, when that desire is threatened or undermined by another that is outside of the dominant libidinal economy, we then see efforts to suppress this rival desire to ensure that it doesn't get out of control. In the case of female non-monogamy in the Yoruba context, the relative economic power of some women means that these (male) efforts are often ineffective and are tacitly contested, which can sometimes lead to male frustration and violence. However, when outcomes are influenced by the Christian theological archetype introduced through the colonial encounter and transformed and reconfigured by evangelical strains in the post-structural adjustment era of the 1980s, the suppression is more successful. Archetypal figures like Eve – the mother of desire in the Judaeo-Christian context and also the originary succubus figure – are often erased in history. When they are not effaced, other accommodating aspects of their personae are highlighted – such as their role as the mother, the nurturer or the fertility goddess, as in the case of Yoruba archetypal figures such as Osun. Contrary to the dominant discourse of Osun as a fertility goddess, there is a sense within the semiotic matrix of Osun that she is also the lodestone of female sexual desire. After all, coitus is what leads to fertility and reproduction, and not the other way round. Osun, as the deity of the water, can be reworked as the archetype of erotic moistness, yearning and plenitude, prior to birthing and regenerative functions. In this respect, both Osun and Eve can manifest alternative ideas about female desire from within the two cultures that birth them. The Oshogbo festival – devoted to the celebration of women's erotic agency and fertility – is still going strong, centuries after Eve has been expunged from the garden.

In many ways, emphasizing the dangerous aspects of sexuality whilst repressing female sexual agency and pleasure becomes an important means for patriarchal reproduction and continuity to reassert itself. It is precisely because patriarchal cultures understand and anticipate the fundamentality of women's erotic desire and pleasure in human reproduction that they must try and suppress its expression. Therefore, each time we focus only on violation and neglect to narrate the fundamentality of ·female erotic desire, we unwittingly align ourselves to an ultra-conservative, theological imperative requiring that women's active pleasure remains hidden.

The founding story of Christianity invokes a sacred form of desire, in the figures of Adam and Eve. But they are immediately cast out of the garden because Eve commits the original sin of bringing desire, both into the sacred space and into the world. An interesting tension at the heart of Christianity is that desire manifests itself at the outset and is immediately cast out. At the moment of desire's coming to presence, it leads to expulsion. Fertility must be excised from any relation to an originary female-centred desire or action. From the outset in Christianity's creation myth, sacred desire is framed as the taboo that must always lead to desacralization; desire belongs to the world of the fallen, not within the realm of the sacred. It therefore becomes imperative that in Christian iconography and discourse, female desire doesn't ever gain coherent meaning or expression. Eve worship is a non-starter within orthodox Christianity; her role as a potential archetype must be masked by the veneration of the Virgin Mary. In order to continue to sustain the myth of reproduction without erotic desire or encounter, it is necessary to build a case for Mary's miraculous conception, free of coitus. Whether through the erasure of Eve, the founding principle of female desire, or via Mary's non-sexual reproduction, we begin to see how patriarchy is hard-wired into Christianity and therefore into the colonial project. The erasure of Eve in Christian discourse amounts to only one thing: the elimination of an originary female desire in favour of patriarchy.

For societies that have been subsumed under the panoptical gaze of Christian colonialism, we begin to see that for female sexual agency to attain coherence, we need to make visible the absence – a female-centred desiring principle – structuring hetero-patriarchal power. If we posit another source of desire or originary desire – the female – it acts as competition and resistance to male originary desire. Occluding female originary desire thus helps to reduce the opportunities for resistance. In other words, if female sexual pleasure and desire is highlighted, the supremacy of male desire, power and control is called into question. Not only are masculinity and patriarchy exposed as unstable, but they are also shown to be a set of iterative performances which must continuously construct a narrative around their own primacy and, in so doing, position women as requiring protection from the excessive desires of other men. This is why many men (across cultures and religion) recoil in the presence of a full-on desiring woman (yet others are turned on specifically by this transgression). It is therefore necessary to repress narratives about female sexual pleasure and deny their full expression.

Focusing on women's sexual pleasure does not erase or negate our quest for social justice, equity, economic rights, political access and participation; nor does it put an end to domination and oppression in all its guises, or 'weaken the critique of sexual danger' (Vance 1984: 3). Rather, what it does is to 'expand the analysis of pleasure' and return us to the erotic embodied agency that is a central part of women's lived experience – a part that patriarchal culture tries to muffle, circumscribe and reduce to passivity through a litany of violations and intrusions. It also allows us to imagine a new way of constituting female sexuality that does not take victimhood and violation as foundational. Instead, the primacy of women's quest for erotic fulfilment and joy becomes the springboard for demanding and creating a safer space and modes of relating across gender difference where violation is not always already inscribed in the body or scripted in how we relate with and navigate the world.

Focusing on female sexuality has the potential to unsettle patriarchal power with its fears about unruly autonomous female desire and action. Patricia McFadden is therefore right to talk about women's erotic pleasure as being potentially more scary and destabilizing than focusing on their violation because it directly challenges patriarchal culture's hostility towards women's sexual agency. To privilege women's pleasure, joy, desire, quest for intimacy and movement towards the other is to flip the dominant script we hear and sometimes find ourselves telling about women's sexual lives. All of this in no way denies the many dangers that many women live through and are confronted with on a daily basis. Nor does it lessen the urgency with which, as activists, we seek to expose the social, economic, political and semiotic violations of women's lived realities. Rather, our narrative shows that there is no inevitability or primacy to the sexual danger script. That script itself can be reconfigured, re-experienced and rechannelled differently when we take control of the kind of story we tell about our sexualities.

Telling stories, thinking with pleasure

Our continued investment in stories (as important as they are) where sexual terror and violation predominate is making us sick and it is erasing the positive and life-affirming sexual experience of many women in the world today. In his book *A Way of Being Free*, poet and novelist Ben Okri wrote, 'A people are as healthy and confident as the stories they tell themselves. Sick storytellers can make their nations sick. And sick nations make for sick storytellers' (1997: 109–10). The kinds of stories we tell about our sexual lives are important. Telling positive stories about women's sexual lives matters because it helps to restore what previously has been maligned and objectified; they can empower and remind us that women's sexual universe is not simply a litany of errors, negations, fears and terrors. The right to sexual pleasure, curiosity, exploration, joy, intimacy, reciprocity, love and longing are all part of what it means to be a sexual being. Sexual negation as the main sexual narrative of women's experience must be resisted and challenged. We must always present it as a violating anomaly in our lived sexual universe, even if its occurrence has taken on the appearance of normativity.

Stories of desire, of pleasure and of love are important narratives for women to hear in a hostile environment because these stories shape us and who we can become. Okri again reminds us that stories 'are the secret reservoir of values: change the stories individuals or nations live by and tell themselves, and you change the individuals and nations' (1997: 112). Telling and circulating women's stories of desiring pleasures and of sexual ecstasy provides the possibility of telling a different kind of narrative that doesn't privilege domination, rape, physical harm, and violation. Such stories make it possible to recontextualize or re-embed negating or violating experiences within a redemptive discourse of new forms of storytelling. If we don't privilege the fundamentality of our capacity for joy, pleasure, love and desire towards one another, then our struggle to end sexual danger becomes futile and we lose focus on why we are doing what we are doing. We become powerless in the face of these powerful violating narratives and experiences. We come to exist in a precarious relationship to our bodies and our desires.

Telling stories about female sexual pleasure, agency and power allows us to uncover a tradition and community of powerful, feisty, indomitable women who will not be cowed by oppression or violation. In this way, we begin to show that violation is not the blueprint for women's sexual experience, rather, it is an example of agency gone awry. By telling a different story, still with the understanding that danger is always a potentiality that

The erotic project: commissioning brief

We know so little about our sexual fantasies. Despite the ubiquity of sex in Africa, our writers have not sufficiently explored it in their writings. Sex is one of the most important and mysterious areas of our lives. What we do and who we are when our naked body is entwined with another is a part of us that we generally don't share with the world. Sex can be and is often the place we go to in search of solace, healing, ecstasy and exploration of our most precious fantasies. The erotic can also be dangerous and traumatic. This is why we are both fascinated and frightened by our own longing for sex. Women's sexual universe has become a cultural taboo, so much so that we try to hide the pleasure and ecstasy we derive from it by pretending that it is dirty, ungodly or reducing it only to its reproductive function or the opportunity for disease. As if it was ever really about that.

We believe that a lot of people are interested in sex and sensuality and they want to read good writing that explores sex in a fun, witty and knowledgeable way.

We are inviting established and upcoming African women writers to contribute stories about sex. Not love or relationships, but tell us the truth about sex in all its forms in an honest and sexy way. We are looking for stories that actively subvert and disrupt our ideas about erotic desire. We want stories that are funny, serious, playful and provocative, ranging in styles and tones. We are looking for stories that will cause arousal, yes, but also stories that explore the joy, pain, pleasure, agony, intimacy, and the ecstasy of sex. We have only three rules a) the stories must appeal to the largest sexual organ – the brain; b) it must be well written; and c) the central protagonist must be an African woman.

must be contested, we are providing a different beginning and therefore a different ending to what it means to be a sexual being in the world. Our sexuality becomes a positive experience of becoming attuned to our own aliveness and mortality in relation to others and the world around us. The quest for joy, intimacy, dreaming and desiring pleasure precedes any form of negation.

This is why Cassava Republic Press, a publishing press I co-founded based in Abuja, Nigeria, is compiling a collection of erotic stories by African women writers. The decision to compile these stories is to provide examples of the interiority of women's erotic imagination, so that other women can reconnect with their own erotic core and begin to see that violation or danger is not the grammar of women's erotic life.

The moment we allow ourselves to see pleasure as preceding violation, it becomes possible to reframe violation into a redemptive discourse or narrative. And once you do so you are taking the sting out of it. So, for example, rather than viewing rape or violation as the dissolution of one's world or as an opportunity to retreat from the world, that experience can be recontextualized in terms of a bigger project of one's life. The subject of rape is invited to think about moments in their life when they have felt joy or try to imagine what a positive sexual encounter might be. It is by privileging pleasure, desire and joy that we come to see sexual danger not as an overarching force that has already happened or is done to women. Negating sexual experience can be reconstituted so that we can return to that place of erotic agency where we take control and ownership of our bodies and the contours of our desires.

If we don't ground our experience in pleasure, desire, eros, intimacy and mutuality, it means that we are locked into a discourse we cannot escape. For example, if we think about the death of a loved one simply as loss and absence, then we experience their death only as finitude and the end of the other. However, if their death is recontextualized in terms of the narrative of absence *and* presence, the absence itself becomes viewed as a form of presence as we remember aspects of their life, the laughter in their eyes, their voice and their passions echoing through our hearts. Death becomes a renewed vitality that becomes an opening towards re-memory, action and being-in-the-world. People who are no longer here can become a form of invigoration for those who are alive. The point of all this is to say that recontextualization and redemption is always possible even in the most harrowing situation. But this redemption can only be possible if there's a prior narrative of positive relationship to one's sexuality or those around us.

Conclusion

There is no necessity and inevitability to violation or danger. To think *with* pleasure allows one to embrace the fundamentality of pleasure in structuring and motivating our embodied experience and erotic encounters. When you think with pleasure first of all you are relativizing the perspective of conscious rational thought in relation to the pre-conscious habitus, the pre-cognitive layers of meaning sedimented within us that inform the way we think and do things before we even do them. Thinking with pleasure allows us to think consciously about the fact that a lot of what takes place around our sexuality comes before thinking.

Thinking with pleasure allows us to see through the patriarchal imprint on our sexual desire that tries to erase the pleasure principle. Thinking with pleasure allows us to see that the individual libido is part of a libidinal economy which tries to impose rules and values on felt bodily experience. What I desire and with whom has implications for the world. It is precisely because what I desire has ramifications for the world that it is considered dangerous and therefore must be repressed. Patriarchal cultures must work to suppress and limit women's bodies by policing women's comportment, sartorial choices, movement in public spaces and participation in political life and the generation of meaning. This patriarchal delimitation includes the reduction of women's sexual agency within discourses framed around fear, violence and safety. This is why asserting the primacy of women's erotic agency and pleasure through new (and rediscovered old) ways of telling our stories can be so powerful.

References

McFadden, P. (2003) 'Sexual Pleasure as a Feminist Choice', *Feminist Africa*, No. 2, pp. 17.

Merleau-Ponty, M. (1962) *Phenomenology of Perception,* translated by Colin Smith, Routledge and Kegan, London.

—— (1968) *The Visible and the Invisible,* Northwestern University Press, Evanston.

Okri, B. (1997) *A Way of Being Free*, Phoenix House, London.

Vance, C. S. (1984) 'Pleasure and Danger: Toward a Politics of Sexuality', in C. S. Vance (ed.), *Pleasure and Danger: Exploring Female Sexuality*, Routledge and Kegan Paul, London.

2

Challenging the Pleasure versus Danger Binary

Reflections on Sexuality Workshops with Rural Women's Rights Activists in North India

Jaya Sharma

Whenever I heard the word sexuality, I used to feel strange.... During the first workshop, I felt shy but excited. I found certain things funny, felt nice inside.... The discussions were so open, about different acts, about our bodies and our lives. I liked hearing about sexuality. I realized that others don't have access to such information. People in our organization used to say these are *sugli-sugli baatan* (bad things). We thought that women in the village would turn around and hit us if we talked about such things! But actually they talk about sex anyway. They sing dirty songs during weddings and *holi* [Hindu spring festival]. They have the freedom to sing such songs on these occasions. But they cannot talk about it openly otherwise.

Kesari Bai is an Indian activist who has been fighting for women's rights and the rights of Dalits (people marginalized on the basis of their caste) for over three decades. She works with a feminist community-based NGO in Rajasthan, a state in the western part of India. Kesari – the woman who had taken on a fierce battle with 'upper caste' people in her village to be able to draw water from the same well, who has led many a rescue operation, literally bursting into homes and getting back children of women who had left abusive husbands – was the same Kesari, who after going through a series of trainings on sexuality, confessed to being very, very nervous about conducting a workshop on the subject with women from the community.

Kesari was one of the participants in 'Younikta aur Hum' (Sexuality and Us), a programme shared by five organizations working at the community level in different states of north India. Aimed at building perspectives on sexuality in a manner both positive and political, the programme was initiated by Nirantar, a women's NGO which has been working on issues of gender and education since its inception in 1993 and on issues of sexuality since 2007.

Kesari's words and experience capture much of why and what I, and Nirantar, would like to share about this initiative. In all, thirteen workshops were conducted in which over 300 women participated: approximately 100 staff members of partner organizations, and 200 rural women linked to village-level women's collectives with whom the organizations worked. The programme constitutes one of the first efforts in the Indian context to build perspectives on sexuality through workshops, with women from rural, poor communities as well as the organizations that work with them, in an intensive manner. The initiative stemmed from a context in which interventions aimed at the rights of women from poorer communities have tended not to address sexual rights. The trainings helped us understand better why players in gender and development fear working on issues of sexuality and the ways in which they relate to women from socially and economically marginalized communities. This chapter presents some of the insights we have gained, based on documentation of the trainings, an external review of the impact, and on my personal experience as a facilitator in the trainings.

Why women's organizations are not engaging with sexuality in positive ways

Women's movements have waged vital and all-out battles against sexual violence and sexual harassment. However, particularly in the global South, they have tended not to engage with more positive aspects of sexual rights. Within the broader realm of sexual rights, dynamic movements for the rights of lesbian, gay, bisexual, transgender and queer (LGBTQ) people have been struggling and growing in different parts of the world. There has not, however, always been a strong synergy either within sections of the LGBTQ movements, or between these movements and the women's movement. An engagement with sexuality and sexual rights – not circumscribed by the logic of any particular other agenda, not linked to particular identities and not limited to its negative dimension – is rare.

There is a need to understand why women's groups and NGOs have not engaged with sexuality, and in particular its more positive aspects. One reason is that rights have tended to be viewed in terms of a hierarchy, with issues related to poverty and violence against women being placed at the top of the hierarchy of rights of poor communities. This perspective does not take into account the significance of each of the dimensions of our lived realities. Considering some rights to be more important than others fragments life into dimensions that reflect this ordering. The framework of a hierarchy of rights fails to recognize the indivisibility of rights. Within this larger problem of fragmenting rights, relegating sexuality to the bottom of the hierarchy reflects a particular attitude towards poor people, which tends to consider them as asexual beings who do not have sexual needs. Yet in other contexts – and this is an interesting reversal – there is a tendency to view the poor as hypersexual.

Many women's movement activists are embarrassed or uncomfortable when talking about sexuality. These 'personal' anxieties need to be understood in terms of the larger 'political' context that constructs sexual desire (other than in the context of reproduction within marriage), and therefore the realm of sexuality, as being 'bad' or 'dirty'. There are also of course patriarchal constructs that ensure that women, including women activists, do not think about their own desires.

One of the fears expressed in our workshops was that talking about issues of sexuality would invite the label of being a 'bad woman'. Within the realm of sexuality, homosexuality was seen as being a particularly tricky subject. As one of the respondents said, 'I was afraid that if we talk about homosexuality my programme will be shaken up.' Others feared that discussing sexuality would challenge hierarchies and upset the relationships that colleagues had built with each other. This fear did seem to be borne out by the trainings. Sexuality seemed to reduce power hierarchies, including those between facilitators and participants. Perhaps this is partly because we all have irrational, unresolved issues of sexuality that we are grappling with. As facilitators we were sometimes anxious about sharing aspects of our sexuality that might be considered non-normative. We found that often it was something that a participant said that gave us the courage to speak about ourselves. As part of one of the introductory activities each of us had to share two examples – a norm that we have challenged in our life, and a norm to which we have subscribed. With respect to the norms that I had challenged, at the first workshop I spoke about how I chose not to get married, despite pressure from the family. At a later workshop, a participant before me, a young woman from a small town who worked at the community level, spoke about desiring a woman as the norm she had broken and this inspired me to 'come out' about being bisexual. At another workshop, it was when a participant spoke about being in a relationship with a man who was also involved with another woman that I decided to share that I was at the time in an open relationship as the norm that I had broken.

Brokering conversations about sexuality and pleasure

Food and sex

One of the most popular and effective ways in which we talked about core ideas related to sex and sexuality was through food. Rural women often described a need for sex as *shareer ki bhook* – hunger of the body. One of the participants spoke, for example, of how if one wants to eat five *rotis* (pieces of bread) and gets only two, one will have to find the other three, even take them from a neighbour if necessary. On the other hand if a woman is forced to eat seven *rotis* she will suffer from indigestion. As facilitators, we also asked participants a series of questions related to food. What do you like eating the most? What do you dislike most in food? Has your taste in food ever changed? Have you learnt how to cook anything new? The patterns in the answers emerged clearly.

First there was the amazing diversity in tastes. Once participants got into the mood, there were elaborate discussions about preferences. Often there was a reason behind a preference – because of where someone lives, what is culturally acceptable or required in terms of religion, gender, caste, region or class. It was also clear that our taste in food changes. Often participants shared stories that made clear why their taste had changed while recounting food memories. Many a time an aversion turned into a preference. Although sometimes there was no reason for a change of taste in food, there were many factors that emerged, such as gender, for example. One of the participants said it was particularly difficult for her to pursue her desires related to food because she started living in a joint, extended family after she got married. She also had to change her style of cooking dishes according to the preferences of members of her marital home. At this point in the discussion, another participant asked whether we cook to please others or ourselves. 'To please our husbands of course,' said someone. Another participant said, 'Even though I cook according to the tastes of others in the family, when it comes to sweet things, I cook according to my own preference.'

The pattern-seeking related to our tastes in food led into a discussion about whether we saw any similarities with sexuality. One participant shared that her mother had told her 'Don't eat good food. If your body is healthy you'll have greater desires, so keep yourself thin.' In one of the workshops, the commonalities that emerged included diversity – 'the possibilities in both are limitless', said a participant in one of the workshops. Another commonality which emerged was 'what I like, you might hate' – just as true for sex as it is for food. Sexual desire and taste in food are both fluid, they can change: this was yet another commonality. We built upon these similarities to argue that although sexuality, like food and taste, seems to be natural and instinctive it is socially constructed. Again like taste in food, sexual desire seems to be located in the domain of the body, the biological, but it is influenced by gender, class, region, and a host of other factors.

Despite the many commonalities, significant differences between food and sexuality also emerged. We can't talk about sex with the ease with which we can talk about our habits and preferences related to food. Differences in tastes related to food are by and large tolerated (although food can also assume great symbolic importance in certain politically charged situations, such as when there is a clash of religious identities). However, differences in sexual tastes can evoke violations ranging from censure in the form of taunts to extreme violence including murder.

Interrogating the notion of 'good' and 'bad' women

One activity that we used in our workshops was a game of snakes and ladders. If the dice thrown by a participant landed on the mouth of a snake, a statement was read out – such as 'You continue your relationship with a man from a different caste despite opposition from the family', or 'You are a widow in a sexual relationship with a lover from your youth' and other statements which represented breaking sexual norms and being punished for them. When players landed at the bottom of a ladder, the statements that were read out included – 'You were attracted to the woman who lived next door but you suppressed your desire', or 'Yet again you do what your husband likes during sex, even if you don't like it.'

We inverted the rule of winning and losing. The player who wins is the one who is the lowest on the board – that is, the one who has been pursuing her desires and breaking sexual norms. The 'winner' was garlanded with a placard – 'Leader of the alliance of bad women'. The expressions on the faces of winners were inevitably confused – there was happiness at winning the game but grave discomfort at being the bad woman who had broken sexual norms. How the winner felt on winning became one of the important points of reflection after the game. Why are we so uncomfortable with being labelled bad women, when all that we are doing is pursuing our desires? This was the question that we left the participants to ponder.

The right to say 'Yes!'

We drew into the programme an important lesson gained during an earlier workshop on gender and sexuality conducted by Nirantar with non-formal education teachers in rural Rajasthan. There had been a discussion on a scene in a documentary film in which a group of young boys talk amongst themselves about their sexual experiences with girls. One of the boys comments on girls' responses and says that even when girls say 'no' they actually mean 'yes'. This was a comment that resonated strongly with the male teachers in the workshop. One of the women teachers, however, said:

> If a woman says 'no' to a man who makes a pass at her, it is common for him to dismiss that by saying 'When a woman says no, she actually means yes.' And if a woman says 'yes' to a man who has expressed interest in her, she will immediately be labelled a 'loose' woman. Women don't have the space to say yes, even when they want to. This opens up the space for men who are rebuffed to invalidate women when they say no.

The discussion concluded with the insight that women will have the right to say 'no' only if they have the right to say 'yes'.

In two workshops there were discussions related to the extent to which heterosexual women are able to initiate sex with men and what happens if they do. In both instances, the discussions began on a negative footing. The tenor of the discussions was that women are not able to initiate sex and, if they do, they suffer negative consequences. As facilitators we tried to open up the possibility for the conversation to take a more positive turn if needed. We found that, in both cases, the discussions turned more and more towards instances of how women do initiate sex, and often find that men tend not to have a problem with this. As one of the participants said, 'They want it anyway, so why will they mind it?'

The programme evaluation found that respondents felt that women should be encouraged to initiate sex if they wanted it. One respondent described her first time initiating sex with her husband after attending the workshops, clearly challenging the idea of the woman being 'passive' and the man being 'active': '*I went to my husband and said to him, "I want to have sex with you." He replied, "Where did the sun rise this morning? How did this happen to you?" … Now, if I have a desire, then I will have sex. Earlier he was the only one initiating sex.*'

An effort was made to build an understanding of social norms as rules laid down by mainstream society, which we are expected to follow but which we have some leeway to negotiate. This was established by evoking and drawing upon personal experiences in different contexts, including but not limited to those concerning sexuality. In one of the workshops, the discussion on desires was on the verge of turning into a victim narrative. It seemed as though sexual norms were dictating entirely the choices that people were making in their lives. At this point one of the younger participants, who was a staff member, turned around and said 'But … we do find a way, somehow, don't we, to fulfil our desires.' Understanding the norms that we were all negotiating created the space for the recognition of agency and not only violations. This was an empowering realization, and much closer to the experiences being shared than a discourse of complete victimization.

The approach, which was not always easy to traverse, of highlighting 'agency' as well as the oppressive nature of social norms was an effort to bridge the binary of 'pleasure' and 'danger'. Usually sexuality is either celebrated as being 'positive' or it gets dominated by a 'negative', violations-oriented approach (Vance 1989). We did not want to fall into this trap. We tried to talk about desire, pleasure and agency and at the same time to analyse why sexual rights are denied and why punishments are meted out to those who break sexual norms.

Overcoming caution with laughter

Although there was a highly open, positive, intimate and often fun-filled atmosphere when we discussed sex, we as participants and trainers did not talk much about our personal sexual lives. We were overly cautious. For example, in the first workshop there was a session on sexual fantasies in which everyone, including the trainers, wrote their fantasies on pieces of paper, which they then put in the middle of the room. As trainers, we made sure to give instructions that participants did not have to write their names. The person doing the documentation was chosen as the one to read out the fantasies. This was to reassure the participants that the person reading the slips of paper would not be able to recognize anyone's handwriting. We need not have worried so much about anonymity because immediately after the activity, during the tea break, many participants giggled and laughed, saying 'I know which one was yours ...', including to the trainers!

Humour played an important role in creating an environment to engage with issues of sexuality relatively free from inhibitions. Humour was not 'adopted' as a conscious strategy but it turned out that we had loads of fun, laughed a lot, and that this helped not just the participants but also the trainers to deal with inhibitions about talking sex and sexuality. I for one was someone who could speak endlessly about issues about sexuality, but sex was another matter. Over the course of the first workshop itself, I found myself laughing uncontrollably about sex and using words related to sex in fun, crazy ways, with participants. This was an empowering experience. The energy we all experienced during the workshops, which participants linked explicitly to empower-ment, owed much to this humour.

Marriage

The workshops addressed ideologies as well as structures, in-cluding the institution of marriage. Participants were asked to list the advantages and disadvantages of marriage. In workshops with community women, one of the advantages listed was that marriage secures housing. A trainer from the partner NGO commented, 'When we commit a "mistake", even a small one, we might be thrown out of the house. If someone from my family, like if my sister, wants to come to stay in my house because of her studies, she can't. After marriage we can't go and stay in our parents' house. The house in which we grew up becomes *paraya* [belonging to the "other"].' The benefits of marriage emerged clearly as being fragile and conditional.

Capturing some of the shifts in perspective with respect to marriage, one participant said, 'In the past I thought marriage was the end all and be all. And I always helped (*sic*) single girls by getting them married without asking them. Now I understand that it's not everything. It should be her wish.'

Sex acts

Another example that might help illustrate how the programme sought to approach sexuality is that of listing sex acts. As part of this, participants were divided into small groups and a competition ensued to list all the possible sex acts that group members could think of. This highly animated activity yielded lists that went up to 50 or even over 60 acts. It also led to discussions about why, when there are so many sexual acts, penile-vaginal sex is the only one that has legitimacy. We introduced the concept of the sexual hierarchy (Rubin 1998), with penile-vaginal sex on top and all other acts at varying distance from the pinnacle of respectability. People participating in acts lower down the hierarchy, including those who enjoy anal and oral sex, evoke a wide range of violations including silencing, censure, taunts and social pressures to conform. Through this, we moved seamlessly from a highly fun, pleasure-oriented activity to talking about these political dimensions.

The instruction given to participants was that only acts, not the sex of the people performing the acts, were to be listed. This enabled participants to see that there is just one act that can be performed only by a man and a woman; that is the penetration of the vagina by the penis. Other sexual acts can be performed between people of the same sex.

Larger lessons from the programme

Violence against women

Sexuality is fundamentally linked to gender-based violence. *Why* women experience violence, *how* they experience it and *whether* they can exit from the violence are all closely linked to sexuality. It is significant that most of the staff members who participated in the programme have been directly involved in dealing with cases of violence against women for around a decade. Time and again participants said that sexuality was at the heart of the vast majority of cases of violence against women that came to their organizations.

In India sexuality has only been recognized as part of violence against women in the case of sexual violence. But sexuality can be a cause of violence – for example, if women break sexual norms, such as single women, widowed women, sex workers, women who desire women and women who have sexual relationships outside of marriage. Sexuality is also a factor that influences women's ability to exit abusive relationships. For example, one participant explained:

> There is a woman I know whose husband sold their house, married another woman and began living with her. He occasionally comes to visit the first wife and continues to be violent with her. Despite this, the woman does not want to leave him. She says, 'My husband beats me a lot, but he also loves me. Physical happiness drives away all the pain.'

An NGO worker gave her analysis:

> In case work, we see that sexuality is a need. Women are told they can experience sexuality only with their husbands. Many women will stand up in court and talk about difficulties in their relationships. But at the end of the day, they'll compromise and go back to husbands

who torture them. Women also have sexual needs. They say, 'We have a need, where will we go?'

Perceptions and socialization also determine what women regard as 'violence'. Non-normative sexual acts that male partners expect women to participate in are often considered by women to be 'unnatural'. Examples that emerged during the workshops included husbands expecting the wife to remove clothes during sex. The man wanting to perform anal sex and to have oral sex performed on him were cited as frequent reasons for seeking help among women who approach violence against women programmes. In many cases, the very expectation of such acts was considered a violation, and in other cases the husband coerced the wife into these acts against her will. Participants explained how when a woman comes to them with the complaint that her husband tries to make her have anal or oral sex, they have counselled both the woman and the man. They have made clear to the husband that he cannot coerce his wife and that it is only if he is able to make the act desirable for the woman that it can be engaged in. They also counselled the woman by saying that there is nothing wrong with any particular act, as long as it involves the consent of those involved and that perhaps she also needs to explore what she might or might not find pleasurable. Because understanding what you find pleasurable is a first step toward achieving that pleasure.

Sexuality is connected to women's empowerment

The workshops helped not only participants but also us as trainers to understand the many and important ways in which sexuality links with women's empowerment. It came as a surprise to us when members of organizations extremely active in women's rights for many years came to the workshop and said that 'finally' they were being able to 'think about ourselves' and not just others. After all, these were activists who have experienced many changes in their lives and being able to 'think about ourselves' is very much part of feminist politics. Why was it that participating in workshops on sexuality was triggering such a comment? To win the battles against other forms of discrimination and injustice, we have perhaps had to maintain our image, and self-image, as respectable activists. These battles have, after all, often been waged at great personal cost, including confrontations with the family and community. Perhaps sexuality represented being able to 'think about ourselves'.

A sense of liberation can be the outcome of creating a space to talk about women's desires. One participant said:

> I'm a villager. I didn't know anything when I came for the workshop. At first I felt angry. I told [my coworker], 'You shouldn't have brought me to such a meeting.' After three days of training I started understanding that this means something. That it's not right that we don't have rights over our body. I began to like it. I learned all these things. Everyone was sharing … we talked about masturbation, oral sex … I didn't know about this, how it happens. When I returned, I said, 'You should have sent me years ago.'

Another reported, 'After this training I felt freer. I feel lighter. If I have to talk to someone, I feel I can do that.' Yet another respondent said, 'The difference is that I did the same thing before – talk to men … but before I used to feel scared of what people would say and whether I am doing the right thing.'

Conclusion

Our work with rural women taught us that there are clear links between sexuality, empowerment and pleasure. The workshops provided the space for an articulation of the linkages between sexuality and a range of women's rights, in relation not only to bodily integrity and desires, but also to rights in areas such as education, health and mobility. In several workshops participants spoke about how a sense of shame, which is strongly inflected by sexuality in terms of parts of the body that are considered to be sexual, prevents women from talking about diseases from which they suffer. In one of the workshops, a participant spoke about how her aunt had felt a lump on her own breast, but did not go to the doctor because of a sense of shame. It turned out to be cancer, from which she eventually died.

Several participants spoke about how girls are forced to drop out of school, typically at the age of ten or eleven, because the next level of school is a few kilometres away from the village. Parents fear that the girl will have sex on the way to school and/ or that she might become pregnant. These fears, in the way that they are articulated (*kahin unch neech na ho jaye* – something 'untoward' should not happen), do not make the distinction between whether the sexual encounter is consensual or not. Women not being allowed to go out at night, in particular, was clearly seen as being linked not only with the fear of sexual assault but also, and perhaps more so, with the fear that the woman might be meeting a man with whom she was sexually involved.

There is more space now for women to talk about violations and for these to be addressed. To reach the stage where women can begin to talk about the violence they face and for this to have legitimacy, has taken the women's movement years of struggle. More NGOs than ever before are working on violence against women. The state, too, has been pushed to enact a law on domestic violence. However it is also true that a majority of women who experience violence are perhaps unable to report it, for a variety of reasons related to gender and sexuality. Therefore it is not as though violence against women has been addressed and we can now 'move on' to look at desire. It is not violence versus sexual desire. Sexuality and violence against women are fundamentally linked and it is essential to address desires in order to address violence against women more effectively.

The work increased our confidence in the possibility and desirability of approaching sexuality in a manner that captures its complexities and nuances. There is no 'dumbing down' of concepts of sexuality required. We worked with ideas of sexuality and gender as being socially constructed, fluid, and as part of a continuum. We sought to build an understanding of 'why' sexual norms exist in the form that they do. Linkages were made between sexuality and structures and ideologies related to gender, caste, class, dis/ability and religion. Participants engaged with the significance of identities based on gender and sexuality as well as the dangers of narrowly defined identity-based frameworks.

The workshops also showed us that it is important not to set up a false binary between 'pleasure' and 'danger'. Even interventions related to gender-based violence, for example, need to be informed by a positive approach to sexuality. It was clear that a positive approach to sexuality is necessary if interventions are to fully understand and be informed by 'why' there is gender-based violence, 'how' violence is being experienced, 'whether' women can exit from the violence and 'who' is currently being included or excluded from interventions arising from violence against women.

If this work is so necessary and powerful, why aren't there more conversations about sexuality and women's empowerment? As feminist activists, we have been able to challenge many forms of discrimination, but perhaps there has been self-censorship at work about issues of women's sexuality, including our own sexual desires. So deeply internalized is the idea of the bad woman that there is often a strong tendency among staff members of community-based organizations to judge each other about these choices; to 'gossip', taunt or laugh at others in the team behind their backs. At one level this might seem trivial. But in fact it has serious implications for solidarity and trust, which are important dimensions of the desired work culture of such organizations. The irony is that even those who themselves are in non-normative sexual relationships judge others in a similar situation. There is a stark contrast between how members of the organization lead their lives and how they respond to others' relationships outside the norm of heterosexual monogamy within marriage. The same is also true of women's collectives at the community level.

But talking about sex and sexuality needn't be difficult. We actually found it easy to speak with rural women about issues of sexuality. Rural participants tended to be more honest and less constrained by worries about whether their responses were 'politically correct' than the more educated staff members. This often made it easier to enter into debate and discussion. Rural participants tended to be less inhibited and more playful about issues of sexual pleasure than us middle-class NGO workers. One reason for this is perhaps, as emerged in the workshops, that there is a culture of expressions of sexuality in the public realm – be it positive, such as sexually explicit songs, or negative, such as public censure of expressions of sexuality that fall outside of the norm. Another factor that might explain why rural women had a greater sense of ease around sex and sexuality is the oft-repeated perception of the need for sexual pleasure as *shareer ki bhook* – hunger of the body. This perception seemed to lend itself to participants being open to less judgemental and less moralistic ways of looking at sexuality, because the recognition of sexual pleasure as a need meant a more matter-of-fact approach to sexuality. There is much that can be learnt from their approach both in India and beyond, and I thank them for the insights and reflections that have informed Nirantar's thinking and this chapter.

References

Rubin, G. S. (1998) 'Thinking Sex: Notes for a Radical Theory of the Politics of Sexuality', in P. M. Nardi and B. E. Schneider (eds), *Social Perspectives in Lesbian and Gay Studies*, Routledge, New York.

Vance, C. (ed.) (1989) *Pleasure and Danger: Exploring Female Sexuality*, Pandora Press, London.

3

Sexual Pleasure as a Woman's Human Right
Experiences from a Human Rights Training Programme for Women in Turkey[1]

•••

Gulsah Seral Aksakal[2]

In Turkey, gender-specific notions of sexuality are instilled in children from a very early age. It is common practice for boy children to be told to show their penises to relatives and neighbours and to be proud of this, whereas girl children are warned that it is shameful to expose, even by mistake, a quick glimpse of their underwear while playing. Girls may be told not to laugh out loud, to sit with their knees together, and often may not even be allowed to ride a bike or play competitive, physical sports. Women's negative associations with their bodies and sexuality are later further exacerbated by the importance given to preserving virginity until marriage and customary practices in some regions such as displaying a bloodstained sheet as proof of the bride's virginity on the 'first night of marriage'. If a woman fails to prove her virginity at the time of marriage, she is likely not only to be disgraced, looked down upon and seen as less worthy, but in some regions she may even suffer the custom-based practice known as 'honour killing'. Men, on the other hand, are allowed, even encouraged, to have sexual encounters prior to marriage and sexual experience is often perceived as proof of 'manhood'.

Women's sexuality remains a strong taboo in Turkey. Most women's access to correct information on the issue is next to none, as it is addressed neither in the formal education system nor within informal information networks such as the family or the community. The closest any adult education programme comes to addressing the topic is in a technical manner through reproductive and sexual health education, without any discussion of the social and cultural perspectives of control and oppression, much less the psychological and individual perspectives of desire and pleasure. What little most women know about sexuality is largely based on misinformation and social myths, all of which serve to support the strict codes of conduct that severely limit or negatively influence women's sexual experience.

Social and cultural constructs around sexuality need to be placed within the context of the patriarchal nature of society, which is riddled with gender inequalities in both the private and public spheres. There is an increasing trend to emphasize women's role as mothers and housewives, and to highlight the nuclear and extended family structures, with women being considered the caretakers of these structures in the private arena of the home. In the public sphere Turkey is currently the only state found in violation of its obligation to protect women from domestic violence by the European Court of Human Rights, as evinced by the case of *Opuz v. Turkey* (2009). In addition, conservatism has been progressively on the rise in the post-9/11 era – both worldwide and in Turkey. Women's participation in the labour force has decreased in the past decade (only eight of the 130 countries listed rank lower). Only a few years ago Turkey's prime minister famously urged all married women to bear at least three children, and publicly stated his belief that it is impossible for men and women to be equal. Moreover, the former state minister responsible for the now-defunct Women's and Family Affairs portfolio, Selma Aliye Kavaf, claimed in 2010 that 'homosexuality is a disease' (*Hurriyet Daily News* 2010), while a study conducted with a national representative sample illustrated the presence and increase of non-tolerance for differences, and community pressure (Toprak *et al.* 2008; Esmer 2009).

In 2011, Turkey's Supreme Court approved the decision of a local court that decreed a 13-year-old girl had engaged in consensual sexual relations with 26 men, and the perpetrators received the lowest possible sentence. In negotiations with the government on the new anti-violence law passed in 2012, strong resistance from the women's movement was unable to change the name of the law; it was enacted under the name 'Law to Protect the Family and Prevent Violence against Women'. More recently, in 2012, at the Fifth International Parliamentarians' Conference on the Implementation of the International Conference on Population and Development Programme of Action on 24–25 May, Turkey's right-wing prime minister said he believed abortion was murder. Pregnancy termination has been legal in Turkey since 1983, provided it is carried out by authorized health professionals before the end of the tenth week of pregnancy. The Turkish Penal Code, which was reformed in 2004, preserved this right verbatim in Article 99. Prime Minister Erdogan's statement, based on personal beliefs, was endorsed by a number of ministers and other officials, including the Minister of Family and Social Policy – the *de facto* minister responsible for women's affairs – and came at a time marked by increased conservatism and infringement of sexual and bodily rights in Turkey. The national women's movement was quick to respond, and international support abounded; marches were organized all over Turkey, a web-based petition reached over 50,000 signatures in just one week, and the government was urged to retract statements that abortion is a crime and call off attempts to further limit, ban or criminalize abortion. Although currently the women's movement seems to have achieved success on this front, as the government later publicly announced it would not draft any proposal on the abortion issue, the social and political environment is growing ever more restrictive for women's freedom to enjoy their sexual and bodily rights in Turkey.

Gendered constructs of womanhood and sexuality are also reflected in social myths and popular sayings, such as 'women are by nature sexually passive while men are by nature sexually active', 'women's sex drive is less than men's', and 'women's sexuality ends after menopause'. The resultant impression is that men need sexual release at all costs, while for women sex is a burden to be accepted quietly, merely a responsibility

Women's voices

This and the subsequent 'women's voices' sections are extracts from discussions held during the course of the sexuality modules of the Human Rights Education Programme for Women (HREP) conducted by Women for Women's Human Rights – New Ways (WWHR).

Childhood

When I was eight years old, I was curious about the sexual organ of the neighbour's son, and wanted to see what it looks like. When my family found out, they confined me to a dark room. After three days of confinement, I was taken to a doctor for a virginity test and taken out of school. The impact of this experience continued after my marriage. I had difficulty in having sex with my husband. I felt pangs of anxiety and shame.

My mother always told me that sex was dirty, that girls and women should never talk about it. I knew nothing of my body until I got married, and it took me years to be able to accept my body, stop being ashamed of it and enjoy sex. But I still find it extremely difficult to talk about it, although I did try my best to at least discuss the basics with my daughter.

Menstruation

I had to undergo psychiatric treatment after having my first menstrual cycle because I lost the ability to speak as a result of the fear I experienced. The impact of this dreadful experience continues to this date, despite the fact that I am now a mother of two children.

I will never forget the day I had my first period and how my mother slapped me across the face when I told her. I still don't know why she did it. [Author's note: Mothers slapping their daughters in the face when they have their first period is an old customary practice in Turkey.]

> *When I had my first period I even considered committing suicide. Why couldn't they have told me what it was and that it was normal, so that I wouldn't have been so afraid. Now I think I want to explain to my daughter such things as soon as she is grown up a bit.*
>
> *When I had my first period I thought that I had lost my virginity, ruptured my hymen. My family had explained to me the importance of the hymen and virginity but told me nothing about menstruation or that I would one day menstruate. I still remember the pain and fear I felt that day and resent my mother for it, but I still can't talk to her about it.*

of procreation, devoid of notions of pleasure. Heterosexual relations and marriage, followed closely by motherhood, seem to be the widely accepted and expected roles for women. When joined with the political environment described above, this social construct works to undermine women's sexuality even more, eliminating, controlling and oppressing it.

The strong codes of conduct that define women's behaviour, including sexual behaviour, are used as an instrument to keep women under the control of their fathers, husbands and brothers, who assume responsibility for ensuring 'their' women retain their chastity; and if women fail to do so it is perceived as an acceptable basis for subjecting them to violence, sometimes with fatal results. In general, sexual codes of conduct serve as a mechanism for restricting women's mobility in the public sphere; and such restrictions are paralleled by the socially expected role of women which consists of marriage, child bearing, and home making – all within the confines of the private sphere.

Modernization initiatives in the Turkish Republic made public space increasingly accessible to women – although primarily to those of the higher socio-economic classes – but codes of conduct for women's sexual behaviour have continued to be used as a mechanism for 'internalized' restrictions on their mobility. Women, who have moved into the public space, have been allowed to do so in return for strict self-imposed codes of conduct regarding their sexual behaviour. Although advocates of modernity and of women's rights have raised the issues of women's unequal status in the family, and in education, employment and politics, they have mostly avoided the question of inequalities in sexuality.

The internalization of negative social messages about their sexuality, and the lack of information on matters pertaining to their bodies and sexuality, has made it difficult for many women to make free and informed choices about their social experiences, thereby limiting their ability to secure a healthy sex life. Many women associate sexuality with a lack of control, violence, and abuse; and certainly not with pleasure.

There is a clear need to empower women to take better control of their sexual lives and to build an affirmative approach to sexuality. As a result, women and sexuality has been one of the priority areas in the outreach work of WWHR, an autonomous human rights NGO based in Turkey. The issue of sexuality is an integral part of WWHR's training programme, its 'Human Rights Education Programme for Women' (HREP). The programme aims to raise women's critical awareness of the laws that affect their lives – whether these are codified laws, customs, traditions or daily practices. Building on the central concept of women's human rights, the training provides participants with the information and skills to put their rights into practice, both as individuals and through solidarity networks, as well as through initiatives pressing for social change.

The Human Rights Education Programme for Women (HREP)

WWHR developed HREP as part of a drive to enable women to exercise their rights in both the private and public spheres, overcome violations of those rights, and collectively mobilize for social, legal and political change. To this end, WWHR trains potential trainer candidates to implement the programme locally. Becoming a certified HREP trainer involves the successful completion of a number of steps, all of which are closely monitored by WWHR. Trainer candidates receive a great amount of support in the form of training materials, regular telephone calls, and supervision site visits during this phase, which involves launching and running a group locally following the trainer training seminar. Once this is completed, they attend an evaluation meeting and receive their certificates, becoming HREP trainers. From this point on, they become part of the Women's Human Rights Action Network and begin to play an active role in the women's movement, some more so than others. Thanks to the dedicated efforts of all HREP trainers, some 10,000 women have been able to benefit from the programme to date, and this number is continually growing.

The training programme consists of sixteen workshop modules on a variety of topics, including legal literacy and democratic means of participation; human rights and women's human rights; civil rights; violence against women and strategies against violence; economic rights; communication skills; gender-sensitive parenting; sexuality; reproductive rights; women and politics; the women's movement; and community organizing. It is currently conducted by specially trained social workers and psychologists at community centres and family counselling centres in 50 provinces in the seven geographical regions of Turkey and in Northern Cyprus, in partnership with a governmental agency. A number of local organizations have emerged as a result of the training, which also act as institutional partners in local programme implementation. Potential trainers from both types of partnerships attend the trainer-training sessions held every two years, then return to their local settings to begin programme implementation. The local training groups consist of women who meet on a weekly basis. The trainers act as group facilitators, leading the participatory exercises and group discussions. Each group discussion follows a structured module that provides information on human rights, women's human rights, and relevant national and international frameworks. As the weeks progress, personal experiences are shared more and more as they pertain to these topics and issues. This ensures that, throughout the process, participants grow ever closer to one another, and in the meantime begin to realize that their personal experiences are in fact common to many other women. In addition, WWHR and a television station, NTV, jointly developed a twelve episode series based on the HREP – *The Purple Series* – in which the 20-minute episodes correspond to the modules of the programme. These episodes are also used during local implementation, further illustrating that the experiences and issues discussed are indeed shared by many other women throughout the country.

Addressing the issue of sexuality within the framework of a human rights training programme is a strategic choice that we justify in two ways. First, a human rights programme for women must include a discussion of sexuality because sexuality is used as a central mechanism in the patriarchal control of women. The holistic approach of the programme provides women with an overview of the systematic violations of their human rights in a variety of contexts, and enables them to trace the interconnections. This allows a shift of the framework from an extremely private, individual context to a social, cultural, and political context that facilitates the discussion of sexuality as an issue shaped by the rules of the patriarchal society at large.

Second, we believe in the indivisibility of human rights and approach the issue as one of *sexual rights*, a human right to bodily integrity. Sexuality is addressed toward the end of the training programme. As a result, the previous discussions of the violations of women's human rights in the family, in public life, and in work life set a framework for approaching sexuality as a 'human rights' issue. The participants' increased knowledge of laws pertaining to women provides them with a feeling of security and self-confidence, which in turn allows them to address some of the taboo issues concerning their sexuality. We believe that it would have been impossible to run the sexuality workshops with the same level of success if they had been self-standing modules rather than part of an integrated programme. In this programme, the participants had already developed a general understanding of human rights and the accompanying skills, and begun to acknowledge the group setting as a safe space to share personal – and sometimes extremely private – experiences.

Women and sexuality within the HREP

The issue of 'women and sexuality' covers a wide range of issues encompassing reproductive rights and sexual violence against women, as well as the more marginalized topics of sexual expression and sexual fulfilment. All of these matters are addressed in different modules throughout the HREP. Sexual violence against women forms part of the modules on violence against women and strategies against violence, and includes a thorough examination of all the codified laws that women can utilize to bring an end to the violence. There is a separate module on reproductive rights, which includes a detailed discussion of all kinds of contraception available to women and men, with a focus on the advantages and disadvantages they entail in terms of protection from sexually transmitted infections, potential side effects, and ease of use. Once all these matters are covered, the two modules entitled 'Women and Sexuality' attempt to facilitate an understanding of sexual rights through the development of an affirmative and empowering perception of sexuality by emphasizing the right to sexual expression, pleasure and enjoyment. Our objective here was to ensure these two modules were committed to a positive perception of the issue, free of both the negative connotations of sexual violence against women and the functional linkages to reproductive sexuality.

Facilitating the development of an empowering perception of sexuality is no easy task; particularly given the internalization of years of social messages enjoining women to suppress their sexual instincts, limit the basis of their sexual experiences to procreation, and emulate a model of female sexuality which is based on passive and quiet acquiescence. This is why we chose to address the issue of sexual violence and reproductive rights in different modules and allow for a separate space for the participants to be able to focus solely on issues pertaining to their sexuality and sexual rights. An example provided by one of the group facilitators is a case in point. One day the husband of one of the participants in her group came to the community centre and said that, initially, he had been opposed to his wife attending this training of 'women's rights stuff'. But it seemed that now he thought differently. He wanted to thank the group facilitator, particularly in relation to the couple's improved sex life. He asked, 'What have you done to my wife to help her relax about sexuality? I used to be driven to despair chasing after her, and she'd always tell me it was shameful and sinful, and that I should stay away from her. Now all that has changed. Please tell me what you told her, so I can tell my friends who are having the same kind of problem with their wives.'

Sexuality is a private matter and many people have difficulty talking about it. The negative social messages that have been internalized by many women in Turkey make it even harder for them to talk about sex, be it in favourable or unfavourable terms. Education level or the extent to which participants consider themselves to be modern can also influence how they approach sexuality. There appears to be a widespread belief and expectation that better-educated women have no trouble enforcing any of their rights, including their sexual rights. This can make it difficult for such women in the group to come to terms with any violation of their rights, feeling they should be able to avert such occurrences. However, acknowledging that the gendered view of women's sexuality is based on social/cultural constructs also seems to lift a burden off their shoulders and enables them to voice their experiences related to sexuality, perhaps for the first time in the group setting.

At the beginning of the sexuality workshops, women often attempt to lead the discussion on to sexual health or the sexual education of their children. Our workshops placed considerable emphasis on creating an environment of security and mutual trust, so as to enable women to talk about their own experiences regarding their sexuality. At the start of the programme, a series of 'group rules of conduct' are established. These include the use of language, refraining from making judgemental comments and confidentiality. By the time the sexuality modules come up, the participants have grown to know each other and the facilitator quite well; and the group rules of conduct have become so well-established that communication amongst the participants is based on mutual respect and care for one another. Given the taboo nature of the issue, group facilitators share some of their own experiences in order to encourage the participants to open up.

The two modules on women and sexuality take the women through a number of steps in order to establish incrementally an empowering definition of sexual rights. The participants begin with a 'free association' exercise where they are given the phrases 'female sexuality' and 'male sexuality' and all the responses that spontaneously come to their minds are put up on a flip chart. Although there are some women in every group who associate pleasurable things with women's sexuality – such as sexual desire, love, attraction, sexiness and sexual pleasure – they are invariably in a minority. More typically, most associate women's sexuality with reproduction, motherhood, virginity, fear, being oppressed, or performing 'a duty'. Men's sexuality, on the other hand, is more often directly associated with sex, pleasure, sexual desire and the freedom to live life to the full.

The group facilitator then asks the participants to review these perceptions and beliefs about the differences between male and female sexuality, and to evaluate whether they are biologically or socially and/or culturally constructed and imposed. This leads into a discussion of what we call the 'social myths' about sexuality such as the ones mentioned earlier. Here it often becomes necessary for the group facilitator to intervene in order to correct misinformation and compensate for disinformation.

As part of the discussion on how various social myths affect the ways in which women experience sexuality, the participants

Women's voices

Lack of information/misinformation

Do we really have one hole for urination and another for the blood to pass through during menstruation and for sexual intercourse? Are they not the same hole? I thought we had only one hole!

What is the clitoris for?

Do girls/women feel sexual pleasure too?

I blame my mother for my lack of information about sexuality. When I was married I believed that I could get pregnant by kissing. My husband and I both suffered very much due to my ignorance. I do not want to repeat the same mistakes with my daughter.

I wish that they had taught us all this information that we are now learning back in school. We all grow up with so little information; and most of it was wrong. I don't want my children to grow up the same way.

are divided into small groups of two or three to discuss how their sexuality has been, and still is controlled/oppressed by their families, partners, society at large, and by the state. The small group context proves more conducive to the sharing of prior experiences and allows each participant to take the time and the space to express herself. As can be seen from the 'Women's Voices' discussion extracts in this chapter, this exercise usually uncovers numerous intense negative experiences of sexuality going back to early childhood memories of punishment for curiosity and exploration, moving into frightful experiences of first menstruation and the first night of marriage. It is important for the participants to have this safe space to speak out about negative experiences, because talking about them out loud often constitutes the first step of the healing process. Moreover, as more women participate in the discussion, similar experiences are repeated again and again; it is through this repetition that the issue moves from the private to the political. This also helps the participants to see that many of their experiences are common to all women, regardless of education, income level or social standing.

This discussion is followed by an information session on the female sexual organs, which includes visual handouts depicting and naming the female genitalia. While this seems like a technical, matter-of-fact type of information-sharing exercise, common levels of disinformation mean that it often culminates in intense discussions. For example, one invariable outcome of this exercise is that participants discover the female sexual organs do not have well-established names in Turkish, and that the existing ones are associated with derogatory meanings as they are often used as swearwords by men. Many participants find it difficult even to say out loud the word for vagina in Turkish in the group setting, openly stating that it is a 'dirty word'. Some resort to telling a 'joke' where the word is used comically, accompanied by nervous laughter from the group. Yet in this way, the participants come to acknowledge how, as women, they have been deprived of even a common language about sexuality, making talking about it even more difficult. Another common discovery is that the majority of the participants are not aware that they have a clitoris, the only human organ whose sole function is pleasure. In one group, a participant humorously pointed out to the group facilitator that when she first heard the word, she thought it was the name of a planet.

At the conclusion of this exercise, the group facilitator encourages the participants to examine their sexual organs with the help of a mirror when they go home. Hence, the participants are encouraged to start exploring their sexuality; and the natural place to start is through getting to know their own bodies.

The modules conclude with a discussion session on 'sexual rights' which include the basic rights to know and like one's sexual organs, the right to seek sexual experiences independent

Women's voices

Virginity, the hymen ('membrane of girlhood') and the first night of marriage

During the first couple of years of my marriage, I was unable to have sexual intercourse with my husband due to the strong internalization of the expectations of my family about virginity. I had to convince my husband that I was a virgin when we got married. I still keep the doctor's reports pronouncing me a virgin, 'just in case' anyone questions this in the future.

On the night of her marriage, a relative of mine fainted when she saw her husband naked in front of her.

My mother never allowed me to climb trees or ride a bike when I was a little girl. She told me girls didn't do such things, that it was bad for my health. I never understood back then, and some of my other friends would ride bikes, so one day I borrowed one from a friend and rode it. My mother saw me that day, caught up with me, slapped me in front of everyone and dragged me home. She yelled at me, saying, 'What if you've lost your virginity now?'

On my wedding night, my husband and I were in a room, and all our relatives were waiting outside the door for us to consummate the marriage, so that the blood stained sheet could be brought out for everyone to see. When this had been done, his mother came into the room, took me to the bath and washed me. I remember this as one of the worst experiences in my life. I cannot stand having sex with my husband. I don't want him even to touch me; I have never had an orgasm.

On my wedding night I did not bleed. My husband cut his finger so there would be blood to show on the sheet. The next morning he took me straight to the doctor to have my hymen examined. Although my hymen was intact, he still sometimes treats me in a condescending manner. Until today, I still had no idea that it is natural for some women not to bleed.

The third time I ever saw my husband was on our wedding night. I was terrified of having sex and did not want to get into bed with him. He forced me so hard he tore me up inside. I had to be taken to the hospital in the middle of the night and get stitched up. I have never enjoyed sex, never understood how women can enjoy sex. But now I see that sex doesn't have to be like how I experience it. So maybe it isn't that I don't like sex, but that I don't like sex with my husband.

A friend of mine who was not a virgin arranged her wedding night to coincide with her period; she even changed the date when she realized it was going to be off by a few days. I think it is an unfortunate way to begin a marriage, but if the man/the family insist that premarital sex is fine for men and not for women, they deserve to be deceived. I think the same thing about women who have their hymens repaired.

For years you are taught that sex and sexuality are the devil to be feared. Then, in one night they are supposed to become an angel to be loved. This is just not possible!

of marital status, the right to orgasm, the right to expression and pursuit of sexual needs and desires, and also the right to choose *not* to experience one's sexuality. This is a process whereby the participants first find the safe space to speak about negative experiences and then move these accounts from the private to the political level for a better understanding of what underlies them and how they can be prevented from recurring. What follows is an affirmative process of physical self-exploration

Women's voices

Pleasure

As I do not get any sexual satisfaction from my husband, despite trying to talk to him about it (and even after seeking therapy), I began to masturbate and give myself pleasure.

We are poor! We can't buy many things that we might enjoy. We can't do as many things as we'd like. But sexual pleasure is something we can all enjoy. So we should make the best of it!

So women also feel sexual pleasure, just like men do! I think it is very important to know this at the beginning of marriage, so that you can also teach your husband about it.

I am married to my third husband. With my first two husbands, I always feared sex and never enjoyed it, never associated it with pleasure. But now I know that it can be wonderful, and I've found that the more I am able to express my desires, the more enjoyable it becomes for both of us.

Instinctively, I've also felt that sex was a natural thing. It is good now to have all this information and to confirm that what I had thought all along was right.

I have a neighbour who talks very openly about sexual pleasure. She was always saying that she could not get enough of her husband and wanted to have sex with him every night. In a few weeks, all my other neighbours began to talk about her, calling her 'Ayse who is on fire' but she doesn't mind and still talks about it!

The men who keep trying to cover women up because they find women inviting and provocative should be told that when they wear tight jeans women find them the same. And so they shouldn't dress up that way either!

and the initial steps towards starting to talk about feelings of pleasure, enjoyment and fulfilment and associating them with our sexualities as women.

For the younger participants, the training also works proactively, providing them with the information and skills to prevent any further damage or misconceptions. For the older participants, who have gone through years of negative associations about their sexuality, it marks only the beginning of a long process of coming to terms with the issue, healing and exploring.

According to some of the findings from two separate impact assessment studies carried out in 2003 and 2011, almost all respondents noted an increase in self-confidence as a result of HREP, and nearly three-quarters began to participate more equally in decision making in the family. Over half were able to end, and nearly one-quarter were able to reduce domestic violence. Again, over half restarted their interrupted formal or non-formal education, and about half began to participate actively in the labour market. All participants, in one way or another, became what we call 'resource women' and spread their new-found knowledge and understanding of sexuality and pleasure to relatives and neighbours, often referring to the handouts and booklets distributed during the weekly sessions. Almost inevitably, in each group there are mothers who affirm their commitment to preventing their daughters from suffering from the misinformation, disinformation, and fearful oppression to which they were subjected. And that is a bright ray of hope for the future.

Notes

1 This chapter is an extended and updated version of Ilkkaracan, I. and G. Seral (2000) 'Sexual Pleasure as a Women's Human Right: Experiences from a Grassroots Training Program in Turkey', in Pinar Ilkkaracan (ed.) *Women and Sexuality in Muslim Societies*, Women for Women's Human Rights – New Ways, Istanbul, pp. 187–96.

2   Gulsah Seral Aksakal is a master trainer and supervisor for WWHR – New Ways' Human Rights Education Programme for Women (HREP). She was one of the writers who developed the HREP Manual, and acted as the national coordinator of the programme from 1998 to 2001. She has implemented HREP locally over the past decade when circumstances allowed, and currently serves as a member of WWHR's HREP Advisory Board. The information presented here is based on these experiences, as well as on two external evaluation studies conducted in 2003 and 2011, respectively.

References

Esmer, Y. (2009) 'Radikalizm ve asiricilik arastirmasi' [A study of radicalism and extremism], Bahçeşehir Üniversitesi, Istanbul.

Hürriyet Daily News (2010) 'Activists Protest Turkish Minister's Remarks about Gays', http://www.hurriyetdailynews.com/default. aspx?pageid=438&n=gay-rights-activists-protest-turkish-minister -2010-04-15 (accessed 9 July 2012).

Opuz v. Turkey (2009) Application No. 33401/02, Council of Europe, European Court of Human Rights, 9 June 2009, http://www. unhcr.org/refworld/docid/4a2f84392.html (accessed 9 July 2012).

Toprak, B., *et al.* (2008) 'Turkiye'de Farkli Olmak: Din ve Muhafazakarlik Ekseninde Otekilestirilenler' [Being Different in Turkey: Alienation on the Axis of Religion and Conservatism], Boğaziçi Üniversitesi, Istanbul, http://www.osiaf.org.tr/images/basin/pdf/ turkiyede_farkli_olmak.pdf (accessed 9 July 2012).

4
Better Sex and More Equal Relationships
Couple Training in Nigeria
•••
Dorothy Aken'Ova

In 1999, I decided to undertake a study on attitudes, knowledge and behaviour regarding sexual pleasure in women. There were, at the time, some projects that took a more positive approach to sexuality and sexual rights. Yet most sexual and reproductive health (SRH) projects chose a more medical/pathological than rights-based approach, and were therefore not as empowering as they could have been. My major concern at this point was that the issues they were tackling – abortion, sexually transmitted infections, HIV and Aids, contraceptives and family planning – were all related to sexual activity, whether directly or indirectly. But the positive and enriching aspects of sexual activity were completely neglected in the process. My conversations with reproductive healthcare service providers and reproductive rights activists revealed that they were influenced by the same patriarchal socialization that vilifies all forms of progressive discourse on sexuality, especially the affirmative and empowering components that challenge the very premise upon which patriarchy is founded – inequality.

The study that I began in 1999 developed into the sexual pleasure project of the organization with which I work, the International Centre for Reproductive Health and Rights (INCRESE). It started as a process of gathering information about issues of pleasure and providing feedback from the outcomes of the study to stakeholders. The project seeks to provide avenues for the beneficiaries to negotiate safer sexual relationships, make choices that are right for them, to be assertive and to demand and negotiate for their needs and desires, including for much-tabooed sexual pleasure.

Studying women's sexual pleasure

In a field that was so new, it was vital to undertake a review to enhance my understanding of the subject matter and sharpen my data collection skills. I therefore began the study by looking at what had been written about the human sexual response. This led me to understand sexual pleasure as an erotic sensation or feeling, that may be physical, psychological, and/ or emotional, and that is derived from sexual arousal. It includes the understanding that sources of arousal may be sounds, smells, dressing, intimate conversation, music, fantasies, a look, a caress or sexual intercourse.

The models I reviewed included those of Masters and Johnson (1966; 1970) who observed men and women mostly having penis to vagina sexual intercourse and masturbation. They monitored and documented the physiological reactions of men and women to stimulation. They concluded that there are four stages in what they called the 'human sexual response cycle' – excitement, plateau, orgasm and resolution. Helen Singer-Kaplan (1974; 1995) introduced desire at the beginning of the cycle developed by Masters and Johnson. Her model of sexual response points out that without the desire to be sexually active, excitement and orgasms are not possible.

David Reed focuses more on the psychosocial aspects of the human sexual response cycle. He proposes four stages in the response cycle – seduction, sensation, surrender, and reflection – and describes what he calls 'erotic stimulus pathways' (Carroll 2007). Seduction is inclusive of all those things we might do to either entice ourselves or someone else into sexual activity – wearing cologne and perfumes, using makeup, dressing sexily, making eye contact, sending love notes, buying flowers, arranging time, sharing feelings and asking for sex. In the next stage, he proposes that we are open to sexual stimulation from all of our senses. Sight, sound, taste, smell, touch, imagination and fantasy all have potential to arouse, depending on our potential to interpret sensations. He, however, concluded that our interpretation of sensations is often influenced by how we were socialized, and what we were taught would be sexually stimulating (or not). Gina Ogden (2000) visualizes pleasure, orgasm and ecstasy as three dancing spheres of energy. She concludes that the circles are overlapping because one may experience all three simultaneously or experience pleasure without orgasm, or orgasm without ecstasy. She also adds the spiritual component to pleasure (Ogden 1999, 2003).

These models, brought together, yield an understanding of the human sexual response cycle, which illustrates the complete potential for sexual pleasure for both men and women, and the various levels and degrees to which pleasure can be experienced.

As a result of lack of time and limited resources, the study was carried out in a semi-formal manner, drawing on in-depth interviews among men and women of reproductive age from all the health zones in Nigeria. Some of the respondents were colleagues in the field of sexual and reproductive health and rights, some of them were clients who came for counselling at INCRESE, others were individuals I met in various social situations. I also obtained information during workshops and meetings, by organizing group discussions in these fora. The study was spread over a period of twelve months, and concluded in 1999. The respondents were told about the objective of the study and asked if they were willing to participate. The interview was conducted only after the respondents had given their consent.

The interview guide consisted of the following questions:

• What does sexual pleasure mean to you?
• What comes to your mind when you hear 'sexual pleasure in women'?
• What do you know about sexual pleasure in women?

- What is your opinion of the cultural/religious perception of sexual pleasure in women?
- Are you aware of health problems or conditions that affect sexual pleasure in women?
- Are you aware of anywhere women could go to if they had problems enjoying sex?
- Would you recommend that services be provided for women who are unable to derive pleasure from sexual activity?
- Who would you recommend to provide the kind of services required to promote sexual pleasure in women?
- What are those services?

The interviews and focus group discussions confirmed that there was reticence to talk about sexuality issues generally, and that, for many respondents, sexual pleasure in women was an even more difficult topic to address. Participants in the focus groups reported that women's sexuality was strictly censored and checked from childhood to adulthood. When I asked why this was so, one of the respondents replied:

> Women are not meant to enjoy it, otherwise they will go looking for it, and that will make them become prostitutes. (Young male graduate, Abuja)

Another respondent said:

> Let us not kid ourselves. Why else do we circumcise women? In fact I should not be discussing this with you. You Beijing women have no respect for traditional values. (A male demographer)

A female respondent, 56 years old, reported that women were bought up to think about their husbands, not themselves, in matters related to sex. She said, 'Our satisfaction came from making the man happy.'

In male-dominated social systems, girls underwent preparations for long periods of time and some painful experiences, including physical injuries to the body, in readiness for marriage. These preparations, which accompanied puberty rites, were meant to develop sex appeal in girls for their husbands. Girls were taught how to satisfy their husbands, but they were not given information or skills in how to obtain pleasure for themselves in the process. Respondents confirmed this by reporting that there was no consideration for such a thing as sexual pleasure for women.

> I knew there was such thing as orgasm in women since childhood. I was fifteen years old when my cousin sister used her finger on me at night when we went to bed. This night, it just happened, I convulsed in pleasure. Now it is funny, I am married and my husband would not touch me there. (Female, 41 years old)

When boys were prepared for adulthood and marriage, giving sexual pleasure to their wives was not part of the preparation. None of the males interviewed received such coaching while growing up, but were aware of the preparations and the grooming the girls were put through on their account. The majority of the men were still of the opinion that all a man is required to do to give a woman satisfaction is perform penetrative sex.

> How can a woman expect an adult like me to suck her breast? That is nonsense. (Male, law enforcement officer, 48 years old)

> Women who like to be fondled and caressed must be lesbians. (Male adult who phoned in during a television programme)

> Men are always in a hurry, they don't give enough time to prepare their partners, then they rush in and in a few minutes, the game is over. (Female trader, 29 years old)

Some of the female respondents reported that a simple touch could be very pleasurable if it was from someone they loved and if they were ready for it. They expressed limited satisfaction sexually in the conditions in which they live.

> In our case, the man comes into your room and clears his throat to warn you to be ready to 'receive him'. Most times you are not ready and it causes pain. But sometimes you are aroused and get a little pleasure. One thing is that the experience leaves you more frustrated because you are not fully satisfied, you do not come. (Female nurse, 36 years old)

Sexual pleasure in women? Enjoy the little you get, you may never go past that little the whole of your life. (Female reproductive health educator, 34 years old)

Women have been punished for daring to express pleasure during sexual intercourse. I recall an experience shared by a colleague about being sent packing in the early hours of the morning because she 'made noises like a prostitute' at night.

My husband beat me up. He accused me of going out. He said I had changed in bed. To tell the truth, I don't know how he did it that night, but I climaxed and shivered all over. Subsequent nights, I was more responsive, working at it, hoping it would happen again. I could not tell him so, but have resolved to be the way I was before. (Female accountant, 41 years old)

In some instances, women are told to be ashamed of them-selves, or admit that something is wrong with them if they experience sexual desire or pleasure, or if they desire to have sexual intercourse.

There is no one; I have not reported my situation. It has always been a battle to get my husband to sleep with me. His mother and his sisters think I am a loose woman to complain that my husband does not have sex with me. Look at me, is something wrong with me? Is it not right for me to ask? I don't know what else to do. (Female school teacher, 38 years old)

Religious perspectives affected the opinions expressed by the respondents. The Christian respondents reported that the religious perspective required 'women should be submissive to their husbands'. I also heard a sermon some time ago where the preacher said, 'Women who do not submit themselves to their husbands are being manipulative. That is witchcraft.'

In a group discussion involving young men and women, all of whom are HIV/AIDS peer educators ranging from ages 22–29, there was heated debate on sexual pleasure in women. The males claimed that women enjoyed sex more than men, that they even have multiple orgasms. The girls argued that the women were lucky if they had any orgasm at all, even though they have the potential for multiple orgasms. Out of curiosity, I asked men why they assumed that women enjoy sex more than men do.

> Women come even before you enter them. A little touch here and there and they release, you find the place wet as you enter. (Male carpenter, 42 years old)

Further probing of this respondent revealed to me that secretion by women during stimulation was what this respondent was mistaking for orgasm, equating it with male ejaculation where seminal fluids are expelled.

> We do all the work while the women just lie back and enjoy it. (Male carpenter, 32 years old)

These are just a few examples of how sexual pleasure in women is perceived and misunderstood. They speak to and challenge those of us who call ourselves feminists and who are service providers, because some of us also suffer deprivation in this area in our own lives.

> He just doesn't know how to do it.... How can I teach him? Do you want him to send me packing? (Female programme officer in an adolescent reproductive health NGO)

The INCRESE Sexual Pleasure Project

Unfortunately, we, the actors in the field of sexual and reproductive health rights, are socialized in the same context – and we have imbibed, over the years, these negative attitudes towards sexual pleasure in women. This is reflected in the way that interventions for women's health and rights have been designed. At the time INCRESE began its work, interventions on sexual pleasure in women were rare. For these reasons we decided to develop a training series on this issue.

We developed trainings that began with a presentation of quotes from the study on sexual pleasure in women, and invited comments and reactions from participants. These were often similar to the views expressed by the respondents of the study.

The facilitator would then go on to discuss the Masters and Johnson and Gina Ogden models to confirm to participants that women are created naturally to experience pleasure during sexual activity. This exercise went further to discuss the programme implications of perceptions of and attitudes to sexual pleasure in women.

In our initial trainings, most of the men wanted more information and asked a lot questions. They were challenged by the sessions and decided to make a change, but were afraid that their partners might think that the change was influenced by a concurrent relationship that they were having. They asked if their partners could accompany them for a repeat of the session so that the women would understand where the change in attitude and practice was coming from. Female members were also asked to bring their husbands and fiancées.

The sessions were repeated. As a result of demand for more information in the question and answer sessions, these were followed by explorations of the anatomy and physiology of the female and male reproductive system. Again the participants asked for sessions on desire, pleasure and seduction. Couples who had challenges in their relationships or were having sexual problems sought help from us and we offered them counselling.

It took two years of periodic seminars and counselling sessions – and thorough documentation of these, and the lessons learnt – to develop a full training curriculum. At the end of two years, INCRESE had put together a training outline for intervention using sexual pleasure as an entry point to promote women's rights and health. I outline this below.

Outline of the trainings

Module 1: Knowledge, attitudes and practices towards sexual pleasure of women. This is the first session taken. It discusses knowledge, attitudes and practices (KAP) towards sexual pleasure in the community. This discussion is wrapped up with the presentation of quotes from the findings of the research on sexual pleasure in women. This session ends in a take-home task – couples are asked to work together to identify similarities and differences between the discussion of the community's KAP towards sexual pleasure in women and those in the presentation. They are also asked to compile a list of rumours and myths on sexual pleasure in men and women in their communities. This session is usually an eye-opener to participants, especially women, who realize that they can make sexual demands.

The next session in this module takes feedback from participants on their take-home tasks. Feedback often reflects that sexual pleasure is circumscribed somewhat in women; that women who ask for sex or express pleasure during sexual activity are seen as women of low virtue; and that experiencing pleasure and daring to show it is an indication that a woman is turning into a prostitute or getting addicted to sex – and that, soon, her sexual urge will become unmanageable and push her into promiscuity. Other rumours brought forward were that sexual activity with women was a field of conquest where masculinity is demonstrated, that men were expected to show prowess, and if a woman derived some pleasure, it was a conquest that added a plus to the virility of the man. Other views included the claim that women were created for the pleasure of the man. The feedback is somewhat contradictory just as we found in the research – on the one hand, women are not expected to ask for or need pleasure; on the other hand sometimes men assume that women experience pleasure very easily with penetrative sex. Sometimes wives are not expected to experience pleasure while girlfriends are expected to. Feedback is discussed and analysed.

Module 2: Life coping skills. Sessions in this module begin by sharing experience with participants reporting on their take-home task. Feedback is based primarily on the comfort level of the couples while undertaking the task. Those who are comfortable doing so share the details of their findings. This provides a basis for discussions of life competency skills spread through several sessions. These include comprehensive sessions with exercises and scenarios to enhance skills, building on self-esteem, values clarification, negotiation, pressure resistance and refusal skills, communication skills and assertiveness. Where necessary counselling is provided for couples who experience communication challenges. This is usually in response to the feedback, for instance, that 'he just won't listen' or 'she was not communicating'. The counselling sessions are aimed at facilitating dialogue.

Module 3: Bodily rights are sexual rights; sexual rights are human rights. This module comprises sessions on sexual rights and reproductive rights which commence with the history of women's human rights. It uses conventions and consensus documents and regional and national legal frameworks as a basis for the sessions. The tool discussed below is used to facilitate the first session.

Participants are asked to look at a drawing of a women's genitals which shows six hands pulling at the surrounding skin. They are then asked to respond to the following questions:

- How did you feel at the first sighting of the poster?
- Read the picture, what's happening in it?
- What are the hands doing?
- Who own the hands?
- What tools and mechanisms do they use?
- How does this impact on women and girls?
- What can we do to stop this from happening to women and girls?

These questions provoke debates and the sharing of experience, which bring to light women's rights abuses within the community. Religious beliefs are also discussed to situate the rights of women within belief systems, and explore belief systems for provisions that protect women's human rights, including their sexual rights. These sessions also establish the fact that human rights are universal and not contradictory, and are therefore a safe framework to use in relationships, policy, laws and programming.

The take-home task after this module is for couples to go and list areas of women's rights violations in the attitudes and practices listed in the first module. They are also asked to identify the rights violated in the issues raised during the use of the tool on bodily rights. Feedback is then taken in the following sessions. Scenarios are used for discussion, to add to the depth of the analytical capacity of the participating couples.

Module 4: Reproductive anatomy and physiology of men and women. With dummies and posters, participants are taught the anatomy and physiology of the female and male reproductive system. They are given a take-home task to do self-examination and, in subsequent sessions, mutual examination. This is with the objective of enabling participants to know their bodies better, what the different parts look and feel like. This has challenged masculinities along with the myth that holds that male reproductive parts are sacred and should not be looked at or seen by women; there are beliefs that this will breed disrespect in the relationship. Men are also often sceptical about visualizing the female reproductive organ. Some couples had never seen each other naked in full light, and this was the first time they were doing so.

Participants are also taught the progression of human growth and development and changes during puberty, as well as the processes of menstruation and fertilization. Reproductive choice, with focus on abortion and contraceptives, is also discussed, along with care of the reproductive organs, and sessions on human sexuality, gender and gender roles. The session on anatomy addresses, at the end, some abnormalities of the reproductive organs and possible remedies, and where to seek help. Various exercises are performed to increase the participants' comfort level with all aspects of the discussion.

Module 5: The human sexual response cycle. All the models of the human sexual cycle are discussed in this module, and how they are all mutually complementary. Thus pleasure is considered at physical, emotional, psychological, mental and spiritual levels, with a list of accompanying common and less common physical changes that occur in both men and women at the different stages of the cycle. All related issues such as seduction, flirting, sexual treats, love banquets, shower shows, setting the stage, teasing, toys and aids, fantasies, sexual positions (their advantages in enhancing pleasure and bonding), and pornography, are also explored, as well as special issues including sexual dysfunctions; pleasure and disability; pleasure and living with HIV; and pleasure after excision (female genital mutilation).

The module provides a safe space, including counselling and sexual therapy sessions for couples. It is a space to discuss what gives them pleasure; just how much pleasure they get and what is missing. This therefore provides an opportunity for women to express how much more their partners need to do for them. Couples are given the task of working together to examine how they have fared, from dating through courtship to marriage. They are expected to practise daily tips given during the sessions, and constantly evaluate themselves to see how well they are faring.

Sessions in this module provide for discussions on safer sex and the intersections between sexual pleasure, safer sex and human rights. Topics include risk reduction and prevention of sexually transmitted diseases including HIV; contraception, including emergency contraceptives; and safe abortion. Couples are encouraged to contact the facilitator individually to seek clarification or help.

Module 6: Patterns of human sexual behaviour. This module commences with an exercise used to clarify values using nine patterns of human sexual behaviour (vaginal sex, oral sex, anal sex, sex for money, sex with the same gender, forced sex, celibacy, bestiality and masturbation), which participants are individually required to rank in order of preference. Each couple shares its ranking, and then discusses and negotiates to agree on a joint ranking. The couples present their ranking, with reasons why they have ranked one behaviour as more acceptable than others;

they also present areas of conflicting ranking or disagreements. The facilitator guides this activity, asking probing questions to enable the participants to question some of the values they have, and takes them through an in-depth analysis. The wrap-up of the exercise consists of giving the participants the human rights framework and health and safety considerations with which to examine all patterns of human sexual behaviour, thus giving them guidance on what is acceptable and what is not acceptable.

The next session examines sexual orientation, sexual and gender identities and expressions, and other patterns of human sexual behaviour. These are discussed using the safety (health and human rights) lenses to assess what behaviour is acceptable or not. This session concludes with a task where each couple works together to discuss what patterns of sexual behaviour they want to try. Participants bring feedback, according to their comfort level, in the plenary or during counselling sessions.

Again, this process provides a huge opportunity for women to put their desires and needs on the table for discussion, and for them to negotiate with their partners in a safe and supervised space, with support systems in place for interventions ranging from counselling through therapy, to referral.

Lessons learnt

In the process of creating this intervention project, we observed that some participants are not comfortable sharing in the group. We learnt that space and time have to be created to address this need for individual support. We learnt that there was need for stand-by counselling, therapy and clinical services. We also learnt that groups and communities are willing to open up to discuss issues of sexuality, including intimacies, contrary to popular opinion among programmers and policy makers, provided the discussions are scientific and not pornographic, serious not naughty.

We learnt that men are prepared to learn to pleasure women once they are carried along by the process of demystifying patriarchy, masculinities and femininities. It ceases to be driven by ego: 'How many orgasms did you have?', and it comes to be about meeting mutual sexual needs and satisfying desires in each other: 'Did you enjoy it; what can I do to improve?'

Even though we started out seeking to address negative attitudes towards sexual pleasure in women, we ended up with some couples reporting outcomes such as a reduction in gender-based violence because, as they reported, they spent all their time practising seduction and flirting and trying to keep communication intimate, transparent and respectful. So, we are hopeful that this strategy can challenge patriarchy and masculinity, bring about mutual respect, and reduce the incidence of gender-based violence.

The project also opened an avenue for feminists to address polygamy, a topic which fear of community and religious sensitivities had hitherto made unapproachable. At the registration point for the project, participants were asked to register as couples, and there are exercises at every level for partners. Those married to more than one wife always brought up the issue of how challenging having more than one wife has been in the context of the project, since they couldn't register their three or four wives. They found it challenging to carry out mutual body examination and other tasks with more than one wife, complaining about the lack of time to do so. We believe that if such knowledge could be gained earlier during the life cycle, such men might be more likely to be monogamous.

In discussing safety and pleasure, issues of HIV/AIDS and STIs were brought up. Partners who were anxious about child spacing had the opportunity to negotiate their concerns with their partners on these. It was fulfilling to watch the women move from negotiating for orgasms to demands for a guarantee of other rights including ones that are not directly related to sexual reproductive health and rights, such as further education, acquisition of literacy skills and jobs. Issues related to divorce, parenting and parent/child communication were also brought up during tasks and counselling.

Implications for programming for women's health and rights

For programming purposes, the important lesson was the fact that the modules could not be followed exactly as planned with all groups. Modifications were necessary to adjust to community needs and comfort level, and it was important to maintain this flexibility. In one community, for example, the participants suggested that women be taken separately from men for the session on reproductive anatomy and physiology, so that is what we did.

INCRESE has also met some resistance to our work. Some key players in Nigeria in sexual and reproductive health, and also in other parts of Africa where I have initiated this dialogue, have argued that lack of sexual satisfaction is not a life-threatening condition. They argue that designing programmes for sexual pleasure in women is a waste of time and a wrong prioritization when we are still battling with issues such as FGM, STIs including HIV/AIDS, maternal mortality and morbidity, and early marriage. Some SRH actors were simply scared of where work on sexual pleasure in women would lead us.

The project taught us that it is often policy makers, rather than participants, who are uncomfortable with the issues we work on, not least because some can already foresee the possibility of self-determination and actualization among women, and the resultant awareness that will culminate in demands by the women for the protection of their rights. From the projects that we have implemented, we now know that work on sexual pleasure in women can lead us to address several issues, some of which require us to clarify our values further, or that we lack the skills and resources to manage. They include the following:

Fear and anxiety. The fear of inopportune pregnancy was often expressed as a counterweight to the idea of sexual pleasure for women, as was the fear of contracting an STI or HIV/AIDS. Therefore, these cannot be addressed in isolation from each other.

Fatigue. Because of our roles, we have a lot of responsibilities. The multiple roles of women cannot be overemphasized and have gained programming and policy attention over the last two decades. Women are the first to wake and the last to sleep. Sometimes they are so tired that the last thing on their mind is sex. Making space for pleasure will therefore also involve addressing the balance of work and responsibility.

Lack of choice. Women may not have the power to choose. Most often, they are not in a position to choose who their partners should be, especially to choose a same-sex relationship as an alternative life style. Even in a heterosexual relationship, women sometimes do not have a choice in the partner they end up with. They are often not given a say in family planning or contraceptive use, even when the device is going to be inserted into their bodies, or ingested by them.

Violence and abuse. Violence, whether it is physical, psychological, emotional or mental, does affect the sexual response of women. Diminishing violence is therefore tightly bound up with opening up space for pleasure.

Addressing any of these issues means taking a strong position in challenging patriarchy, and therein lies the strength of this intervention strategy. It provides the space to deconstruct male-dominated value systems, and replace them with a system built and driven on feminist principles; a system that upholds the principle of erotic justice; a system where female agency is visible, protected and promoted; a system where pleasure pays!

References

Carroll, J. L. (2007) *Sexuality Now: Embracing Diversity*, Thomson Wadsworth, Belmont, CA.

Masters, W. H. and V. E. Johnson (1966) *Human Sexual Response*, J. and A. Churchill Limited, London.

—— (1970) *Human Sexual Inadequacy*, J. and A. Churchill Limited, London.

Ogden, G. (1999) *Women Who Love Sex: An Inquiry into the Expanding Spirit of Women's Erotic Experience* (revised edition), Womanspirit Press, Cambridge, MA.

—— (2000) 'Sexuality Overview', in C. Kramarae and D. Spender (eds), *International Encyclopaedia of Women*, Routledge, New York.

—— (2003) 'Spiritual Dimensions of Sex Therapy: an Integrative Approach for Women', *Contemporary Sexuality*, Vol. 37, No. 1, pp. i–viii.

Singer-Kaplan, H. (1974) *The New Sex Therapy: Active Treatment of Sexual Dysfunctions*, Routledge, New York.

—— (1995) *The Sexual Desire Disorders – Dysfunctional Regulation of Sexual Motivation*, Brunner Mazel, New York.

5
Building a Movement
for Sexual Rights and Pleasure

Xiaopei He

At the end of 2007 I was sitting in a meeting in Beijing discussing how gay men in China could utilize the law to protect themselves. The purpose of the meeting was to collect evidence from gay men who were being bullied, and to mobilize lawyers, journalists, researchers and writers to help produce new and enabling medical and juridical guidelines. There were about 40–50 participants from all over the country. Most of them were gay activists, gay writers, lawyers, sexologists and journalists. In the middle of listening to many gay men's testimonies of being abused by the police or family members, I heard a woman's voice gently saying: 'I am not a gay; I am an ordinary heterosexual woman....' Participants were stunned, wondering what story a heterosexual woman would bring to this meeting.

The woman, whose name is Wen,[1] began her story. She talked of dating her fiancée, the ideal husband with a good job and looks. Although they never held hands or kissed, she believed that this was because he was being gentle and polite. Months later, they got married. There was still little intimacy between them, but soon she got pregnant. After their child was born, there was no physical contact: 'He even avoided looking into my eyes.' He beat her up a few times, and on one occasion he pushed her over, stamped on her, and she felt he was going to kill her. At this moment, her three-year-old son walked in on the scene, screamed, and fainted – and that 'woke him up and made him stop'.

Wen survived. But she suffered very low self-esteem and felt that she was not attractive. Soon that turned into depression. During the nine years of their marriage, the husband had been bringing his male friends home for food, to watch porn films and to share a bed with him. Little did she understand the nature of their relationships. Wen could not imagine her husband was homosexual because it is so stigmatized. She had been prescribed anti-depressants to help her with what she believed to be her own mental problem. Then one day she found on the computer that the websites her husband always browsed were gay dating websites, and that he had been using them to date men. The word 'homosexual' on the websites eventually made her realize that her husband was gay.

Wen said that since homosexuals suffer from a great deal of stigma and discrimination in society and within their families, they might indeed have to disguise their sexual orientation by marrying women. But, she said, gay men should not pass their hardship on to women and make them suffer. Wen said that she would support same-sex marriage, which could avoid straight women suffering together with gay men.

Wen's speech received different responses. A well-known sexologist said that Wen's experience was not representative, as in her studies over several years on Chinese gay men, she had never heard of married gay men beating their wives. A gay activist stood up and simply said that Wen's story was off-topic and that people should focus on the subject of the meeting, which was the abuse and suffering of gay men.

Since China began its economic reform and open door policy in 1987, Chinese society has seen many changes. Legal reform in 1997 eliminated from the penal code the so-called 'hooligan offence', which could be used to sentence homosexuals to death. In 2001, the new Chinese classification for mental disorder (with diagnostic criteria) was issued, and homosexuality ceased to be seen – legally – in that light. From then on, being homosexual has no longer been treated as a crime or sickness by the authorities. However, medical treatment for 'correcting homosexual behaviour' is still provided by some medical professionals and police harassment still happens occasionally at gay bars, gay clubs, parks and cruising places. It is estimated that there are 20 million gay men in China, and 80–90 per cent of them get married at some point, more often under social or family pressure than by their own desire. This leaves at least 16 million gay men's wives, who live their lives with a certain degree of pain and sorrow, as well as health and HIV risks.

This incident made me think. First, are sexual rights just for people who are gay or are straight women too entitled to sexual pleasure? Second, marriage normativity pressures people into relationships that they do not desire. Both gay and straight people can suffer from this. Could we not form a united movement aimed at challenging marriage normativity and compulsory heterosexuality? Third, I considered how pleasure approaches could empower people who are deprived and help to build understanding and solidarity for a united sexual rights movement. Over the last few years, Pink Space, the NGO I co-founded, has been working on these issues, trying to form a movement which includes pleasure as a means as well as a goal, which makes people happier along the way as well as happier in the end.

Pink Space NGO: uniting marginalized sexual identities, organizing beyond identity politics

In the eloquent words of Scott Long:

> Sexual rights are not a privilege, nor the property of a minority. They are everyone's birthright and everyone's concern. The man who faces arrest and torture in Egypt because he fell in love with a man; the lesbian in South Africa whose family believes that rape will 'cure' her; the transgender woman in the United States harassed and brutalized on the street – these people share, despite their differences of geography and detail, a common cause with the woman confronting a death sentence for adultery in Nigeria; with the mother ostracized and shunned by her village community in Jamaica because she contracted HIV/AIDS from a sexual partner;

and with the woman in Pakistan whose parents can take her life with impunity, because her behaviour supposedly strikes at the family's 'honour' – and her safety is unprotected by the state. All these people endure abuse, and are denied their basic rights, because they have claimed their sexual and physical autonomy in ways the state condemns and society fears. We must stand together in asserting that our bodies are our own; that our pleasures like our pains are part of us; that our privacy and integrity and dignity cannot be bargained away. (Long 2004)

As Long vividly drives home, many people are abused and denied their sexual rights because they diverge from gender and sexuality norms. Gender and sexuality norms restrict women in general and women with stigmatized identities in particular, holding them back from organizing and from accessing basic rights, and from expressing sexual desires and seeking sexual pleasure. There is a need to gather together different disadvantaged identities and unite our struggles, fighting for basic rights that have been denied.

With this in mind, five lesbian and bisexual activists in Beijing together set up the Pink Space NGO in 2007 and we began our mission for 'Sexual Rights to Pleasure for All'. We believe that sexual rights are a basic right for everyone, for women, men and transgender people, married or not, young or old. We decided to work with different groups of people marginalized by gender and sexuality norms to empower these people, and to collectively challenge these norms that cause so much injustice. First of all, we identified marginalized groups of people to work with. We found that women living with HIV, female sex workers, and lesbian and bisexual women had very few organizations, and these had little power. Women married to gay men, and female-to-male transgender people had no organizations or representation at all!

We began to reach out to these groups through existing organizations and contacts. Lesbian organizing began in the 1990s, and now a few lesbian organizations exist in urban areas of China, including lesbian discussion groups, bars, and internet and telephone hotlines. Female-to-male transgender people do not identify as lesbians or bisexuals, but lesbian organizations sometimes make connections to transgender individuals. Women with HIV were also beginning to organize, so we started to communicate with a Beijing-based women-with-HIV group, 'Happy Faces', who organize meetings now and then. I had previously run trainings for female sex workers through the governmental body, China Family Planning Association, which promotes condom use and safer sex among sex workers in different cities and provinces. So I got in touch with some of my former trainees.

We learned much from the encouraging experience of gay men's organizing: there are hundreds of gay organizations in China, either registered or grassroots-based. A gay magazine, *Friends*, has been running for more than ten years, and many websites actively represent Chinese gay men's voices and experiences, providing services for the community and promoting gay culture. Gay organizing has empowered many gay men, won male homosexual desire some degree of social acceptance, and also secured funding opportunities for some gay organizations to work on preventing HIV/AIDS.

The most difficult group to reach was gay men's wives, as few people come out with this identity. First of all, it is a newborn identity; and second, those who know their husband's sexual orientation often feel either ashamed or threatened, as homosexuality has always been linked to sickness, perversion and criminal offence. Third, many gay men's wives want to keep their marriages for a variety of reasons: some for the sake of their children, as single parenting is believed to be bad for child rearing; some to protect family honour, as divorced women are socially shamed; some for housing reasons, as houses are usually held in their husbands' names; and others maybe for economic reasons, as husbands may still be breadwinners. All these factors contribute to the silence of gay men's wives.

In order to find gay men's wives, Pink Space launched a gay men's wives hotline. We also wrote down one gay man's wife's story and published it on the website, in a newsletter and later in a popular magazine, the China edition of *Marie Claire*. This process resulted in many people calling the hotline self-identifying as gay men's wives.

In 2008 we started to organize exchanges between the different groups. The purpose of these meetings was to create spaces for people with marginalized gender and sexual identities to come forward and discuss their own needs, desires and pleasures, to find and share commonalities, and to build a common goal of realizing sexual rights and finding more pleasure.

By 2010, around 200 people had participated in our exchanges. Most lesbian and bisexual women we work with are from lesbian organizations or bars. They are mostly middle-class, urban-based and educated to university or high school level. Women with HIV are mostly farmers from rural areas, or working-class people with lower levels of education, but they include a few activists with high levels of education who work for AIDS organizations. Gay men's wives who access our hotline are mostly urban-based, with high levels of education and white-collar jobs. Female sex workers have less education, and are mostly originally from rural areas but working in urban areas. Most of the people we work with are between 17 and 50 years old. Our exchanges brought together people of different ages, classes and sexual identities.

An exchange between lesbians and women living with HIV: finding common ground

The very first Pink Space meeting, held in 2008, brought together women with HIV, lesbians and bisexual women. For many of the women with HIV, this was the first time they had knowingly met a lesbian, and vice versa. So I first encouraged the women with HIV to ask any questions they had about lesbianism and bisexuality, and also urged the lesbian and bisexual women to answer the questions.

Many candid questions came out, such as: Why do women love women? How do women have sex with women? Can women have orgasms without a penis? What is bisexuality? Can lesbian women love women with HIV and have relationships with them? How about children? Lesbians and bisexual women shared their feelings, experiences and practices of sex, love, relationships and desiring women or men.

A bisexual woman told us how she had thought of herself as straight before she accidentally entered a lesbian bar in Beijing and fell in love with a woman. She told us that she finds both men and women attractive, and follows her own feelings when it comes to romance or sexual relations. A lesbian couple who were seeking a sperm donor spoke of their hope of giving birth to a child. A woman with HIV told how she had in the past sometimes had feelings for other women.

One woman with HIV, Hong, spoke about how she still dreamt about having sex with her late husband, who had passed away over six years ago. She told us about the discrimination she faced as a widow, and how she had to remarry, this time to a man for whom she had no feelings. She had refused many times to have sex with her new husband, but ultimately this led to domestic violence, injuries to her arms and legs, and broken locks and windows in her house.

Hong also shared some of her sexual pleasures with everyone at the meeting: she said she found a boiled carrot wrapped with cling film could be used as a dildo, and she liked to wear rubber gloves while using this. Boiled carrots are softer, and felt authentic; often she reached orgasm calling out her late husband's name. Her new husband, finding the carrot lying in her bed and hearing the noise she made, asked her about it but she did not tell him.

A young woman, Qingyun, said it is very difficult for women with HIV to find lovers and have relationships, as society expects positive people to tell their partners about their HIV status. But since people often equate HIV with death, coming out as HIV-positive means most partners will leave. Qingyun used to date a man and they lived together. Although she carefully used condoms with him every time they had sex, she constantly felt it her duty to come out to him about her HIV status. For some time, she did not dare. But one day he decided to end their relationship, and as he drove her back to her own place, she told him that she was HIV-positive and urged him to get a test. The man said nothing at that time. A couple of months later, he called Qingyun and told her that he had done the test and the result was negative. He also said that when they were in the car and he heard that she was HIV-positive, he nearly drove the car into a truck to end their lives together, as he thought he must be infected with HIV and about to die anyway.

Participants found that the Pink Space meeting created a safe place to express their desires, feelings and experiences. Some women with HIV told us that sharing sexual desires and pleasures made them forget the social and physical sufferings that HIV had brought to their bodies, and gave them a moment of joy and happiness, which is hopeful and empowering. One lesbian woman said that before she left for the meeting, her girlfriend had told her not to eat with positive women in case she got infected with HIV. But now she feels that positive women are as healthy as anyone else, in contrast to the representations of sick and dying people often depicted in the media.

Many of the women with HIV, and the lesbian and bisexual women also, talked of the social pressures they face: having to get married, or having to come out as HIV-positive or as lesbian/bisexual, both of which can cause fear, rejection, disturbance and social discrimination. Many participants expressed the desire for children, but this is rarely fulfilled as they face too many social obstacles, either as women living with HIV or as lesbian women. Positive women told how difficult it is to find sexual partners because the social pressure to disclose their status means potential lovers and partners are often scared off. Doctors and health workers are unwilling to support women with HIV to conceive; rather they usually strongly suggest that positive people should not have sex or get pregnant. Many doctors are reluctant to provide information on the medicines that can reduce and prevent mother-to-child transmission. Lesbians also explained how the family planning policy only allows married couples to give birth to children, which means gay men, lesbians and unmarried people are all excluded from pursuing parenthood.

In the course of these discussions, marginalized groups began to realize that disallowing them from parenthood takes their rights from them. Whether HIV-positive or lesbian, people should have the right to pursue parenthood, which is a basic human need or desire. Being denied parenthood is to suggest that these people have less ability for parenting, that their sex is non-legitimate, and that they are second-rate citizens. The groups therefore came to realize that the status quo denies their right to be parents, denies their right to have sex, and denies their right to be human. On the basis of these realizations, we arrived at the fact that it is not only straight, married couples who have the right to love, sex, children and relationships, but unmarried people, LGBTQ and people with HIV have these rights too. In this way, the business of forming strategies to claim these rights came to be on the agenda.

These meetings gave Pink Space the confidence to create more spaces and opportunities for marginalized people with diverse gender and sexual identities to share their sexual desires and practices, articulate their sexual needs, express themselves, and get a chance to claim their sexual rights.

Exchanges between gay men's wives

Pink Space organized some meetings specifically for gay men's wives, but with some others present such as gay men, HIV-positive activists, and lesbians/bisexual women. At one meeting, Jingyun, a gay man's wife, said that she had been married for eight years. She could count on her fingers how many times her husband had sex with her. She had always welcomed the many men her husband brought home, without realizing her husband had any sexual interest in them. When she discovered his sexual preference, she was devastated, as her dream that their relationship could one day improve was shattered. She felt she had nowhere to go to talk about her suffering, as nobody would understand homosexuality and people would question how she could have had a child with a gay husband.

Jingyun said that her everyday life was torture, like having a blunt knife constantly cutting her heart. She saw no escape, and felt she was in a 'living death' or that she had a 'death sentence'. After their child was born, she quit her job, gave up her small business and became a housewife. Now she had no income, no job and if she left her husband she would have nowhere to live and would have to leave her child behind. However, after attending the first Pink Space meeting, Jingyun said she felt that her 'death sentence' had become a 'life sentence', as she found people there who are allies, who understood her and could share her feelings. After her second meeting, she felt that her 'life sentence' was further reduced to a 'fixed-term imprisonment', as her head had become clearer after venting about those many years of suffering, and she realized she might one day be able to change her situation. She began to look for jobs, and volunteered to support other gay men's wives, and share her life stories with others. She started to smile again.

Some gay men's wives talked about the difficulties of getting divorced, because they feel they have to give acceptable reasons to their children and families for the divorce. They said the fact of their husband's homosexuality could not be the stated reason because of the shame and stigma attached to it. Very few people understand how homosexuals feel and what they do. Some lesbian and bisexual women brought their lovers and partners to the Pink Space meetings, and they were there holding hands, and showing their intimacy and feelings in public. These simple gestures between lesbian women made the gay men's wives understand a little better the nature of homosexual relationships.

Yingying, 54 years old, from Jinan city of Shangdong, had never heard the word 'homosexual'. She had always treated her husband's male 'friend' nicely, cooking him food, buying him presents and paying for his tickets to visit her husband. When she learnt that her husband is gay, she was disgusted and could not understand how men can have feelings for other men. She felt that homosexuality is shameful and a disgrace, and pitied her husband. But seeing lesbian women lovers openly showing their love and emotion at the Pink Space meeting changed her mind. She commented: 'Look how happy they are! It does not matter whether people are homosexual or heterosexual, as long as they are happy. They live better lives than we do.'

For the young lesbians under family and social pressure to get married, hearing the gay men's wives' stories gave them conviction. They constantly encouraged each other: we must fight; we must insist on not getting married; we must not give in.

The very first gay men's wives' meeting resulted in participants identifying a list of fifteen needs to work on in the future. They also launched eight self-help hotlines and set up the self-help group 'Gay Men's Wives' Garden'. After the meeting, Pink Space helped the group by providing them with training to run the self-help hotlines and the Gay Men's Wives' Garden, as well as by mobilizing many gay men's wives to write and publish their stories.

Developing an analysis: marriage normativity and compulsory heterosexuality

Some gay men's wives said their husbands treated performing sex as a responsibility, therefore forcing themselves to go through the process to serve their wives' sexual needs. According to a gay activist who works with married gay men, some married gay men have to take Viagra to be able to have sex with their wives. One gay man admitted that while having sex with his wife he has to close his eyes and imagine she is a man, or he would feel sick and dizzy. The suffering is on both sides.

However, sex in these circumstances, according to some gay men's wives, is like rape. There is no foreplay, no talking, no intimacy and no communication. Weiwei said it would be better not to have sex at all. A divorced gay man's wife, Dou, who was in her mid-20s, was extremely worried she might catch HIV, although she and her husband seldom had sex. She divorced him after one year of marriage, but was severely beaten a couple of times during that year. Two years after the divorce, Dou still trembled with fear when she remembered those violent episodes. Eventually she ran away from home, asking for an unconditional divorce. Although she got nothing from the divorce and lives alone in a smaller and simpler room, she said she missed nothing from her marriage, neither the fancy flat, nor the man she was married to. She felt her life is much safer and calmer now than it had been then.

Many gay men's wives did not dare to divorce or run away from their gay husbands. Some felt that their children need fathers; others said that their parents or parents-in-law would be hurt too much by it. Shengying, 43, from Dalian, a metropolitan city of Jilin Province, said that in her family, among her relatives, and among her colleagues at work, no one is divorced. It is still shameful to be a divorced woman.

These discussions and the sharing of stories made people understand how the institution of marriage and compulsory heterosexuality work together to control and regulate people's sexual desires and practices, to shame and stigmatize certain human feelings and behaviours, to make gay men as well as their wives suffer, and to keep both men and women in unhappy marriages. The system celebrates certain sexual behaviours which fit the norms, and suppresses those that do not. Within this system, it is not only gay men who are blamed, but also their wives, lesbians, bisexuals, and transgender people. People living with HIV face pressure to get married, but are excluded from the marriage system and from society if they are open about their status. Single people lose rights to sex, love and children. Sex workers face high levels of violence, and are seen as immoral and disorderly, threatening marriages by tempting men away from their wives, instead of organizing their sexuality properly by getting married as society requires.

How we worked with pleasure

Pleasure and positive approaches are both a means and an end for Pink Space. We want to create a world where people are happier, more fulfilled, and have more pleasure, whether that pleasure is sexual or not. We believe that the struggle to create such a world can often itself be an enjoyable struggle, that we can attract more people to join such a movement, and that this movement can be more empowering if a positive approach is taken. Below I describe some of the elements which were part of our positive approach.

Seeking pleasure without overlooking the pain

At the same time as taking a positive approach, it is very important to make enough space for people to vent their many bitter experiences of marginalization, discrimination and even despair. This requires empathy and patience, and may take some time.

In the gay men's wives' meeting, for example, it was extremely important at the beginning for people to pour out their pain and sorrow. Many of the gay men's wives suffer low self-esteem and depression, and many felt that they were alone in the world suffering this misery and distress. A few even felt suicidal. Most of them cried and sobbed in the meeting while talking about experiences of coping with coldness, violence, asexual lives or non-intimate relationships.

This first meeting was structured to allow as much time as needed to share feelings and experiences. The accommodation was in dormitories or big apartments for four or five people to stay together, because sharing rooms also allows for sharing feelings and experiences. Because of this, when the meeting started on the second morning, one participant, a divorced 'gay wife', suggested that we should talk about the future, not the past: 'We have had enough tears and it is the time we should move on and form our strategies.' But other participants carried on sharing more tears and sorrow regardless. Only after sharing tears could people begin to think of change and be ready to move on to think about positive ways forward.

Building solidarity instead of victimhood

Marginalized people need to validate their own identities and feel good about who they are. Many people, for example, have never heard of female-to-male transgender people. Some of the transgender people who came to our meeting self-identified as 'patients'. One said, 'I always call myself a patient, a sick person, but I am not sick, I am healthy, and now I am a healthy "trans"' (跨性别). He was very interested in mobilizing female-to-male transgender people and forming a community.

Gay men's wives had never been recognized by society. For many participants, meeting and hearing the stories of tongqi, or 'gay's wife', was a new experience. Women married to gay men often knew so little about homosexuality or heterosexuality, or sex at all, that they felt the coldness or lack of sex in their marital relationships must be their own fault, and when they found out their husbands were gay, they still felt shame and were unable to talk openly about it. Thus being able to admit to being a gay man's wife or former gay man's wife was in itself an important step in moving beyond shame and confusion.

To some extent, the Pink Space meetings helped create positive identities for different desires, from which people could gain power. But we also tried to move beyond identity-based organizing by bringing people with different identities together. One aim in linking them up was to get beyond identity politics, where each group thinks they suffer the most and that the solution is simply a better deal for their own group. We aim to get beyond feelings of victimhood, to gain the insight that many different groups face obstacles due to marriage normativity, compulsory heterosexuality, and other sexuality and gender norms. Collective action can help us all overcome these obstacles and challenge these norms.

Exchanges between the different groups generated such insights. After hearing gay men's wives' stories, one HIV-positive woman said that gay men's wives' lives are much harder, as they are subject to domestic violence, linked to social stigma, and little social support is available. On hearing the story of a gay man forced into marriage, unable to get divorced due to his wife's and family's opposition, suffering from depression and eventually suicidal, one gay man's wife said gay men have more difficult lives than their wives, as the wives can escape the stigmatized identity by leaving their husbands, whereas gay men have to hide their secret, and bear stigma and discrimination all their lives. Some activists from more organized lesbian and gay groups also realized that sex workers, transgender people and gay men's wives are especially marginalized, as these identities are more hidden and therefore need support to get organized. Activists from two lesbian and gay organizations stated that they are getting sex workers and transgender people involved in their groups and also offering support for their own organizing.

People come to realize that other people may be worse off than them, and that they have a role in empowering others as well as saving themselves.

Talking about sexual pleasure

Equally important to this mutual solidarity in overcoming victimhood is a positive approach to sexuality. We do not focus only on discrimination and violence faced by those who break sexuality norms, or negotiate the power dynamics of relationships. We also take a positive approach to sexuality, and create opportunities for sharing experiences of pleasure, to enable people to find affirmation in their sexual feelings and interactions.

Our meetings always encourage people to discuss what people enjoy about sex and how to make it happen. Sharing sexual pleasures can make people shy and embarrassed, so we organize games and structured activities to help participants relax and loosen up.

Meetings with sex workers have been quite successful in terms of exploring sexual pleasure as well as promoting safer sex and condom use. Social discrimination against sex work, which makes many people in the sex industry live in shame and stigma, usually silences sex workers' experiences of joy and pleasure in sex, paid or unpaid. But in the discrimination-free environment of Pink Space, people could begin to express the pleasure some of them experienced at work, while also providing sexual pleasure for clients. One participant said that in her next life she would 'want to be a sex worker again'!

A woman with HIV told us that missing her partner and waiting for him to come to her home was the most exciting moment, sometimes better than the sex, as the strong emotional feelings could really hit her. A lesbian woman said the first sex with her girlfriend had made her feel the whole world had changed before her eyes. Gay men's wives also are encouraged to share their experiences of pleasure. One said: 'I knew what sex should be, I had a boyfriend before I married my husband. It was completely different. We should encourage young people to have sex before marriage, then they would be able to tell if their husbands are gay.' Another gay man's wife said: 'I divorced my gay husband. Now I have a new boyfriend and we have great sex. I often lie in bed like a slut, seducing him.'

Talking about sex can also bring much laughter. In one meeting, a positive woman sighed with emotion: 'This meeting has brought us laughter, which does not happen so often.' Laughing can release tension and pain, and give people courage and confidence.

The purpose of exploring pleasurable sex is not only to make sex joyful, but also to liberate and empower people with marginalized identities such as sex workers, in a culture that depicts their work as immoral, and people with HIV, for whom having sex has come to be about transmitting the virus to others. Having a space to discuss sexual pleasure openly is to affirm the right to enjoy sex and that sex is our right, which should not be withdrawn. People began to recognize that enjoying sex is a basic right for everyone, regardless of gender, sexual orientation, health status, marriage status, and whether or not money is exchanged along with emotion.

A sex-positive approach is also powerful as it makes people more active and willing to act, not just sexually, but in mobilizing. One of the HIV-positive women, Xixiang, hardly spoke at all at the first Pink Space meeting. But only a couple of meetings later, she actively joined in a photo project to share her life, started her life diary, started a blog on the internet, and launched a positive women's hotline. The positive approach encouraged and empowered her immensely. Few positive women had dared speak in public before, but Xixiang did so several times. With the assistance of Pink Space, she went to the Lala Salon, a lesbian community in Beijing, to talk to lesbians about living with HIV. Most extraordinarily, Xixiang and a UNAIDS official were our two distinguished guest speakers in a Pink Space seminar open to the public. In front of over 50 people, mainly journalists, academics, NGO workers, students and people living with HIV, the official talked for 10 minutes about female HIV transmission in Asia and Xixiang talked for over 40 minutes about her story of living with HIV. Their talks generated a good deal of discussion, and attracted media attention. She later accepted an invitation, together with an UNAIDS official and an UNAIDS ambassador, to talk about the epidemic live online on Sohu.com, one of China's biggest search engines.

Conclusion

In our few years of working with women living with HIV, sex workers, transgender people, lesbians and wives of gay men, we have found that it is not difficult for people to share their privacy, emotions or sexy experiences, as long as a safe space is created and trust is built. In the process of sharing experiences, people – male, female and transgender, straight, gay, or bi – begin to realize that we are all human beings; that we all have feelings and rights to enjoy what our bodies and minds desire; and that social norms should not stop any of us from pursuing these.

People with marginalized gender and sexual identities can be empowered and encouraged using pleasure approaches. These can enable the sharing of joy, the articulation of desires, the communication of practices and emotions. They can make people proud to be themselves, leaving the fear and shame behind and thus pushing the movement forward. Sharing experiences helps people who are marginalized to realize that social and cultural norms such as marriage normativity and compulsory heterosexuality oppress not only women but also men; not only LGBTQ people, but also straight people. With this realization, a united struggle to change social norms becomes possible. These exciting stories, erotic desires and colourful lives of our participants from different marginalized communities – and the boundary-breaking good humour with which they are often shared – motivate Pink Space to continue the collective struggle for rights to pleasure.

Note

1 All the names in this paper have been changed to protect the persons concerned.

Reference

Long, S. (2004) 'Lesbian, Gay, Bisexual, and Transgender Rights Project, Human Rights Watch', 11 July, http://transdada2.blog spot. com/2004/07/lgbt-rights-project-human-rights-watch.html (accessed 10 August 2011).

6

Enabling Disabled People to Have and Enjoy the Kind of Sexuality They Want

●●●

Lorna Couldrick and Alex Cowan

> Policy and provision around disability often neglect to consider
> sexuality as one of the basic human needs. While housing, transport,
> education, and other needs are dealt with, albeit inadequately,
> consideration of social and sexual factors is not high on the welfare
> agenda.... This failure to prioritize matters which are highly signifi-
> cant to most adults, including most disabled adults, reflects a failure
> to consider disabled people as fully human. Just like elderly people,
> disabled people are not seen as having sexual needs, and provision
> consequently neglects this. (Shakespeare *et al.* 1996: 87)

It is almost forty years since this asexualization of disabled people
was first documented. Seminal works such as *Not Made of Stone*
(Heslinga *et al.* 1974) and *Entitled to Love* (Greengross 1976)
were published. In the United Kingdom in 1972, a committee
on the Sexual Problems of the Disabled (SPOD)[1] was convened
(Christopher 1991) and in 1974 the Sex Information and
Education Council of the United States published its first lead
article on 'sexuality and the handicapped' (cited in Calderone
1981). These publications and organizations highlighted the
endemic asexualization of disabled people and campaigned for
the recognition of disabled people as sexual beings entitled to
express their sexuality.

These efforts coincided with an international drive to improve
the education of all health practitioners, including those working
with disabled people, to ensure the inclusion of sexual health
within service provision (World Health Organization 1974). They

proposed that all health workers should be able to provide sex information; carry out elementary counselling; and refer on more complex cases to specialists (World Health Organization 1974). By the 1990s in the UK, sexual expression, as a determinant of health and well-being, entered National Health Service (NHS) policy (UK Department of Health 1992). The close of the decade saw the introduction of new drug treatments for impotence, with Viagra becoming available on the NHS for men with specific, listed, clinical conditions including multiple sclerosis, Parkinson's disease, spinal cord injury and spina bifida (UK Department of Health 2000).

Health and social care for disabled people are increasingly delivered through multidisciplinary teams (UK Department of Health 2005). National guidance indicates that the integrated assessment and care planning provided by these teams should include sexual health (National Institute for Clinical Excellence 2003; UK Department of Health 2005). For example, clinical guidelines for the management of multiple sclerosis identify the need for a thorough, systematic assessment, to consider any 'hidden' problem such as impaired sexual function (National Institute for Clinical Excellence 2003). It recommends that men and women should be asked if they experience any sexual dysfunction and, if so, whether it is a concern to them; or if they have any difficulties in establishing and maintaining wanted sexual and personal relationships (*ibid.*).

Despite these recommendations and guidelines, progress over the last forty years appears erratic. In 2009, the World Health Organization reported that, worldwide, the sexual and reproductive health of disabled people is often overlooked or neglected (World Health Organization and United Nations Population Fund 2009). Based on our experiences in the UK (Alex as a disability consultant and trainer, who now uses a wheelchair due to multiple sclerosis, and Lorna as a health practitioner, educator and researcher), it seems progress has been made in some regional specialist rehabilitation services, particularly in spinal cord injury. However in many settings, sexual health is not on the health or social care agenda. In their book *The Sexual Politics of Disability*, Shakespeare *et al.* (1996: 182, italics added) included amongst the barriers to change: 'Government policies, *professional ways of working*, media representations and public attitudes'.

In particular, this chapter focuses on professional ways of working. Our experiences suggest that, albeit unwittingly, the very delivery of health and social care may undermine the sexual health of disabled people and perpetuate the myth that if you are disabled, intimacy and sex no longer matter. We begin the chapter with a little information on the context of our experience, which underpins our position. Then, after defining sexuality and sexual health, we explore why any discussion of disability and sexuality must encompass intimate relationships and sexual pleasure and not be limited to sexual dysfunction. We will then highlight some of the issues, grouped around themes: the awareness of professionals working with disabled people; improving the comfort, knowledge and skills of those professionals; and developing service policies. These are drawn together with the introduction of a new model of sexual health practice: the Recognition Model. The aim of this model is to develop competence and confidence, enabling services to work in sexually affirming ways. This approach promotes positive sexual self-esteem and identifies those service users who would like help where disability impacts on intimacy and sexual health. Finally, sexual surrogacy is briefly considered. Surrogacy could be a valuable resource for some disabled people but it is not formally available in the UK. Therefore the legal framework around the use of sex workers' services is discussed.

Disability, illness and treatment can undermine sexual health through neuro-physiological damage, psychosocial processes or attitudinal and physical barriers. However, physical disability is not synonymous with sexual problems. Indeed some disabled authors indicate a richness and diversity of sexual expression, born out of the necessity for good communication and creative problem solving, that many non-disabled people may not achieve (Shakespeare *et al.* 1996; Shakespeare 2000; Zilbergeld 2004). This chapter therefore is not about the sexual problems of disabled people. Rather it is about supporting holistic, integrated, multidisciplinary team practice that encompasses the sexual health needs of service users. The focus is on how disabled people can be enabled to have and enjoy the sexuality they want.

The context of our experience

> There is quite an industry producing work around the issue of sexuality and disability, but it is an industry controlled by professionals from medical and psychological and sexological backgrounds. The voice and experience of disabled people is absent in almost every case. (Shakespeare *et al.* 1996: 3)

With this in mind, we have chosen to start with Rachel's story as an introduction to the experiences that permeate our thinking. The story is not fabricated – it happened, and we have Rachel's permission to reproduce it here (using a pseudonym).

Rachel's story
I was experiencing bladder incontinence and using pads to deal with it. It had got to the point where I was cancelling meetings and not going to social events because I might need the loo and I couldn't change my pads when I was not at home. I was also rationing my drinking but this was negatively affecting my health. So my urologist suggested a supra-pubic catheter. I didn't really like the idea of it. I'd seen pictures and didn't like the thought of having a tube coming out of my bladder, through my stomach! I was really worried about how I'd look; whether my husband would still find me attractive; my sense of myself as a woman. It was hard to see the benefits when I was just so afraid of losing my husband's desire to have sex with me and whether I could really be an attractive person. I talked with my husband. He was really honest, which I appreciated, and said he wasn't sure how he would feel but he didn't think it would affect our sex life or his feelings about me sexually, and certainly it wouldn't affect how he felt about me. Reassured, I was then able to look more realistically at the impact on my day-to-day living. I made the decision to have the supra-pubic catheter.

I did raise some of my worries with my continence nurse. She was open and approachable which helped but we didn't talk about the position of the catheter. At the hospital no one, the nurse, the surgeon or anybody, asked me about that. Since no health professional discussed the site with me, I assumed the catheter could only be put in one place and would be located taking everything, including sex, into account. But, as I learned later, this wasn't the case.

When I woke up I was really worried because the catheter seemed so close to my vagina and clitoris. I was worried whether I'd be able to have sex again let alone have an orgasm. Healing took six weeks; all the while I was worried but nobody talked to me about it and I didn't bring it up. I was embarrassed and I thought: if it had been something that other people had experienced, one of the health practitioners would bring it up with me.

The first time my husband and I had sex I was worried about whether it would be painful or something awful would happen. Luckily everything was fine during sex but, when I became more disability-confident, I realized the catheter wasn't in the best place for me and that a discussion should have taken place before the catheter was inserted. When I spoke to the surgeon about this, he said he hadn't thought about the siting of the catheter in terms of sex. He had assumed that as a woman I wanted to have it below the bikini line so that I could sunbathe without it being seen. But funnily enough sex is more important to me than sunbathing! He admitted he was wrong not to have consulted me about the position of the catheter. He has apologized and has since re-sited it. The catheter is now in a place that is much more convenient for my sex life and my husband and I really like that.

Everyone has the right to a consensual sex life including disabled people. Health professionals need to talk with their patients about the issue of sex when they are doing anything that may affect a person's sex life. I was not given this choice and I really should have been. I know there is discomfort, awkwardness or reluctance among some health professionals to talk about the issue of sex with their patients. This needs to change. Health professionals need to find ways of making themselves more comfortable and confident about discussing this issue.

The catheter, for me, has been one of the best decisions I've made. It has really freed up my life and improved my health. My husband and I still have sex and he still finds me attractive. This is really important for me. I do feel that at the beginning of this whole process it was not considered: I was not really seen as a sexual being. It was as though, as a disabled person, I would not have a sex life.

Rachel's story exemplifies some themes we wish to explore: lack of awareness of disabled people's sexuality; the difficulties of raising the subject, and the consequence of not doing so. But it is only one story.

Rachel, like us (Alex and Lorna), is a member of SH&DA:[2] the Sexual Health and Disability Alliance. SH&DA, formed in 2005, is an informal network that brings together professionals (practitioners and managers) in health, social care and education; disability organizations and disabled people; sex workers; policy advisers; and others. Its vision is a more inclusive society where every disabled person's unique sexuality is respected and accepted, enabling its expression and celebration. Meetings are held twice a year where stories like Rachel's may be shared; or organizational barriers discussed, and specific issues investigated.

This chapter also draws on Lorna's extensive qualitative research study, 'Sexual Expression, Physical Disability and Professional Practice', which explored professional ways of working (Couldrick 2007). The supervisory team included a disabled person, Dr Michael Rogers, who was appointed as an adviser. The research, conducted within a contemporary critical theory paradigm (Kincheloe and McLaren 2005), was developed in consultation with 18 national disability organizations and 40 people with direct experience of disability (Couldrick 2001).

Based on this consultation, the practice of three community physical disability teams was investigated. The teams, located in south-east England, provided rehabilitation, support or advice with the specific aims of enabling people to remain in their own homes, promoting independence, and improving quality of life. Participants included ten occupational therapists, seven physiotherapists, four nurses, four speech and language therapists, three psychologists and two support staff. Data were gathered through focus groups with each team, and in-depth interviews with some team members. The emerging thematic analysis (Holliday 2002) was shared with participants at second focus groups and interviews. This encouraged deeper exploration, particularly of the tacit, often unconscious, perspectives they held in relation to the sexual health of service users. Findings indicated that, for these disability teams, sexual health was a very uncertain area. There was a theory–practice divide. All but one of the 30 participants said sexual health should be within their team's remit, yet it was either virtually not addressed (two teams) or very difficult and inconsistently addressed in practice (one team).

Thus our experiences are UK-based and mostly focused on physical disability and community care. There may be some additional concerns for other service areas, such as in mental health, the care of older people, and those for people with learning disabilities, for example, around the capacity to consent to sex. Apart from these, we suspect the issues discussed here in relation to sexuality are probably broadly similar in other services. Likewise, there may be common ground in other settings, such as intensive rehabilitation units or for staff teams working with disabled people in schools, colleges and residential homes. In resource-poor countries the organization and delivery of healthcare and rehabilitation undoubtedly will be different. It will be for readers in these settings to reflect on whether sexual health and sexuality are encompassed within the disability services provided: are disabled people enabled to have and enjoy the kind of sexuality they want?

Defining sexuality and sexual health

The World Health Organization (WHO) is developing working definitions of sex, sexuality, sexual health and sexual rights. Although not representing the official position of WHO, these definitions provide some international consensus to aid understanding. Some people may disagree with them but, in terms of improving healthcare, they provide a useful foundation for practice. Sexuality is defined as follows:

> Sexuality is a central aspect of being human throughout life and encompasses sex, gender identities and roles, sexual orientation, eroticism, pleasure, intimacy and reproduction. Sexuality is experienced and expressed in thoughts, fantasies, desires, beliefs, attitudes, values, behaviours, practices, roles and relationships. While sexuality can include all of these dimensions, not all of them are always experienced or expressed. Sexuality is influenced by the interaction of biological, psychological, social, economic, political, cultural, ethical, legal, historical, religious, and spiritual factors. (World Health Organization 2006: 5)

Drawing on this definition it can be argued that no one is asexual. Sexuality is uniquely personal and may influence how we dress; present ourselves to other people; the activities we engage in; and the life roles we undertake. For some it is of little significance, for others it is a priority concern. We may express our sexuality through heterosexual, gay, lesbian, bisexual and transgendered identities. It may be expressed in a rich variety of behaviours alone or with others. This may be in monogamous or polygamous relationships and through publicly acknowledged or clandestine encounters. Some may select sexual partners with whom they have no emotional intimacy. For others, emotional intimacy is an essential prerequisite to sexual intimacy. Some people, single or partnered, express their sexuality through celibacy. We argue that celibacy is not the same as asexuality.

Similarly, the WHO provides a broad definition of sexual health:

> Sexual health is a state of physical, emotional, mental and social well-being in relation to sexuality; it is not merely the absence of disease, dysfunction or infirmity. Sexual health requires a positive and respectful approach to sexuality and sexual relationships, as well as the possibility of having pleasurable and safe sexual experiences, free of coercion, discrimination and violence. For sexual health to be attained and maintained the sexual rights of all persons must be respected, protected and fulfilled. (World Health Organization 2006: 5)

Thus sexual health is considerably more than the absence of disease and the prevention of unwanted pregnancy. It is closely allied to powerful themes of pleasure, self-esteem, intimate relationships and connectedness. Sexual health is therefore integral to quality of life and should be framed in terms of strategies for fulfilment and pleasure rather than only with reference to sexual acts like penis/vagina penetration.

Sexuality and sexual health can be more simply explained. Using the clear language principles of Easy Read[3] these definitions might be given as:

> Your sexuality is part of who you are as a person. It is part of being alive and being human. Being sexual and having sex can be very enjoyable. You can do this in lots of different ways. For example, you can think or dream about having sex with someone else or enjoy touching parts of your own body. This is all part of sexuality. Having sex is a nice thing to do. You can have sex with someone else if they agree and it would make them happy too. The way you feel about sex and your sexuality can be different depending where you are from and what you learn when you are growing up. It is affected by the world around you and what you believe in. Your sexuality is about how you feel about yourself and how you feel about other people.
>
> Sexual health is feeling well in your body and mind about your sexuality. Sexual health means looking after yourself when you have sex. People can have sex in many different ways and with different people. Whatever sex you are having you need to make sure you are safe and happy doing it. Also any person you want to have sex with must have told you he or she wants to have sex with you as well.

We have offered these simplified definitions for two reasons. We wish to highlight that we are talking about straightforward concepts even though many people, including health professionals, find them difficult to talk about. Secondly, we wish to emphasize that meeting the sexual health needs of service users, to enable them to fully express their sexuality, is relevant to everyone including people with intellectual or developmental disabilities.

Valuing sexual pleasure and intimacy

At a pan-European conference on intimacy and sexuality in multiple sclerosis, several eminent neurologists and urologists described innovative medical treatments for sexual dysfunction. It was not until a man with multiple sclerosis and his wife spoke that the audience had that 'ah-ha' moment: the realization that the focus of the conference was too narrow, too medicalized. They spoke of what sexuality meant for them. They said,

> It is not just erectile dysfunction. It is life giving and life affirming. In our relationship, it has been about having children but much more besides. For us it has meant affirmation, reconciliation, celebration and healing. (Golding and Golding 2001)

Focusing on sexual dysfunction, as classified in the International Classification of Diseases (ICD-10) (World Health Organization 1992) and the Diagnostic Statistical Manual (DSM IV) (American Psychiatric Association 2000) – with their precise cataloguing of problems of desire, arousal, orgasm and pain – is problematic. First, this is because these classifications are phallocentric. They revolve around penis/vagina penetration with orgasm as the goal. On this criterion, many disabled people may be inappropriately labelled as sexually dysfunctional. The man unable to have an erection or the woman unable to have an orgasm, due to physical impairment, by these classifications have a sexual dysfunction even though they may have rewarding and satisfying sexual lives. Sexual satisfaction may be relatively independent of sexual function (Tepper 2000). For example, painful intercourse ceases to be a problem for those who enjoy non-penetrative sex.

Second, for many disabled people sexual dysfunction may not be the issue at all. The WHO definition of sexual health includes emotional and social well-being in relation to sexuality. This can include issues like self-esteem, relationships and social inclusion. For example, negative attitudes to disability, plus the media obsession with the body beautiful, may damage concepts of attractiveness and sexual self-esteem, and contribute to social exclusion. Shakespeare (2000: 164) indicated a danger in overstating the importance of sex as opposed to relationships, suggesting that most people are not seeking sex *per se* but 'intimacy, warmth, validation and connectedness'. Therefore the social opportunity to establish and maintain relationships, and move them toward intimacy, has to be part of sexual health.

It should be remembered that intimacy and sexual expression are not synonymous. Intimacy can exist without sex and sex without intimacy although, for many, the two are inextricably linked. Intimacy has been described both as a need for, and a capacity to, experience emotional closeness to another human being, and to have that closeness reciprocated (Esmail *et al.* 2001). Intimate relationships may also foster perceptions of value, competence, connectedness and belonging (Hammell 2004).

In considering the role of health professionals in enabling disabled people to have and enjoy the sexuality they want, intervention is better focused not on the reduction of sexual dysfunction, but on increasing the subjective experience of intimacy, pleasure and satisfaction. In recounting the benefits of sexual pleasure, Tepper (2000) describes the power it has in making one feel alive and adding meaning to life. Or as one man with multiple sclerosis said,

> Sex can be a wonderful reason to keep going when everything else seems bleak. It can be a way of connecting with someone we love, of giving our bodies attention, of relaxing, even of mild exercise. It is good for fatigue and excellent for pain relief. And there really is no disability that makes sex impossible, if we define sex not as intercourse, but as physical contact for the purpose of sharing intimacy and pleasure. (Spero 2003: 1)

Importance of practitioner awareness

Alex's own experience of dealing with different health professionals over the years is that for many it does not enter their heads that disabled people not only have relationships but also a sex life, and can have a very active sex life. This perceived lack of awareness was echoed by the disabled people who emailed, phoned or wrote to Lorna during the research consultation. A consequence of this disregard is that many disabled people feel they have no one to talk to about sexual concerns and no clear avenue for help and advice. In the consultation, a few disabled people had reported seeking help through generic relationship and sexual health services. These were usually described as good, but limited, as they lacked knowledge and skills around disability. Some were inaccessible. The consultation highlighted the importance of sexual health to personhood, self-esteem, quality of life, confidence and psychological well-being. For some individuals it was the highest priority concern even at the point of trauma: as one respondent said, 'Within hours I was asking how will this affect sex, not will I go to the loo independently!'

Lack of awareness by practitioners was demonstrated in the focus groups conducted with the disability teams: the majority of participants had not considered the issue before. Others avoided it or assumed it to be of little importance. There were several examples of what became labelled as 'first case scenarios' where participation in the research appeared to trigger the very first inquiries received by the team. For example, one team had said the subject was never raised by service users, yet in the interim between focus groups at least three people in the team were approached. Subsequent discussion indicated that taking part in the research had raised their awareness, helping them present a more accepting approach, or had helped them recognize and respond to a sexual inquiry being made. Sometimes practitioners ignored sexual questions. For example, one physiotherapist described a spinal patient that she was working with in the gymnasium, 'And he suddenly said that he'd had an erection that morning, for the first time'. He wanted to know if it meant he was improving. This was 'out loud in the middle of the gym with other patients near'. When questioned by a colleague she acknowledged that she had not responded: 'I just didn't want to go further with it.' Even when service users' sexuality was acknowledged it could be dismissed as low priority: 'They have more important things to worry about.' One practitioner suggested it was dismissed as 'an optional extra' because it was not essential to independent living. There were also some examples where older or severely incapacitated people were assumed not to have sexual needs or desires.

For most participants in Lorna's research this was a new and unfamiliar area of practice: an unseen issue. In the focus group discussions, all three teams said more should be done, but many practitioners felt they lacked skills and knowledge. However until practitioners become aware that sexuality is important for disabled people and appreciate the positive role they could have in supporting sexual health, they will not begin to develop comfort, knowledge and skills.

Practitioner comfort, knowledge and skills

There were examples of good practice in the focus groups, particularly from one team. A speech and language therapist shared a picture book of activities of daily living, which included relationships and sex, with service users who had little or no speech. This ensured they had an opportunity to discuss their sexual concerns should they wish. One physiotherapist did not ask service users about intimacy or sexual expression but was aware that sexuality was an issue for 'nowhere near the majority [of our service users] but it is a substantial number'. This awareness, plus the nature of her work which often crossed norms of physical contact, seemed to trigger sexual disclosures: 'Sat right up close you can almost feel something kind of bubbling up and then a question comes.' An occupational therapist in this team was the only person amongst the 30 participants who had attended a course on sexual issues in disability since qualifying. She gave examples of problems that had been resolved. One was of working jointly with a physiotherapist to improve a woman's spastic contractures that made sexual intercourse difficult. Another was obtaining charitable funding for a double profiling bed which was not available through existing equipment services. This team had good referral resources but most inquiries and concerns, they said, were managed through the skills within the team.

However, even in this team many felt uncomfortable when addressing sexuality. Their first focus group opened to a discussion about their initial screening assessment. Some two years earlier SPOD had been invited to a team meeting. This made them aware that, 'It was a question we should be asking, and so we put it onto that very first assessment.' However this became a section 'hardly ever completed or filled in and people found it quite difficult to ask'. So eventually it was left off the form. This was explored in depth in the discussion that followed. As in the other two teams, the research revealed that there were powerful deterrents that made addressing sexuality more sensitive than other aspects of care.

Deterrents included uncomfortable emotions, like anxiety and fear, which could lead to avoidance. There was a fear that the service user could be offended and this might jeopardize the therapeutic relationship, or perhaps the practitioner would be misunderstood and accused of professional malpractice. Another fear, if they opened a conversation, was, 'Would I be able to deal with it?' With little or no training, participants only had their own limited experience of sexuality to guide them. They were fearful about disclosure of sexual behaviours outside their experience, knowledge or comfort.

In part, discomfort can be linked to professional education. Of the participants only two, a psychologist and an occupational therapist, qualified believing that sexual health was part of their role; and only one, the psychologist, said her training on sexual health was adequate. So, although participants espoused a theoretical role, several had had no training around sexuality at all. For others, training amounted to a single lecture or a half-day workshop in a three-year programme. Pressures of covering curricula may dictate that many topics are dealt with briefly. What emerged in the research was that training on sexual health was encapsulated. It was managed as a discrete entity, delivered by a specialist in a single session, and did not pervade the curriculum.

Tutors on the educational programmes were not personally involved and therefore offered no role modelling. Additionally, whatever learning occurred in college, it was not seen to be applied when out on clinical placements. This reinforced the separateness of sexual expression from other areas of practice. Discomfort was also due to the private nature of sexuality and people's ideas of what is normal in society. The majority of participants had qualified with no exploration of their personal beliefs and values.

Education to address attitudes, skills and knowledge in sexual health is essential and more texts are becoming available (Sipski and Alexander 1997; Cooper and Guillebaud 1999; Wells 2000; White and Heath 2002; Butler *et al.* 2010). At the very least, we suggest that all practitioners working with disabled people should have the opportunity to discuss values they bring to training, including potentially asexualizing attitudes. They need to understand the importance of sexual health to quality of life and well-being. *The International Classification of Functioning, Disability and Health* places the ability to participate in relationships, including intimate and sexual relationships, on a par with mobility, communication and self-care (World Health Organization 2001). Educators may wish to evaluate whether their health and social care programmes reflect this.

Developing service policies

In this section we wish to highlight the advantages of sexual health policies for both disability teams and the wider organizational contexts. We believe clear policies will support practitioners who work in this sensitive area. A sexual health policy provides a clear, public statement identifying what and how sexual health can be facilitated. It can clarify role responsibilities and establish that this work is supported by the organization. Ideally, policies need to be drafted before a sexual inquiry is received. Otherwise, as the director of one disability organization said: 'Jo Bloggs quietly raises a concern with a nurse, the nurse raises it with the ward manager, a protocol is demanded and Jo Bloggs's intimate and private issue is now the property of a grand committee/consultation exercise' (Couldrick 2001: 15).

Other authors have stressed that all members of a multi-disciplinary team should have awareness, knowledge and skills to ensure a positive approach to sexual health (Glass 1995; Tepper 1997; Mona *et al.* 2000). The professional roles in the disability teams investigated were ambiguous: not one of the five professions represented consistently included, or excluded, sexual health from its remit. The psychologist who confirmed it was very much part of her role saw her expertise around emotional and interpersonal issues but biomechanical issues were outside her remit. She did not receive many referrals related to sexual health. This is because she relied on her colleagues for referrals but they had not considered sexual health before and did not know this was an area of her expertise. In another team, the psychologists focused on cognitive deficits and assumed other members of the team were addressing sexual health. Another team incorrectly assumed that sexual health was routinely screened by the nurse. So within each team there was confusion about whose job it was. It could be everyone's job, but more usually it was not addressed by anyone.

Possibly of a greater concern for several participants was the sense that either the organization that employed them or their professional body would not support them to address sexual health. As one nurse said, 'I don't know how far, from the Trust's point of view, I've got backing to do that sort of work.' An occupational therapist said that as sexual health was not overtly on his organization's agenda, 'It's almost giving you permission to avoid it.' At the time of the research only one of the professional bodies, the Royal College of Nursing, had a clear policy document indicating, with examples, the role of nursing in sexual health and rehabilitation (Royal College of Nursing 2000). This kind of discussion document helps to define practice. This is especially important where sexuality has not been an integral part of professional education.

From our SH&DA experience, we also suggest that the negotiations and discussions required to develop a policy are beneficial steps in moving services toward a sexually affirming and enabling approach. We would urge managers to involve service users in these discussions. Writing the policy helps communication and team development, which in turn can address many anxieties that deter practice – for example, the complex legal issues, or how sexuality can be approached sensitively in a way that respects privacy. It also ensures other activities, like appropriate training and supervision, are in place.

The Recognition Model

The Recognition Model is designed for use by disability teams to ensure that the sexual health of all service users is supported. It is summarized in Table 6.1 and has been presented fully elsewhere (Couldrick *et al.* 2010). This simple five-stage model allows discussion about the strengths and skills of team members and helps to identify any support and training necessary to develop confidence and competence. Some practitioners may be unable to work at all stages of the model, but a team approach means that all service users who wish to can discuss their sexual concerns. They can then be supported through the existing skills within the team and be referred on to other agencies where necessary.

The first stage, recognition and awareness of the sexual needs and desires of disabled people, negates asexualizing attitudes and should be essential learning for every practitioner working with disabled people. It encourages a sexually affirming approach and also helps practitioners to hear, and respond positively to, service users' sexual enquiries. Ignoring such enquiries may be interpreted as, 'You are disabled therefore sex no longer matters.' An affirming response might be:

> This is an important question (*affirmation*). It is a concern other service users have raised with me (*normalization*). Perhaps we could book some time and a quiet room where it would be easier to talk.

Table 6.1 The Recognition Model*

Stages	Description
1 Recognition of the service user as a sexual being	This requires placing the disabled person as a fully human being with sexual needs like any other, at the centre of service planning. It requires skills of validation, normalization and affirmation, acknowledging the importance, relevance or priority the service user may attach to sexual expression. It includes their broad concerns like appearance, social opportunity and privacy. All disability practitioners, regardless of role, should be able to respond positively to direct questions raised by the service user as well as to more subtle inquiries.
2 Provision of sensitive, permission-giving strategies	This requires skills to invite disclosure whilst respecting an individual's right to privacy. Techniques include indirect questions, printed service information, posters and user group leaflets. Where team members, for religious or personal reasons, are uncomfortable about providing permission to discuss sexual issues, arrangements need to be made within the team to proactively ensure every service user is given the opportunity to disclose relationship/sexual concerns.

* Reproduced with kind permission of the *International Journal of Therapy and Rehabilitation*.

3 Exploration of the sexual problem/concern	This requires obtaining sufficient information to understand the impact of the disability on the development and maintenance of intimacy and sexual relationships. The team could encourage all members to develop these skills but, if this is not possible for whatever reason, the stage of exploration could pass to practitioners in the team who are more experienced. This could be a designated sexual health practitioner in the team, the psychologist or those team members who are comfortable about seeking deeper exploration.
4 Address issues that fit within the team's expertise and boundaries	This requires skills of analysis, treatment planning and goal setting; working always within the professional competencies of the team. Although the psychologist may have particular skills with relationships, all team professionals have a valuable contribution. It may require a clear understanding of the different professional roles and might require inter-professional working.
5 Referral on when necessary	Referral is required for any goal that does not fit within the team's professional competence. It requires knowledge of the wide range of referral resources. It includes advocacy where resources are unavailable or inaccessible. It may include offering disability expertise to generic services.

(*Or, for the practitioner not confident to move to stage 3*) It is not my area of expertise (*acknowledging limitations*) but I can ask my colleague to speak with you.

Recognition also helps practitioners discuss the impact that their actions may have on service users' sexuality. For example, in Rachel's story appearance and sexual identity were as important as function. Recognition of sexuality is the foundation of a positive respectful approach to sexual health.

The second stage is about providing clear and direct permission to talk about sex, thereby identifying all those who wish to discuss their sexual concerns. Like Rachel, many service users will not share their sexual worries. Sexuality is a personal and private part of life for most people that usually would not be discussed openly. The privacy afforded to sexual expression also means that it is not possible to know who has sexual concerns. It is essential therefore that *every* service user is given a clear and direct invitation to disclose his or her concerns. Sensitive strategies are advocated, such as indirect questions or statements that invite service users to respond only if they wish to, without seeking any personal information. This could be done quite simply during any screening or initial assessment, for example:

I find some people (*normalization*) also want to talk with me about their relationships or have questions about sex (*acknowledgement*). I am happy to discuss these if you do have any concerns. (*Or, for the practitioner not confident to move to stage 3*) If you wish, I can ask my colleague to speak with you.

This approach respects individual privacy yet invites people to proceed if they wish. Providing permission to discuss sexuality, of itself, is insufficient because of its multi-faceted nature. Exploration is necessary to understand how disability impacts on sexual health. It may be about social opportunity, sexual identity, or the service user may seek to explore how the consequences of impairment can be managed during intimacy, for example using a hoist, having a stoma or not being able to undress. It could be about role changes between sexual partners because of the care needed, or how fatigue, spasticity or pain can be managed. It is feasible that all practitioners could help service users explore their sexual concerns. However where, for whatever reason, this is not possible, exploration could be assumed by specified team members.

The fourth stage is addressing issues that fall within the team's expertise and boundaries. Practitioners are familiar with a problem-solving approach to address identified needs. We suggest asking the service user about the problem and what they would like to happen. The practitioner and service user are then able to work together to find solutions and remove barriers. In essence the task is to ask, listen and act (where an 'act' can be broadly defined as responding respectfully and appropriately). Many emotional, social and physical aspects of sexuality could be resolved through the existing skills of the nurse, psychologist, occupational therapist, physiotherapist, and speech and language therapist. Emotionally it is important to allow a service user to express their sadness and anger when a sexual function is not possible, or is now lost. Recognizing, and affirming, grief may be the first step in starting to look at sex differently: in ways that focus on achieving sexual satisfaction and pleasure. Emotional adjustment may be necessary especially with regard to body image and self-perception. Other goals might include increasing social opportunity or improving levels of privacy. Or a person with impaired speech may value assistance to communicate their sexual concerns with their partner. The team is also able to address many physical issues. Examples include: biomechanical problems that cause discomfort during intercourse such as positioning, management of pain and spasticity; advice on fatigue management; information on sex toys like a long handled vibrator or masturbator[4] and the provision of disability specific sexual health literature. Goal setting should also include enabling access to all services available to the non-disabled population.

Always some issues will fall outside the disability team's role, and hence the fifth stage is referral: that is, providing information on, or referring service users to, appropriate agencies such as the doctor for a review of medication or for contraceptive advice. Referral could be to a relationship counselling service or to a psychosexual health service. For some, referral on may be to a telephone help line, like that provided by the Sex and Disability Help Line[5] or to disability-specific organizations.

Sex work, surrogacy and the legal framework

In Lorna's research some practitioners expressed considerable anxiety about discussing sexual concerns with their service users in case they might be asked to do something illegal or even be asked to assist physically in a sexual activity. Yet there was confusion and misunderstanding about the legal framework. We do not intend to cover the law in depth here, but we do wish to explore three important issues: the use of sex workers[6] by disabled people; limitations for health and social care staff where employing a sex worker may be helpful; and the potential value of surrogate sexual partners. These themes are considered in relation to adults who have the mental capacity to understand and consent. It should be remembered that our experiences are based on UK (and more specifically English) law supplemented by some dialogue with sexual surrogacy services in the Netherlands (Couldrick 2009).

In the UK it is not, and never has been, an offence for someone to engage in a sexual activity for payment. There are both men and women who have made an informed and voluntary decision to become independent sex workers. They are not trafficked or controlled by others (Pottle 2009; TLC Trust 2010).

There are, though, some very real abuses that take place within the sex industry and many activities surrounding sex work, like soliciting, pimping and running a brothel, are illegal. Recent legislation, aimed at discouraging demand, has been introduced making it an offence to pay for the services of a sex worker who is the subject of any form of force, coercion or trafficking (Home Office 2010). (How this is to be established by the customer is not explained!) Personal beliefs, risk of coercion, plus the many prostitution-related offences has led some to see sex work as distasteful or synonymous with organized crime. Also, in the UK, sex work is unregulated and usually clandestine.

A disabled person may wish to pay for sex for the same reasons as his or her non-disabled counterpart – in the last national survey of sexual attitudes and lifestyles 4.3 per cent of men reported paying for sex (Johnson *et al.* 2001). This may not be problematic where they can arrange it themselves privately. Where they cannot, for example if they have severe communication difficulties, or their privacy is compromised by high levels of care, the attitudes of the staff supporting them can present barriers.

The furtive nature of sex work may make locating an independent and skilled sex worker onerous and the TLC Trust has taken steps to provide help and guidance both to disabled people and to the staff supporting them.[7] Additionally, contrary to popular belief, it is not illegal for care staff to book the services of an independent sex worker for a service user. This should not be confused with the offence of procurement where a person, who is not a sex worker, is obtained with the intention of making them a sex worker. It is also not illegal for staff to drive a disabled person to the sex worker's premises whereas, for example, kerb crawling in a public place to find a sex worker would be an offence. It is not illegal for an independent sex worker to see their client in a nursing home or residential setting. Clearly, to protect the privacy of the client and to ensure other residents' feelings are considered, this needs to be managed discreetly. Importantly, it does not make the premises a brothel. Even if different sex workers visited regularly at different times, there would still need to be someone keeping, or managing, the premises as a brothel to constitute an offence.

Health practitioners and care staff are in a position of trust and have a duty of care to service users. Therefore, in almost every situation, it is clear they cannot be involved in any direct sexual relationship or activity with the service user. Such activity is not only proscribed in law but also by professional codes of ethics. Yet there are moments, although rare, when direct help may be desirable. Three examples are explored.

The first is where a man or woman, not in a relationship, is unable to masturbate due to their impairment. In the Netherlands, in these circumstances, the disabled person can receive government funding for sex (10–15 times a year) through commercial companies (often a coalition of sex workers).[8] At present, in this situation in the UK, one recourse to avoid continuing frustration is to find an independent sex worker. In which case, care staff may need to minimize any potential risks of exploitation not only for the sex worker but also for the disabled person.[9]

Another example is a disabled couple we know of who need help with positioning during sexual activity: the UK legal framework, although untested in case law, makes it virtually impossible for care staff to remain present. The solution in this case has been to employ an independent sex worker to assist them.

Finally, a leading charity, Sense, has documented how people who have complex communication and support needs, due to multiple sensory impairments like deafblindness, can be helped to learn about sexuality (Sense Scotland 2008). In the absence of sight and hearing, touch becomes incredibly important. Sense has highlighted sensitive areas where a professional's duty of care conflicts with the needs of the disabled person. They have suggested, until the law is clarified, using an independent sex worker as the safest course of action.

In the UK, the negative climate surrounding sex work may encourage some practitioners to ignore the sexual needs of their service users, rather than grapple with these contentious issues. Health and social care staff need to weigh this complex legal framework and negativity against the policies and legislation supporting social inclusion and equality. Equality of opportunity means disabled people have a right of access to all services available to non-disabled people (United Nations 2006).

Likewise this negative climate may lead some disabled people to shut out their own sexuality. One disabled man in the research consultation described how, unlike his friends at university, he dismissed any thoughts of sexual relationships: how could he get a girl into his bed when he could not even get himself into his own bed! It was years later, after finding the opportunity for rehearsal with his paid personal assistant (who understood his disability needs like dressing, hoisting and bladder management), that he discovered what he could do and what he could enjoy. Only then did he open his mind to sexual pleasure and recognize that he could participate in a reciprocal sexual relationship.

We suggest that it is time for a debate about sexual surrogacy. There are disabled people who would value more direct opportunities to learn about, and rehearse, how they can achieve sexual pleasure. In the Netherlands, in addition to the regulated services of sex workers, there are organizations specialized in supporting the sexual health of disabled people. One such, De Schildpad,[10] is a not-for-profit organization employing a small team of specialist care staff (both men and women) recruited to provide practical and emotional support. They receive training to help them understand disability and to develop the practical skills needed to support everyday activities. The aim is for the worker to assist disabled people develop their social skills and confidence in building and maintaining desired intimate relationships. Involvement in a direct sexual relationship may be included within their work, where appropriate, but it is not the primary role. The focus is on encouraging independence and helping the disabled person to build their skills and confidence: to grow beyond needing the service. There is nothing similar in the UK.

Conclusion

> Sexuality is an integral part of the personality of *every* human being. Its full development depends upon the satisfaction of basic human needs such as the desire for contact, intimacy, emotional expression, pleasure, tenderness and love. (World Association for Sexual Health 2010)

Sexual health has been identified as an important contributor to health and quality of life (World Health Organization 2001). This includes the well-being derived from a positive sexual identity;

building intimate relationships, in all their diversity; and the pleasure experienced in expressing sexuality. Disabled people do have sex, want to have sex, and have a right to a good sex life. However they can feel asexualized by society (Milligan and Neufeldt 2001); have concerns about developing and maintaining relationships; and sometimes are worried about sexual function due to disability. It is especially important therefore that their sexual health is not ignored; their sexuality and intimacy concerns not left unheard and unseen. Unwittingly, practitioners may contribute to the asexualization of disabled people by giving the impression that sexuality no longer matters.

Although our experiences are based in a resource-rich country we believe the message is universal. At the heart of all service provision should be the recognition of disabled people as fully human with sexual needs and desires like any one else. Health and social care services already providing rehabilitation and care for disabled people are ideally placed to support the sexual health of their service users and redress damage caused through negative social attitudes. We therefore urge all health and social care practitioners to be alert to, and appreciate the important role they have in supporting, sexual health. There are some disabled people for whom this may not be an issue, but there are others where it will be: so the opportunity to discuss sexuality must be offered to all. Practitioners need to find ways to become comfortable with talking about the issue with their service users.

Our aim in this chapter has been to provide some ideas and resources for this. They include better professional education: sexuality pervades all our lives it should therefore pervade practitioners' education. We have proposed a model of sexual health practice that takes a team approach, allowing team members to work at different skill levels. It demonstrates how issues of sex can be raised during a consultation and identifies how practitioners can use their core skills to address issues that rightly fall within their professional roles. We have indicated the importance of service-wide policies and the value of developing these through discussion with both practitioners and service users. This helps not only to clarify and ensure the organization's support but also to identify training and supervision that may be needed. We have also opened a discussion on the use of sex workers and the potential value of sexual surrogacy.

Recognition of, and support for, the sexual health of disabled people can be applied in any setting. The key is to look at sex as encompassing a much greater variety of expression than just penetration, and being open to however the service user would like to define or express their sexuality. The really important thing is not to assume, but to ask, and work towards enabling disabled people to have and enjoy the kind of sexuality they want.

Notes

1 Later renamed the Association to Aid the Sexual and Personal Relationships of People with a Disability, it always retained the acronym SPOD. It closed in 2003.

2 See www.shada.org.uk for further information.

3 Easy Read is a way of presenting information in a clear and easy-to-read format. It is mainly used by people with learning disabilities but can also work well for older people and those who speak other languages. It can be produced as a print document, in a web page or as an accessible PDF using various combinations of text, pictures and audio. See Raincharm, www.raincharm.co.uk/easy_read.php (accessed 31 March 2013).

4 See, for example, www.beecourse.com or www.spokz.co.uk (accessed 31 March 2013).

5 See the Outsiders website at www.outsiders.org.uk (accessed 31 March 2013).

6 We use the less pejorative term 'sex workers' rather than the legal term 'prostitute' (accessed 31 March 2013).

7 See the TLC Trust at www.tlc-trust.org.uk (accessed 31 March 2013).

8 See FleksZorg at www.FleksZorg.nl (accessed 31 March 2013).

9 Some guidance is available from the TLC Trust at www.tlc-trust.org.uk (accessed 31 March 2013).

10 See De Schildpad at www.deschildpad.nl (part of Stichting Handicap en Seksualiteit) (accessed 31 March 2013).

References

American Psychiatric Association (2000) *Diagnostic and Statistical Manual of Mental Disorders: Text Revision* (4th edition), American Psychiatric Association, Washington DC.

Butler, C., A. O'Donovan and E. Shaw (eds) (2010) *Sex, Sexuality and Therapeutic Practice: a Manual for Therapists and Trainers*, Routledge, London.

Calderone, M. (1981) 'Sexuality and Disability in the United States', in D. Bullard and S. Knight (eds), *Sexuality and Physical Disability*, The CV Mosby Company, St Louis MO.

Christopher, E. (1991) *Psycho-Sexual Problems*, British Association for Counselling, Rugby.

Cooper, E. and J. Guillebaud (1999) *Sexuality and Disability: a Guide to Everyday Practice*, Radcliffe Medical Press, Abingdon.

Couldrick, L. (2001) 'A Preliminary Inquiry to Establish the Consumer Perspective in Defining the Research Question in Preparation for a Study into Sexual Expression, Disability and Professional Practice', unpublished report, School of Healthcare Professions, University of Brighton.

—— (2007) *Sexual Expression, Physical Disability and Professional Practice*, unpublished dissertation, School of Health Professions, University of Brighton.

—— (2009) 'Disability Sexual Health Services in the Netherlands', report presented to the SH&DA meeting, 12 October, http://www.shada.org.uk/sites/default/files/Netherlands.pdf (accessed 28 August 2010).

Couldrick, L., G. Sadlo and C. Vinette (2010) 'Proposing a New Sexual Health Model of Practice for Disability Teams: the Recognition Model', *International Journal of Therapy and Rehabilitation*, Vol. 17, No. 6, pp. 290–9.

Esmail, S., Y. Esmail and B. Munro (2001) 'Sexuality and Disability: the Role of Health Care Professionals in Providing Options and Alternatives', *Sexuality and Disability*, Vol. 19, No. 4, pp. 267–82.

Glass, C. (1995) 'Addressing Psychosexual Dysfunction in Neurological Rehabilitation Settings', *Journal of Mental Health*, Vol. 4, No. 3, pp. 251–60.

Golding, J. and E. Golding (2001) 'Personal Observations on Sexuality of People with Multiple Sclerosis', paper presented at the European MS Platform Congress, Oslo.

Greengross, W. (1976) *Entitled to Love: the Sexual and Emotional Needs of the Handicapped*, National Marriage Guidance Council in Association with the National Fund for Research into Crippling Diseases, Rugby.

Hammell, K. W. (2004) 'Dimensions of Meaning in the Occupations of Daily Life', *Canadian Journal of Occupational Therapy*, Vol. 71, No. 5, pp. 296–304.

Heslinga, K., A. Schellen and A. Verkuyl (1974) *Not Made of Stone*, Stafleus Scientific Publishing Company, Leyden.

Holliday, A. (2002) *Doing and Writing Qualitative Research*, Sage Publications, London.

Home Office (2010) 'Provisions in the Policing and Crime Act 2009 that Relate to Prostitution (Sections 14 to 21)', http://www.homeoffice.gov.uk/about-us/home-office-circulars/circulars-2010/006-2010/ (accessed 27 August 2010).

Johnson, A., C. Mercer, B. Erens, A. Copas, S. McManus, K. Wellings, K. Fenton, C. Korovessis, W. Macdowall, K. Nanchahal, S. Purdon and J. Field (2001) 'Sexual Behaviour in Britain: Partnerships, Practices, and HIV Risk Behaviours', *The Lancet,* Vol. 358, No. 9296, pp. 1835–42.

Kincheloe, J. and P. McLaren (2005) 'Rethinking Critical Theory and Qualitative Research', in N. Denzin and Y. Lincoln (eds), *The SAGE Handbook of Qualitative Research* (3rd edition), Sage Publications, Thousand Oaks CA.

Milligan, M. and A. Neufeldt (2001) 'The Myth of Asexuality: a Survey of Social and Empirical Evidence', *Sexuality and Disability*, Vol. 19, No. 2, pp. 91–109.

Mona, L., J. Krause, F. Norris, R. Cameron, S. Kalichman and L. Lesondak (2000) 'Sexual Expression Following Spinal Cord Injury', *NeuroRehabilitation,* Vol. 15, pp. 121–31.

National Institute for Clinical Excellence (2003) 'Multiple Sclerosis: Management of Multiple Sclerosis in Primary and Secondary Care', Clinical Guideline No. 8, developed by the National Collaborating Centre for Chronic Conditions, NHS National Institute for Clinical Excellence, London.

Pottle, H. (2009) '"Sex Worker's Rights are Human Rights!" Takin' it to the Streets on the Las Vegas Strip', *Research for Sex Work*, No. 11, pp. 4–5, http://www.nswp.org/resource/research-sex-work-11 (accessed 5 October 2011).

Royal College of Nursing (2000) 'Sexuality and Sexual Health in Nursing Practice', Discussion and Guidance Document, Royal College of Nursing, London.

Sense Scotland (2008) 'Batteries Not Included', http://www.ckuk.org. uk/index.html?pid=211 (accessed 9 September 2010).

Shakespeare, T. (2000) 'Disabled Sexuality: Toward Rights and Recognition', *Sexuality and Disability*, Vol. 18, No. 3, pp. 159–66.

Shakespeare, T., K. Gillespie-Sells and D. Davies (1996) *The Sexual Politics of Disability*, Cassell, London.

Sipski, M. and C. Alexander (eds) (1997) *Sexual Function in People with Disability and Chronic Illness: a Health Professional's Guide*, Aspen Press, Gaithersburg MD.

Spero, D. (2003) 'The Healing Value of Sex', *Open Door,* May, pp. 8–9.

Tepper, M. (1997) 'Providing Comprehensive Sexual Health Care in Spinal Cord Injury Rehabilitation: Implementation and Evaluation of a New Curriculum for Health Care Professionals', *Sexuality and Disability*, Vol. 15, No. 3, pp. 131–65.

—— (2000) 'Sexuality and Disability: the Missing Discourse of Pleasure', *Sexuality and Disability*, Vol. 18, No. 4, pp. 283–90.

TLC Trust (2010) 'Sex Workers', http://www.tlc-trust.org.uk/profiles/ index.php (accessed 11 December 2010).

UK Department of Health (1992) *The Health of the Nation: a Strategy for Health in England*, HMSO, London.

—— (2000) 'Consultation on the Current Statutory Framework for the Treatment of Impotence on the National Health Service by GPs', www.doh.gov.uk (accessed 12 January 2010).

—— (2005) 'The National Service Framework for Long Term Conditions', http://www.dh.gov.uk/en/Publicationsandstatistics/Publi cations/PublicationsPolicyAndGuidance/DH_4105361 (accessed 16 July 2010).

United Nations (2006) *Convention on the Rights of Persons with Disabilities and Optional Protocol*, http://www.un.org/disabilities/default. asp?navid=13&pid=150 (accessed 4 August 2010).

Wells, D. (ed.) (2000) *Caring for Sexuality in Health and Illness*, Churchill Livingstone, Edinburgh.

White, I. and H. Heath (2002) 'Addressing the Challenges: Agendas for Education, Research and Practice Development', in H. Heath and I. White (eds), *The Challenge of Sexuality in Health Care*, Blackwell Sciences, Oxford.

World Association for Sexual Health (2010) *Sexual Health for the Millennium: a Declaration and Technical Document,* http://www.world-sexology.org/millennium-declaration (accessed 5 September 2010).

World Health Organization (1974) 'Education and Treatment in

Human Sexuality: the Training of Health Professionals', Technical Report Series No. 572, World Health Organization, Geneva.

—— (1992) 'The ICD-10 Classification of Mental and Behavioural Sisorders: Clinical Descriptions and Diagnostic Guidelines', World Health Organization, Geneva.

—— (2001) 'International Classification of Functioning, Disability and Health (ICF)', World Health Organization, Geneva.

—— (2006) 'Defining Sexual Health: Report of a Technical Consultation on Sexual Health, 28–31 January 2002', http://www.who.int/reproductivehealth/publications/sexual_health/defining_sh/en/index.html (accessed 21 September 2011).

World Health Organization and United Nations Population Fund (2009) 'Promoting Sexual and Reproductive Health for Persons with Disabilities: WHO/UNFPA Guidance Notes', Department of Reproductive Health and Research, World Health Organization, Geneva.

Zilbergeld, B. (2004) *Better Than Ever*, Crown House Publishing Ltd, Carmarthen.

7
Desires Denied
Sexual Pleasure in the Context of HIV
• •
Alice Welbourn

> Rape involves an invasion of the parts of a woman's body preserved
> for chosen intimacy, for communication of her deepest feelings, for
> pleasure of a deep and exquisite kind, for the creation of life. It is a
> violation which rages against women. (Kennedy 2005: 138)

This chapter isn't about rape, but about what it means for a
woman to learn that she has HIV and to believe – and be told
– that she can no longer have sex or children. Yet the words of
British human rights lawyer, Helena Kennedy, in her groundbreaking book *Eve was Framed*, evoke the nearest analogy I have
found to what, as a woman, having HIV can feel like.

I am not trying to pretend that rape and having HIV are one
and the same. I am extremely fortunate never to have been raped.
But as someone living knowingly with HIV for the past 21 years,
these words struck a particularly strong chord for me. Forced sex
and forced asexuality are opposite sides of the same coin: they are
both rooted in control over women and over our rights to choose
what to do or not do with our bodies. Both forced sex and forced
asexuality deny women our rights to our own autonomy with
regard to our sexual – and reproductive – pleasure.

This chapter seeks to explore HIV in the context of a widely
held and wholly false assumption that women's rights to sexual
pleasure – and to having (more) children – should be withdrawn
if she has HIV. This is not just about invasion, violation and rage.
It is also about survival, resistance and agency. There are many

of us women with HIV who have managed to restore our self-esteem, our deep belief in our fundamental rights to our sexuality and the sexual pleasure and well-being that go with those rights, as there are also many women who have become rape survivors. I admire all the more the many women who have had to deal with both in their lives.

In this chapter I will show how Western Judaeo-Christian belief systems have framed a fear of uncontrolled women's sexuality. I go on to illustrate how Western legal and medical traditions were constructed on this basis, preserving and projecting the same erosive fear at their core. Through the historically widespread reach of the British Empire especially (and, more recently, of the US regime, also based on the British system)[1], these legal and medical systems were exported to many corners of the world, through the imposition of the British colonial system of government, legal and health services. Thus these early legal and medical traditions have had international influence. This is an issue not just for the West.

I then go on to explore the consequences of these policies and practices for women with HIV around the world – most of whom are citizens of former British colonies. Finally, I explore how human rights frameworks can change policies and practices of law and medicine, to help make the good effects of these disciplines more common and their bad effects less common. I conclude that women's rights to sexual and reproductive pleasure – if and when we want it – need to be upheld by and not undermined by governmental, legal and medical frameworks globally.

Women in their place: opposite sides of the same coin – forced sex and forced asexuality

When I was diagnosed with HIV in 1992, no treatment was available. I and my partner (now my husband) assumed that this was a death sentence for me – and for him too. I was pregnant when I had this news, and full of deep joy at the prospect of having another baby. Thus the HIV diagnosis felt like a death sentence not just for me: upon medical advice, I decided to have a medical termination, for fear that going to term would put my own life at risk and leave my older children motherless. Miraculously, we soon learnt that I hadn't passed the HIV to my partner, despite my having become pregnant by him. I was also extremely fortunate in that he took it for granted that he would stay by my side and that we would continue to have a loving, fulfilling relationship together, including an active sex life, thanks to the use of condoms and (later) female condoms. Here we are still together, 21 years on, and he is still HIV-negative. We had no more children and I still grieve for the second son I lost. Nevertheless, we have been most blessed with our other children and in other ways in our lives.

One could – and should – argue that this relationship is, in principle, my right. And so it is. But my experience is pretty uncommon. Many positive women have been subjected to violence from their partners upon disclosing their HIV status to them (or, even worse, upon their HIV status being disclosed to their partner by health workers without their own permission). I also know many positive women who are yet to find loving, caring partners, whom they so richly deserve, because their positive HIV status has scared the potential partners away.[2]

It is also rather more common than I had assumed for women to experience both rape and HIV. In a series of audio interviews which I conducted with 12 HIV-positive women activists from around the world in 2008, some told me about also having been raped. I found this quite shocking, since I had previously been unaware of this additional trauma in their lives. I did already know that in South Africa women have their daughters injected with depo-provera, in anticipation of their being raped, so they will at least escape an unwanted pregnancy. Yet I had not realized that levels of rape associated with HIV seem more common elsewhere also.

How do we make the uncommon good things, which I have

experienced with my partner and my healthcare, common? How do we make the common bad things, which so many of my positive friends and colleagues around the world have experienced, uncommon?

Belief systems, sex and women

In all belief systems globally, sex, new life and death are events which are closely linked (Susser 2009; Coakley 2002; Douglas 1988). This is hardly surprising since, without sex, we would (until very recently) have had no life. And childbirth in many countries is still a time of high mortality for women and children alike. For women, being raped, getting divorced, becoming-HIV positive or becoming a widow all seem to be viewed as events of symbolic death for themselves. Some societies promote the practice of sex at these times, others promote asexuality in response. For instance, in some societies marriages and funerals are seen as times when it is *good* for people to have sex – with multiple sexual partners also – as a part of the process of the ritual. In some societies, if a newly widowed woman *refuses* to have sex with the next stranger who enters the community, she is endangering the well-being of that whole community. She must have sex with this particular stranger in order to protect everyone else (Barnett and Parkhurst 2005).

By contrast, in other societies, including the UK, for example, widows are expected to become asexual. I have various friends, colleagues and close relatives who have told me of the cloak of asexuality which society ascribes to them once they have lost their husbands. It is as if widows[3] – and divorcees also – might become rampantly sexual in their new status and might pose a temptation – or threat – to others around them. In the UK, as in many other places, widows and divorcees are still seen as potential rivals by other women and quietly excluded from many informal social networks as a consequence.

As soon as a woman steps outside the social norms ascribed to her by society in any way (in this case marriage), whether through her choice or not, her sexuality – and her rights to that sexuality – are suddenly in question also. Indeed, in the UK just a hundred years ago, a widow was sometimes quickly married off to a male relative of her husband, so that she could step back in to the 'fold' of 'belonging to' a man. This happened to my own paternal great-grandmother when her husband died. She married her late husband's paternal first cousin. This practice is still widespread in many parts of the world and women are rarely given a choice in the matter of to whom they are remarried (and I use the passive tense advisedly here). Indeed its very name, ascribed to the practice by social anthropologists, 'widow-inheritance', illustrates its roots in the legal obligations of the passing on of possessions from one (male) to another (male).

Other powerful examples of how women's lives historically have been controlled with regard to their sexuality are rife. Katherine of Aragon, Henry VIII's first wife, was divorced because she did not produce a surviving son for him, thereby causing the break from Rome and Catholicism and the establishment of the Church of England (Elton 1991). Much more recent were the Magdalena convents in Ireland, for girls who had been raped, or who had become pregnant through relationships before marriage (often with an older, married man in whose house they were serving as a house girl).[4] Both the girls and their babies were consigned to the opprobrium of deep disgrace, living in these convents for the rest of their lives – whilst the men involved were untouched. The assumption was always that it was the young women who were at fault and who had led the men astray, rather than any recognition that there might be equal agency, let alone the possibility that a woman might have had sex against her will.

Kate Adie's book, *Nobody's Child* (2006), which documents the stories and circumstances of foundlings and adoptees, presents another chilling analysis of the history of 'illegitimacy', interwoven with society's ideas of 'morality', and the long-term crushing effect that many practices had both on the (mainly young) women concerned and their children – in the UK and beyond.

All the attitudes and practices towards women and our sexuality described above from Western examples are rooted in the Judaeo-Christian tradition. There are similar attitudes in other belief systems. However, the Judaeo-Christian tradition is the one I know best since it is the one in which I was raised, and is also the one which has been exported around the world through the British, Spanish and other colonial systems. Therefore the roots of attitudes to women in this belief system warrant analysis, to help us understand and challenge them more clearly.

The image of woman as potential threat to stability is highlighted in the Judaeo-Christian (and Muslim) Creation story – the story of Adam and Eve (Crawford 2007). Eve is seen as the serpent-like temptress of Adam in the Garden of Eden, who seduces him into 'biting an apple', whereupon they both realize that they are naked and are banished by God from paradise. This apple is traditionally believed to have been a pomegranate, which is also known in English as a 'love apple'. In the Christian tradition, the dichotomous image of a woman either as 'perfection' or as a 'sinner' is personified by the Virgin Mary, the mother of Jesus Christ, and by Mary Magdalene, whom Jesus 'saved from sin'. The Virgin Mary, according to Christian tradition, conceived Jesus immaculately – in this case, without having sex with anyone – and thus without sin[5] – and God was Jesus's father.[6] Thus attitudes towards women and asexuality, purity and goodness – on the one hand – and women and sexuality, temptation, evil, sin and badness on the other, are notions which run very deep in the Christian tradition.

In Britain, from the eleventh century, when England first began to be unified, the Norman kings sought to validate their leadership through identification with the Christian belief system and all that this involved. There are still buildings standing in Britain built at this time: enormous stone churches,[7] full of brightly coloured stained glass and other artwork depicting Bible stories.

These stories are also widely represented in the great artwork of Europe, with images such as the Madonna del Prato,[8] and of Mary

Magdalene.[9] Indeed, one could best describe mediaeval religious art as the precursor of the modern-day multi-million advertising industry. These images adorned churches, monasteries – and places of political power also, since monarchs were keen to validate their supremacy by asserting their close allegiance to the Bible and all it stood for. These images used symbols of colour to enable people to identify key players in the scenes quickly. The Virgin Mary was always depicted wearing a blue robe, whilst Mary Magdalene was shown wearing red – if anything at all. In one fanciful nineteenth-century French painting of Mary Magdalene, she was portrayed languishing naked outside a French cave, where she was reputed to have spent the rest of her days after the events of Jesus's life. Blue was good, pure, asexual; red was bad, sinful and sexual. What the images conveyed stuck in the minds and psyches of all, just as advertising does today. Ironically, it was probably a bad idea to have the ribbon that symbolizes AIDS coloured red. But then hindsight is always a wonderful thing.

So attitudes towards women and 'female sex out of place' have had a strong negative impact on many different aspects of women's lives. Since medical and legal traditions in the West are both rooted very firmly in Christian principles, in the next section we will explore the strong influences of this religious belief system on these professions. The influence of British colonization in many parts of the world on laws, missionary activities and Western medical practices has played a major part, too. For example, homophobic laws brought in by British imperialism are still on the books in many former British colonies,[10] although they have thankfully been repealed in India recently, thanks to Justice A. P. Shah.[11] It also seems unlikely to be mere coincidence that 72 per cent of all women with HIV in the world, in 2005 at least, were citizens of Commonwealth countries, formerly colonized by Britain (Welbourn 2005). In what follows it should be borne in mind that with HIV we are talking not just about sexuality, but about birth, the spilling of blood, and death also – all events hedged with ritual in all societies globally; dangers (Douglas 1988) for society to deal with.

Influences of belief systems on the law

Doctors and lawyers may be shocked to read the above and may feel this has nothing to do with them and their practices. This is because the great power of cultural belief systems is that many are so deeply embedded that we rarely, if ever, think about or question them. We assume that they are the natural order, if we do ever think about them, and it is challenging for us to analyse and question them. I still remember the deep shock and amazement I experienced when, as a young student, I first read anthropologist Lévi-Strauss's slim volume (1963) in which he openly questioned the possibility of Mary's immaculate conception. So deeply entrenched had this belief been in my own upbringing, which I thought to be relatively liberal, that I remember looking up and around me in the university library to check if anyone was watching me, as if I was trying to hide a pornographic magazine under my study books. Yet, if we look at the Magna Carta,[12] for instance, signed by King John of England in 1215, and recognized as a precursor to the English mother of parliaments, we can see how God and the church were invoked from the very first phrase to support his leadership and uphold the legitimacy of the document. We can see also how women's roles in society were firmly placed in legal subordination to men in this document (for example, in clause 54). The subordinate role of women in society is explicit in this first document of 'modern' law.

As Helena Kennedy has clearly argued in *Eve Was Framed*, the Magna Carta was just the beginning of many centuries of female subordination to the legal system in England. As Kennedy eloquently explains, the legal system in England and Wales has been framed by male academics and political leaders who have had little or no experience of women's subservient role in our society. This groundbreaking book was at first ridiculed by the legal profession in England – and some older (male) judges still speak very disparagingly of its author in private today. Thankfully, however, it has now become a standard textbook for first-year law students and Kennedy's views are highly respected.

Thus the Western legal profession – and the faith communities also, both steeped in the male hierarchy and traditions of their structures – find challenges to the role of women and women's sexuality deeply threatening to the status quo.

Influences of belief systems on medicine and health care

Medical traditions in England also stemmed from the belief system of Christianity and inevitably inherited its attitudes to women, our sexuality and our role in society. The earliest hospitals were housed in and run by religious communities and were also set up along the Crusaders' routes.[13] Most of the London teaching hospitals[14] have saints' names. From the outset the role of women in healthcare was considered to be one of everyday caring, whilst the role of physician and healer was considered to be a male role. Even the role of women in childbirth was from the early days of the Church seen as a time of women's defilement and, until the mid-twentieth century, the 'churching' of women, in the Book of Common Prayer,[15] was used in England to purify women – even those who were married – after childbirth. This harks back to the assumption that childbirth was associated with sex and is therefore something sinful and dangerous, which has to be redeemed through a religious service.

Medical traditions, scientific advances and the tyranny of belief systems

So what implications do all these traditional connections have for women with HIV in relation to their sexuality? It is now possible for an HIV-positive woman, if she is stable on her medication, has no other sexually transmitted condition, has an undetectable viral load and a good CD4 count, to have unprotected sex with a partner without danger of passing on HIV.[16] It is also possible for her to conceive and give birth naturally (that is, without a caesarean) with less than 1 per 1,000 babies being born with HIV.[17] This is a giant scientific leap – and yet even family doctors in London are as yet unaware of it. A workshop organized by Positively UK in 2009, with some London family doctors, by contrast, showed that they were advising women with HIV not to have *any* sexual relationships and that they believed that 50 per cent of all babies born to women with HIV would be HIV-positive. This latter figure is completely wrong, because even without medication, the rate of transmission from a woman to her baby is around 33 per cent. Such is the gulf between scientific advances, on the one hand, and belief systems and practices on the other.

A lot of attention is paid to women's reproductive systems globally – rightly, considering the levels of maternal mortality. When it comes to HIV, this is intensified because of the high rates of vertical transmission between a mother and her baby without medication. However, while this is a sex-differentiated approach to medical care systems it is a distinctly *gender-in*sensitive approach. Pregnant women with HIV are rarely referred to as 'women' but rather as 'mothers', 'patients', 'PWAs' (People with AIDS) – anything to avoid somehow identifying them holistically beyond the immediate clinical issue. Ultimately they are seen as vectors of disease and vessels for producing children. Women's *feelings* about the pregnancy, the shock of a positive diagnosis during pregnancy – which, thanks to their own lack of knowledge and lack of support from medical staff, they think is going to be fatal – just do not appear in medical literature.

An HIV-positive diagnosis is an extremely traumatic experience. After trauma, individuals can react in very different ways. Nine months after 9/11 for instance, there was a great leap in the number of babies born in New York City, presumably as an emotional response to the horrors of that day. Not only did people resort to sex for comfort; they were also presumably intending to conceive and bring new life into the world. This was their right. By contrast, I have myself experienced a huge sense of asexuality after the trauma of loss of life, a sense which

I know to be shared by others also. This can last for weeks or even months, as if having sex is somehow disrespectful to those who have died. Thankfully in my case, my sexuality returned in its own time. But for me at least I had the *choice* to decide if and when to return to being sexually active. This was also my right and I was fortunate in being able to assert it. Yet for many, as I will discuss below, they have no *choice* over whether to express their sexuality with someone else or not, if their HIV status is seen as a cancellation of such rights.

I believe this attitude stems, at least in part, from attitudes towards women held traditionally by the medical profession also. In his book *Making Doctors* (Sinclair 1997), which analyses the undergraduate medical teaching at University College Hospital (UCH), London in the early 1990s, psychiatrist turned social anthropologist Simon Sinclair shows an illustration from *Gray's Anatomy*, which portrays a womb with a baby curled up in it, entirely cut off from a torso and missing most of the legs. This image, above all others, symbolizes the professional distancing traditionally imbued in all trainee medical students, in order to objectify those in one's care as much as possible – and perhaps also as a part of their distancing from the distastefulness of the sexual act that must inevitably have taken place for the baby to exist. The doctor was seen as master of all he surveyed, whose word and opinion about what was best for a patient was law – and beware all those who crossed his path. Sinclair is at pains to add that his participant observation of UCH in the early 1990s was at the end of an era – and that medical training over the past 15 years or so has transformed beyond recognition and become far more person-focused. Sadly, however, as I discuss below, other health centres in the UK and elsewhere have not yet changed – and we are still left with many senior doctors around the world for whom this tradition of the doctor being the all-knowing seer about what is best for anyone was the normal and the right way to behave towards those in one's care. Of course, there have always been notable exceptions to this rule, my own consultant being one of them. But the fact that these exceptions exist proves my point all the more – you can still have exceptionally good doctors who are *also* entirely sensitive to one's needs as a woman, in all manner of respects.

This global medical teaching tradition, in one of its most recent ramifications, has meant that HIV-positive women in Namibia are being coerced whilst in labour into signing documents that give the hospital the right to perform a sterilization after delivery. Once the women come round to realizing what they have signed, the deed is irreversible. The doctors responsible for this in Namibia have openly defended their actions, explaining that 'these' women already have too many children and should not be risking the spread of HIV. A court has since ruled that these women were unlawfully sterilized but failed to find that this was due to their HIV-positive status.[18] This practice is not limited to Southern Africa, but has also been recorded in Papua New Guinea[19] and Chile.[20]

A further dimension to medical interventions around pregnancy, HIV-testing and women is the likely gender violence that can erupt as a consequence of a woman's partner discovering her HIV-status.[21] This can take the form of physical beatings, sexual abuse and psychological abuse, including fear of loss of custody of their children. Women are also thrown out of their homes, rejected by their families and communities, and may lose out on any inheritance. Yet healthcare services are not renowned for taking these issues into account, in their pursuit of global AIDS-free generation policies.[22]

When you are a young, pregnant, newly diagnosed, HIV-positive woman, or one who has just given birth and has now been sterilized, and you are also dealing with violence at home, and deep fear for your child's future well-being, especially if she will now be your last, it is hard to focus on your own rights to sexual pleasure, much as it is absolutely your right to do so.

Legal approaches to asexuality of women with HIV

Just in case the negative effects of probably well-intended – but desperately ill-conceived – medical policies and practices are not enough to ruin the quality of life of women with HIV, legal steps have also been taken in many countries in the past three years to add to their challenges. In Sierra Leone, for instance, a proposed law contained language explicitly criminalizing mother-to-child transmission of HIV. According to this bill, a woman could be fined or jailed for knowingly placing her foetus at risk of HIV. Amazingly, this provision of the proposed law has been rescinded, thanks to the work of the International Community of Women Living with HIV/AIDS and Aziza Ahmed.[23] However, to have such drastic transformation in a bill so quickly is extraordinarily rare and is, to date, the only example we know of. At the 'Living Tomorrow' conference of HIV-positive people in Mexico in 2008, just before the International AIDS Conference, delegates from the USA described how their social workers were advising them, if they wanted to start a new relationship, to take the prospective partner with them either to see their consultant or an attorney, so that they could disclose their HIV status to this individual with a witness present, in order to avoid potential future legal recriminations. Hardly a great vote-winner compared to a romantic candle-lit dinner.

Joking apart, the criminal prosecution of people with HIV – both male and female – for transmission has, once again, struck at the hearts of those of us with the virus. Indeed in a court in Germany in September 2010 (conveniently held two months after the International AIDS Conference in Vienna, the theme of which was human rights), a young popular singer, Nadja B,[24] was served an 18-month suspended sentence for exposing someone to HIV when she was 17. She had been very publicly arrested by a posse of armed police officers before a concert and was held in jail for some time before being released on bail. This sentence has since been praised by Western Cape Premier and Democratic Alliance Party leader Helen Zille[25] in the South African press. Once more, our sexual pleasure becomes something scary for us to think about, let alone realize, as it is couched not in terms of what is our right and how we can be supported in this, but in terms of our evil intent, as if we *wanted* to go out and spread this virus to others.[26] For women especially, potential legal prosecution also masks all kinds of reasons why women may not feel that it is safe for them to disclose their status to their partners – and yet, once more, the law acts as a blunt 'one size fits all' instrument, unable to distinguish between different issues affecting sectors of a population. The fact that some women may fear that if they *don't* have sex with their partner they – and perhaps their children also – may experience gender violence or homelessness does not even enter into the legal equation.

Consequences of these policies and practices for women with HIV

Here are some words from Susanna, a close colleague of mine:

> Sometimes I feel lonely. I feel lonely when in the middle of the night I roll around the bed and the sheets on the other side are cold, the space too wide. I feel lonely when pots look too big for the one-person dinner I am cooking. I feel lonely when I realize I have been talking to my cat aloud most of the evening, calling him 'Amore' which means 'Love' in Italian, my native language, and it is a word that we only use between lovers, or mother and child. I find myself even lonelier in the company of friends with children and long-term partners. I wonder how it feels to experience that kind of love and intimacy. I try to cope by making sarcastic jokes, buying far too many high-heel shoes, or booking another holiday. Those may seem all clichés. How many women in their mid-40s are childless and single? Many, right? Why should I blame having HIV for my solitude?

Susanna goes on to describe how she learnt about her HIV diagnosis and about the massive effect it had on her life. She also critiques the huge gap in support from most medical and social services for younger women, especially when they are diagnosed. She continues:

> I think my story highlights some important issues. Women who become HIV-positive are often young vulnerable women, just as I

was, with mental health issues, low self-esteem and problematic drug or alcohol use. Once you find out that you have HIV those issues don't suddenly improve or go away. However, society expects you from now on to take all the responsibility of managing your intimate relationships with openness and assertiveness. It was very hard for me to learn, and had I not become part of a collective of women living with HIV I don't know if I would have even survived. There is much more to living with HIV than swallowing a handful of pills. I have had the privilege of accessing high-quality psycho-social services which have not only enabled me to cope with my difficult relationships but have also inspired me to become part of a group of women who challenge stigma around HIV by speaking publicly and by openly advocating for the human rights of HIV-positive women. I am extremely worried that in the current economic climate high-quality peer-led services for women with HIV will not be a priority and will not get funding. Without those services many women will face terrible isolation, poor mental health, poor physical health, and will lack the support necessary to develop the skills and confidence to negotiate safe and pleasurable sex. Without the appropriate support most of those women will remain silent, and society as a whole will lose the contribution of our voices.

How can Susanna's fears be prevented from unfolding? How can we make the uncommon good a common good for HIV-positive women, so that our sexual pleasure can be expressed in all its manifold ways?

Human rights: reframing the medical and legal landscape

Thankfully there is a chink in this armour of repression, a small light guiding us to a way forward. This takes the shape and form of human rights.

Sofia Gruskin and Laura Ferguson (2009)[27] have argued cogently and persuasively recently for a human rights approach to public health. They spell out clearly how, just because there is not a formal evidence base to indicate the immense and complex challenges faced by women with HIV on receipt of their HIV diagnosis, this is no reason to ignore them. They argue clearly that there is no such thing as a neutral, objective evidence base,[28] and that medicine is as much subject to the views of those who have asked the questions and gathered the data as any other branch of enquiry.[29] This is important because it enables us to recognize that it is not enough just to create policies, without also looking long and hard in the side mirrors for the juggernaut about to plough you down as you change lanes – as Helena Kennedy puts it. Gruskin and Ferguson also argue that new indicators need to be introduced into public health work, which reflect the human rights implications of policies and practices. They are arguing persuasively that policies and practices that damage the quality of women's lives are plain wrong – and that the medical profession, as well as policy makers, should be held accountable for these damages.

Similarly, when it comes to the law, as Helena Kennedy has so eloquently argued:

> There is no hierarchy of human rights and women cannot be relegated to a second division in the protection of their rights; instead the state has a duty to ensure that women are not treated as second-class citizens or subjected to violence even within the private domain of the home. There is no sovereignty of home or nation when abuse is actually taking place. (Kennedy 2005: 290)

Laws which criminalize women with HIV, for any reason, because of our status are entirely unjust laws. Laws and practices which make us fearful of even thinking about our rights to sexual pleasure, let alone acting on them, are unjust and harmful to women.

There are so many extraordinary women like Susanna out there. In the words of Helena Kennedy once more: 'The symbol of justice may be a woman, but why should we settle for symbols?' (Kennedy 2005: 290). It is high time for both the medical and legal professions to heed the wisdom and compassion of women like Susanna, Gruskin and Kennedy. I believe if they did so, the world would be a better – and safer – place for us all.

Acknowledgements

Thanks to Aziza Ahmed and the editors of this chapter for their comments on earlier versions.

Notes

1 For a particularly insightful study of the politics of the AIDS response in South Africa in relation first to British colonialism and more recently to US global politics, see Susser 2009.

2 See for instance http://www.positivelyuk.org/docs/2010summer. pdf.

3 See Widows for Peace through Democracy website: http://www. widowsforpeace.org/.

4 Their plight was highlighted by a film in 2002 (Peter Mullan, http://www.imdb.com/title/tt0318411/plotsummary).

5 In southern Spain visitors to a convent are traditionally greeted with the words 'blessed be the Virgin Mary' to which they are supposed to reply 'born without sin'; see Boyd 2004.

6 Similarly, according to Catholic dogma defined by Pope Pius in 1854, the Virgin Mary herself was conceived 'immaculately', or free of 'original sin'. This meant that, although Mary's parents were understood to have had sex to conceive her, she had no 'original sin' in her when she was born. This is by contrast with the rest of us, all of whom are believed to be born with 'original sin' in us. See http://www.catholic.com/library/Immaculate_Conception_ and_Assum.asp.

7 http://www.canterbury-cathedral.org/history/stained-glass.html.

8 Giovanni Bellini, National Gallery, London, http://www.national gallery.org.uk/paintings/giovanni-bellini-madonna-of-the- meadow.

9 Mary Magdalene by Carlo Crivelli: http://www.nationalgallery. org.uk/paintings/carlo-crivelli-saint-mary-magdalene. See also: Tinagli 1997; Lehmann 2009; http://www.bible-art.info/Mary Magdalene.htm.

10 See http://aids-freeworld.org/Our-Issues/Homophobia/AIDS- Free-World-Urges-the-Commonwealth-to-End-Its-Silence-on- Homophobia.aspx.

11 See http://economictimes.indiatimes.com/news/politics/nation/ one-giant-leap-for-gay-community/articleshow/4731073.cms and

http://www.aidsalliance.org/includes/Publication/Enabling-legal-environments-for-effective-HIV-responses.pdf.

12 See http://www.bl.uk/treasures/magnacarta/translation/mc_trans.html.

13 See http://www.britannica.com/EBchecked/topic/272626/hospital/35526/History-of-hospitals.

14 http://www.bartsandthelondon.nhs.uk/aboutus/history/barts.asp.

15 See http://cofe.anglican.org/worship/liturgy/bcp/texts/24-thanksgiving-of-women-after-childbirth.html and http://www.orthodoxytoday.org/OT/view/wehr-the-churching-of-women.

16 See http://www.salamandertrust.net/resources/WelbournIWD March09.pdf.

17 See http://i-base.info/htb/1865.

18 See http://www.opendemocracy.net/5050/jennifer-gatsi-mallet-aziza-ahmed/sterilisation-fight-for-bodily-integrity; http://www.bbc.co.uk/news/world-africa-19044569.

19 The audio interview with Maura Mea of Papua New Guinea is at http://www.salamandertrust.net/motherhood/mother hood.swf.

20 See http://www.opendemocracy.net/5050/francisca/dignity-denied.

21 See http://www.sophiaforum.net/index.php/Events/Health_and_Safety:_Women,_HIV_and_gender_violence and https://sas.elluminate.com/p.jnlp?psid=2010-10-27.0746.M.2DD2F5468818 ACF401D20DDBBA6353.vcr&sid=voffice.

22 See http://www.salamandertrust.net/index.php/Projects/The_HIV,_Women_and_Motherhood_Audio_Project/.

23 Announced at the satellite session on criminalization, organized by the ATHENA Network at the Commission on the Status of Women, 2010, New York City Bar Association.

24 See http://www.bbc.co.uk/news/world-europe-11097298.

25 'Zille said the recent court case against a German pop star for failing to disclose her HIV-positive status was an example to emulate', in 'Charge those who Knowingly Spread HIV', Babalo Ndenze, *The Cape Times*, South Africa, 13 September 2010: 3.

26 See http://www.sophiaforum.net/index.php/articles/HIV,_Women_and_the_Law.

27 See http://www.who.int/bulletin/volumes/87/9/08-058321/en/.

28 See http://www.womeneurope.net/resources/LauraFergusonEvid encebaseslidesWNZTownHallSessionJuly2010.pdf.

29 See also Lakoff and Johnson 1999.

References

Adie, K. (2006) *Nobody's Child*, Hodder, London.

Barnett, T. and J. Parkhurst (2005) 'HIV/AIDS: Sex, Abstinence, and Behaviour Change', *The Lancet Infectious Diseases*, Vol. 5, No. 9, pp. 590–3.

Boyd, A. (2004) *The Sierras of the South*, Santana, Malaga.

Coakley, S. (2002) *Powers and Submissions: Spirituality, Philosophy and Gender* (Challenges in Contemporary Theology), Cambridge University Press, Cambridge.

Crawford, K. (2007) *European Sexualities, 1400-1800* (New Approaches to European History), Cambridge University Press, Cambridge.

Douglas, M. (1988) *Purity and Danger: an Analysis of the Concepts of Pollution and Taboo*, Ark Paperbacks, London.

Elton, G. R. (1991) *England under the Tudors,* Routledge, London.

Gruskin, S. and L. Ferguson (2009) 'Using Indicators to Determine the Contribution of Human Rights to Public Health Efforts', *WHO Bulletin*, Vol. 87, No. 9, pp. 714–19.

Kennedy, H. (2005) *Eve was Framed*, Vintage, London.

Lakoff, G. and M. Johnson (1999) *Philosophy in the Flesh: the Embodied Mind and Its Challenge to Western Thought*, Basic Books, New York.

Lehmann, A.-S. (2009) 'The Rising of Mary Magdalene in Feminist Art History', in R. Builema and I. van der Tuin (eds), *Doing Gender in Media, Art and Culture*, Routledge, London.

Lévi-Strauss, C. (1963) *Structural Anthropology*, Basic Books, New York.

Sinclair, S. (1997) *Making Doctors: an Institutional Apprenticeship*. Berg, Oxford.

Susser, I. (2009) *AIDS, Sex, and Culture: Global Politics and Survival in Southern Africa*, Wiley-Blackwell, Chichester.

Tinagli, P. (1997) *Women in Italian Renaissance Art: Gender Representation Identity*, Manchester University Press, Manchester.

Welbourn, A. (2005) 'Gender, HIV and the Global Tsunami: Some Essential Steps for Survival', speech at Parallel Symposium of Commonwealth Heads of Government Meeting, Malta, 22 November, http://www.para55.org/reports/22November05/Wel borneNov05.ppt.

8

Sex is a Gift from God

Paralysis and Potential in Sex Education in Malawi

• •

Anaïs Bertrand-Dansereau

This chapter looks at sex education as it is done in Malawi, where both secular and religious organizations have been engaging in HIV prevention, and thus find themselves intervening in the regulation of sexual practices. This chapter is based on research conducted in the central and southern regions of Malawi in 2008, with professionals working in youth and HIV programming in government, civil society and the religious sector. A diligent literature review on sex education had prepared me to find kindred spirits in NGO workers and polite conflict with Christians, but reality turned out to be surprisingly different. Secular initiatives tend to be paralysed, in both the public and private sectors, by moral and cultural perceptions that sometimes limit the information presented to young people and that almost systematically operate a moral hierarchy among the prevention options. On the other hand, some religious initiatives offer sex-positive and comprehensive approaches that show great potential for helping young people not only to protect themselves from STIs and unwanted pregnancies, but also to develop a healthy relation to their own sexuality.

In a way, the term 'sexuality education' may be an overstatement, as most programmes funded in the name of HIV prevention would be more accurately described as 'disease prevention education'. Their narrow focus on physiology avoids most thorny questions about sexuality, and instead they repeat *ad nauseam* the ways in which HIV can and cannot be transmitted, and remind young people that being sexually active always poses risks. They take for granted that the 'young people' to whom they speak are heterosexual, able-bodied and not engaging in any kind of sex work; they also take for granted that boys are libidinous, sex-seeking creatures, and that girls are not. Thus, in this chapter as in most sex education in Malawi, pleasure will be noticeable mostly for its absence – until it crops up around unexpected corners.

Scaring the desire out of them: secular initiatives

In Malawi, secular sex education initiatives can be broadly divided between the life skills education (LSE) classes that are taught in public schools, and the myriad projects and programmes that civil society designs and implements. While some NGOs have been able to take a non-judgemental approach, most secular sex education that I encountered was fear-based, and constructed a heavy hierarchy of prevention options presented to young people.

Life skills education in public schools[1]

LSE is a mandatory subject that is taught in public schools across the country, both at primary and secondary levels.[2] It was first implemented as a pilot project for Standard Four pupils in 1997, three years after the first multi-party elections, and eventually made mandatory for all grades. The curriculum was based on other African LSE initiatives, and replaced a patchwork of information that was given in different classes such as biology, health and Bible studies. It identified different themes that are linked to HIV transmission (for example, adolescent development, alcohol and substance abuse, gender-based violence or harmful cultural practices) as well as sixteen psychosocial skills (for example, communication, decision making, self-esteem, assertiveness). LSE has a unique reach, as most children and adolescents attend the first years of primary school, and as both children and parents have high levels of trust in teachers (Wittenberg *et al.* 2007: 19).

There are, however, serious problems in both content and implementation of the LSE curriculum. In accordance with the Ministry of Education's policy, abstinence is the preferred prevention method that is promoted in schools:

> In schools, it is accepted to discuss condoms as one possible way to prevent HIV, but never as a preferred way or as a 100 per cent safe prevention. Teachers and schools cannot deny children and youths access to information. However abstinence has to clearly be the first choice that is imparted to learners in primary and secondary schools. If pupils want more information on condom use, or want to access free condoms, they can do this in clinics and hospitals. There is no demonstration or distribution of condoms in schools. (Gerald, education worker in the public system)

The curriculum does not plan for lessons that provide information on condoms, but teachers may answer questions from pupils on the topic, and refer youths to the local clinics. This policy comes from a country-wide consultation with parents, which showed that there was widespread support for sexuality education and HIV prevention, as long as there was no mention of condoms. Talking about condoms, it was felt, would encourage children to become sexually active right away,[3] even though all studies show that sex education tends to delay sexual debut, a fact known by education workers:

> The problem is that we think if we give them correct information, they will be able to use it and make informed decisions – that's what we think. But the community doesn't think like that. The churches don't think like that. Because the Ministry of Education is trying to go along with what the community wants, that's why there is that policy: in primary and secondary school, no teaching the condoms. (Takondwa, education worker in the public system)

Because of perceived cultural taboos, the information that is given in LSE is limited. For example, although it is labelled as a 'sexual and reproductive health class', at no point is there an explanation of what sexual intercourse consists of. Youth are taught of ways to avoid 'it', of the dangers 'it' poses, but are expected to figure out for themselves what 'it' is exactly.

These policies may seem to make sense – why give detailed sexual information to young children in primary school, a majority of whom are not yet sexually active? The pupils in primary schools are not, however, all young children. The government considers normal primary school going age to be 6–13 years old; however, 16 per cent of pupils were older than this, and 'the Malawi school system is highly characterized by the under and over-aged pupils particularly in primary and secondary education' (National Statistical Office of Malawi 2010: 18). What's more, the very idea of sex education is to provide information to youths before they become sexually active. At age fifteen, about 20 per cent of adolescent girls have been sexually active at some time, and close to 10 per cent have already had a child (Wittenberg *et al.* 2007: 11). Even the later years of primary schools are too late for many: marriage and pregnancies cause girls to start dropping out in large numbers around the age of thirteen, a phenomenon which only increases in subsequent years (National Statistical Office of Malawi 2010: 16, 25).

Another set of problems with the LSE relates to implementation. First, some teachers have strongly resisted teaching LSE, which tends to make pupils excitable and brings questions that are deemed 'embarrassing' by many teachers. In addition to discomfort with the content of LSE, there is the problem of teachers' workload: especially in primary schools, teachers have large classes and the addition of a subject was seen as an extra burden. Moreover, teachers are under pressure to focus on the subjects that are necessary for pupils to pass the national exams, such as maths, language and science classes – and do not see self-esteem and negotiation skills as a priority. All of these factors combined mean that unless a principal or a teacher personally sees LSE as a priority, it is common for the subject not to be taught at all.

Civil society: independent dependency

While in theory the public schools' LSE reaches the largest number of youths in the country, civil society also produces a variety of prevention programmes that focus on sex education and life skills (LS). In Malawi, associations of all kinds were extremely rare under the Banda regime, but came alive following the 1994 multi-party elections, and their number has exploded with the increase in outside funding since the early 2000s. Seen as an antidote to both the corrupt and rigid public sector, and the heartless profit-driven private sector, civil society has been touted as something of a magic solution to most development problems (Chandhoke 2007: 608). I'll use the term to talk about the vast array of NGOs, community-based organizations, youth clubs and youth centres, women's groups, post-test clubs, AIDS service organizations, and other local associations.

Although it is made up of independent organizations, civil society is very much donor-dependent, and is at times reduced to the implementing arm of the development industry.[4] The organizations I met generally organized their work around the various administrative requirements of donors, and constantly struggled to find a meeting ground between their members' needs and a donor's funding priority. With the exception of one organization, which got 20 per cent of its revenues from income-generating activities, most organizations I met generated between 1 per cent and 5 per cent of their own funding – which means 95 to 99 per cent of their funding came from donors. One informant did not mince words in his analysis of the generalized dependency that is found in Malawi:

> Instead of looking at our priority as a nation, we say, 'Oh but the Global Fund will not accept that' – it's the problem of the Global Fund? It's our own problem! The priorities are being set in Geneva, yet we have our own issues here. What are the priorities in Africa?... Our priorities are being set over there, and we're just being told what to do. For example, you want to fund my organization; you'll tell me your priority areas, the thematic areas that you are into. You'll say ... 'Here's $25,000, go back and review your strategic plan so that it includes these things.' I hastily go back to review my strategic plan, present it to you and

you'll say, 'Oh! This is just what we have been looking for!' You pump millions of kwachas into my programme and say things are working, but in the first place, as a case worker on the ground, I had my own priorities. But you've dangled a juicy carrot before me, and I couldn't miss the call. (Gabriel, regional coordinator for an HIV/AIDS umbrella organization)

With regard to prevention messages, organizations are limited both by donors and by national policy. Donors have their preferences, generally organized along the lines of the condoms vs abstinence opposition, and organizations who work with them must go along with these. In addition, the National AIDS Commission produces a compendium of approved public messages about HIV and AIDS, from which organizations must choose when they produce materials.

HIV prevention targeting young people may take many forms, but some activities were especially common in the organizations that I met. Most organizations will offer life skills classes through peer education. One youth organization, YouthNet and Counselling (YONECO), also offers an anonymous helpline where young people can call during the day to ask questions, report abuse or simply get a supportive ear. Other common activities include: special events on the 'edutainment' model; drama clubs that put up short plays about HIV, which then tour neighbouring communities to spread health messages and generate discussion; sports tournaments, featuring football for boys and netball for girls. Fewer organizations have youth centres, physical spaces where young people can hold activities or simply spend their free time, and where some sexual and reproductive health (SRH) information is made available. A whole set of prevention initiatives focuses on economic activities, notably vocational job training and income-generating activities, which are often collective business ventures to help young people have a small income. The sheer number of organizations, notably the ubiquitous youth clubs, means that these activities reach many young people.

Paralysis in sex education

The sex education that is provided by most civil society initiatives is not without its challenges: there are problems with regards to approach, content and implementation.

The approach used by most civil society organizations and in the public schools can be described as fear-based, where the purpose of sex education is to instil in young people a fear of the consequences of sexual activity. While unprotected and coerced sexual activity certainly poses serious dangers, adolescent sex in itself is not harmful when it is protected and takes place among consenting people (Santelli *et al.* 2006: 74). Grounding sex education in fear is the exact opposite of what is recommended in the Sexual Health Model, which advocates 'exploring and celebrating sexuality from a positive and self-affirming perspective' as the most effective way to help people avoid sexual risk by making them feel comfortable with their own sexuality (Robinson *et al.* 2002: 50).

This is compounded by the heavy imposition of hierarchy among prevention options that I found in most discourses about prevention for youth. While most organizations do provide the complete ABCs to young people,[5] these are rarely presented as equally valid prevention methods. For young and unmarried people, most interventions promote abstinence and present condoms as a solution for 'those who cannot abstain', as illustrated by these few quotations:

> If you can abstain, it's better to abstain until you are married. As young people you are future leaders so when you are young and productive you should abstain. But sometimes you feel you cannot abstain, then you should use a condom. (Dorothy, project manager in an HIV/AIDS umbrella organization)

> You'll see an organization implementing activities related to abstinence, encouraging people to abstain from sex. But they know for sure that not the majority abstains from sex, so they say, 'OK, abstinence is good because it's 100 per cent sure, if you abstain from sex there's no way you'll get HIV/AIDS. But if you cannot, then use condoms.' (Arthur, project manager in the public sector)

> Sex workers would be targeted with message of condom use. Young people should get messages of abstinence, but again some young people may not really abstain so they should use a condom. For families, you can use faithfulness. (Jonas, project manager in a HIV/AIDS umbrella organization)

Hence the problem is not that condoms are absent – indeed, they are mentioned even by organizations dedicated to abstinence promotion. However, their use is presented as a failure, while abstinence is presented as the correct, normal thing for young people to do. Being sexually active is perceived as something that happens because of a lack of will, or a loss of control.

Rarely did I hear of young people who chose to be sexually active, even from informants who recognized that abstinence was extremely rare. Instead, sexual activity seems to be always presented as something that takes over young people against their will. Such a vision of sexuality – a hostile exterior force that contaminates previously pure people – is not unique to Malawi or Africa; indeed, it is extremely common in the West as well (Real Reason 2008: 12). It is, however, a problem in so far as it detaches sexual desire from the rest of an individual, which does not promote a coherent sexuality. Also, it allows a silence to fall over the other reasons why young people become sexually active: pleasure, intimacy, love, curiosity – and not just coercion, poverty and peer pressure.

A last problem is that of implementation. Some organizations do have remarkably complete, non-judgemental approaches to sex education and service provision for adolescents and young adults. For example, this national coordinator for an NGO explains their perspective:

> The provider has to ask, 'Can I help you? What do you want me to do for you?' If somebody hasn't come for a lecture, why do you force your lecture on them?... They don't have to judge anybody. If a young person says, 'I want a condom', regardless of their age, they have to get that condom, without being asked questions. This is how we have already lost a lot of young people.... The moment you start

judging them, they'll do it anyway and they'll end up getting a lot of problems. (Esther, coordinator for an NGO)

While this seems like a laudable approach that avoids the pitfalls of moralizing prevention options, the discourse I got from a local worker from the same organization was rather different.

There are some [young people] who come here accessing the condoms simply because they don't know how to abstain, so we normally stress abstinence, how they can abstain, those particular techniques [like reading a book about mathematics or taking a cold shower]. They come in here accessing condoms, but they may not know there are other ways how they can prevent it, or that they can run away from sex. So we give them counselling on abstinence and faithfulness. And still, if they really insist, we give them [condoms] with counselling, to say how you have to use a condom effectively, following the procedures, the steps. (Arnold, local worker for an NGO)

In this specific case, the likelihood of an adolescent 'really insisting' on getting condoms seems to be relatively low. While this was but one particular example of a gap between programme design and implementation, it seemed to reflect a real problem. No matter how carefully designed and evidence-based the approach, if it goes against some fundamental elements of the social and cultural norms that frame discussions of sexuality, it remains very hard to implement.

Sex is a gift from God: the potentials of faith-based prevention

In a country as religious and donor-dependent as Malawi, it is not surprising to find a vast array of religious organizations working on HIV-related programming. Faith-based HIV prevention interventions are numerous and diversified, and include a wide range of attitudes, approaches and discourses. It was in this somewhat unexpected milieu that I found an alternative to the paralysis of secular sex education.

The religious landscape of Malawi

In Malawi, religion is a social fact that cannot be ignored; while most Westerners consider religion to be a private, and even an intimate matter, many Malawians bring up the subject upon meeting people, and love to discuss their faith, even with strangers. Faith is at once wide and deep in Malawi: the vast majority of people are fervent monotheists, and religion occupies a central place in many people's lives.

> In Malawi, wherever you go you'll find a church and people worshipping God. There's a high consciousness of God. This is different from the West. Over 80 per cent of Malawians identify as Christian, then there are 15 per cent Muslims, and 5 per cent who don't have a God. Actually, you won't really find people who don't believe in God; and if you tell them you don't believe in God, they will tell you: 'You are stupid.' (Edwin, coordinator for an association of churches)

The Christian majority is spread across many denominations, both in mainline and in Evangelical churches.[6] As is the case elsewhere in the developing world, and especially in sub-Saharan Africa, Evangelical churches have mushroomed in size and in numbers in the past twenty years (Freston 2001; Daneel 2004; Gifford 2004; Robbins 2004; Ranger 2008). These churches are sometimes home-grown from one of Malawi's larger cities, and sometimes they are branches from other African countries or from Western countries, usually the USA. While religion is central to people's lives, it is often lived with a certain fluidity, and it seemed fairly common for people to change churches, denominations or even religion.

Churches not only take care of people's spiritual life; they are also important social hubs. Both types of churches tend to have a development arm; mainline churches have been running hospitals and schools since colonial times, and more recently many Evangelical churches have created NGOs to run development projects with outside funding. Also, many churches have smaller groups: women's groups, youth clubs, choirs, and sometimes men's groups. In addition to the churches themselves, there are two major youth-oriented, faith-based organizations (FBOs): Scripture Union for primary school children, and the Students Christian Organization of Malawi for secondary and post-secondary students. Both organizations have been active since the 1960s in Malawian schools; since the late 1990s, they have become active with regards to HIV/AIDS. Overall, churches and FBOs can be important places for young people to socialize; the respectability of the church gives them a certain freedom to be with their peers, away from the suspicion of parents.

The very existence of faith-based HIV prevention initiatives is fairly recent; for the better part of the epidemic, churches contributed to stigma by relaying the idea that AIDS was a just retribution for having sinned (Samson, youth FBO coordinator). Things started changing in the late 1990s when the very same church leaders who denounced immorality themselves started dying from AIDS – at which point churches had to recognize that the epidemic was not just the lot of the unsaved, but had to be addressed from within (Clifford, FBO coordinator). The move towards HIV programming was gradual for most organizations, and started with caring for the sick and fighting stigma, then moved to encouraging HIV testing for everyone, and eventually got to prevention activities for youth and adults alike. Most of this is done through the smaller groups within churches:

> Local congregations are doing youth activities, and HIV/AIDS activities are mainstreamed in most of them. For example, the youth section of a congregation will be devoted mainly to spiritual development, but will include discussions of HIV/AIDS. It's the same for Sunday schools, which include LSE and HIV/AIDS topics.... This mainstreaming is not limited to youth groups, as women's guilds also hold monthly meetings where HIV/AIDS issues sometimes come up, and cover prevention, care and support. (Herbert, HIV/AIDS coordinator in a Christian church)

For young people, prevention activities often take the form of formal LS sessions in Sunday school, in Bible clubs or in youth groups within the church; they can also be in the form of peer discussions in the same settings, or one-on-one mentoring with a youth pastor or with a church leader who takes a special interest in young people. Prevention is often part of the promotion by churches of a Christian lifestyle for young people, whose primary aim remains the salvation of the soul, but whose 'side effects' are health and material success through education and hard work.

Sex is a gift from God

Two elements made some religious sex education initiatives stand out: their sex-positive approach, and their openness in communicating about sexuality. While most secular sex education programmes start with the inevitability of physical development in adolescents, the religious approach often starts with the idea that 'sex is a gift from God'. Sexuality, they say, is not only normal, it is beautiful – an idea which is often new for many young people.

> Many young people see some of the teachings from the Bible where sexual desires are looked at as sinful, so they think anyone who has sexual desire must be thinking evil thoughts. But that's not what the Bible says! God created us sexual beings with sexual desires, it's a gift from him. So if I acknowledge that my sexuality is a gift from God, then I'm not going to see it with negative feelings. I'm going to cherish it, to value it because God gave me that gift for a purpose. (Samson, youth FBO coordinator)

> I say, 'It's ok to have sexual feelings! If you have them you are a normal person. If you don't have them you have a problem, I must pray for you.' It's like you take them out of their cocoon and they begin to realize it's normal.... So we have to bring them to a level when they know it is normal to have sexual feelings, that's how God created us. (Lucy, church worker)

While many secular programmes seek to inspire a fear of the consequences of sexuality, this religious approach seeks to inspire a respect for one's own sexuality as a healthy source of joy and pleasure. Sex is not only an unavoidable part of life; it is presented as being part of the divine, no less than God's gift to every person. It seems difficult to underline just how important this is in helping adolescents accept their own sexuality. Of course, the religious message does not end there: sex may be a gift from God, but it must be used at the right time, within the bonds of monogamous heterosexual marriage. 'They must understand that if I'm not careful with this gift, it can lead me to self-destruction. If I contract STIs, the same gift that was supposed to be celebrated, to bring me enjoyment, can bring me destruction in my life' (Samson, youth FBO coordinator).

Religious interventions do promote abstinence to their young believers, but they do it differently to the education or NGO sector. While secular interventions present abstinence as the 'natural', default-mode way to behave for young people, many religious interventions name it as the hardest path to follow, and in doing so also name the flip side of the abstinence coin: sexual desire.

> Young people must acknowledge the fact that they're sexual beings, with sexual desires. Because when I acknowledge that I'm vulnerable, it's easy for me to take precautions. If young people acknowledge that they're vulnerable to premarital sex, then they will be careful how they live…. But if I say, 'No I'm not, I don't have sexual desires' – many find themselves in doom because they ignore the warning signals until it is too late. (Samson, youth FBO coordinator)

> That's what I tell young people: abstinence is not easy but it's worth the sacrifice. The moment you tell them that, when the going gets tough, they know! But when we just say, 'Abstain! Pray to God to help you'…. I pray so much, but it's not enough to tell a young person to pray, there's certain measures they need to put in place for abstinence to work. (Lucy, church worker)

Such measures are very concrete: never being alone in a private place with a boyfriend or girlfriend; keeping oneself busy with other things when sexual feelings arise. Abstinence is not presented as passive, as the absence of 'immoral behaviours'; rather, it is a constant effort to behave according to one's moral convictions, even when the most 'natural' thing to do might be to become sexually active.[7] It is not the normal path from which a few will deviate out of personal weakness; it is a choice that is morally right, but extremely difficult to achieve. This fits in with the general Evangelical discourse in which leading a Christian lifestyle sets one apart from the crowd, and which warns that young Christians will face ridicule, contempt and hardship because of commitment to their faith. This may seem ironic in a country where almost everyone seems vocally Christian, but it is part of a wider Christian worldview entrenched in ideas of spiritual warfare:

> [A]lthough Born-Again Christianity has become an increasingly hegemonic social and cultural form, at both an individual and collective level the notion of rupture and difference remains particularly strong, and the community continues to project itself ... in direct struggle with prevailing norms and the dangers they carry. (Marshall 2009: 84)

Even the promotion of abstinence is presented as going against the grain, as a form of resistance to donors and a culture of permissiveness – even though, as we have seen, it is part of the national education curriculum.

While discourses on condoms were often almost Manichean – separating out 'good' and 'bad' in simplified terms – in practice some religious interventions were remarkably realistic. They were certainly not condom-positive; indeed, as is the case in most religious discourses about sex education, condoms were presented as something that should not be needed.

> My approach as an adviser to religious leaders is to say that, 'We want to promote A and B to the extent that the need to have condom use is no longer there. This is our goal. We want to promote these so that the use of condoms doesn't exist anymore. If somebody is abstaining and is faithful, there will be no need for condom use and this is what we want.' (Clifford, FBO worker)

However, the religious workers that I met deal with the issue of condoms through a fine balance of ideals and pragmatism. They do promote abstinence, yet they are aware that young people need condom information as most are sexually active.

And we know that a number of our members are sexually active. And many of them use condoms because they have that information. But it's not what we promote. We wish it was otherwise. But we also realize that we are living in a world where the pressure is so much, and it requires a lot of determination, commitment, for someone to remain sexually pure. So we don't want to be naïve, but at the same time we don't want to take the word of God for granted. (Samson, youth FBO coordinator)

Acknowledging reality while working towards an ideal, accepting young people as they are while encouraging them to behave differently, 'hating the sin while loving the sinner': this is the delicate position that I saw in many religious youth workers. Concretely, religious organizations will not actively encourage condom use,[8] but many recognized the need and the rights of youth to have information, and either provide the information themselves, or refer the youth to health services. The only exceptions are the religious hospitals, which distribute condoms to anyone who requests them.

An interesting aspect of this position is the way that religious interventions deal with parents and communities. In many instances, they have decided to trust young people with condom information, but to do it discreetly so as not to arouse suspicion from the parents.

We even train [our young peer educators] on issues of condoms, but we make sure the church leaders don't see us do that. What we are saying is, give young people choices. We train them, we don't encourage them to use condoms because we feel abstinence is the issue and we promote abstinence. But at the same time, I think we'd be silly and ... not helpful to our young people if we don't train them, if we don't teach them about condoms. They need to know and it's up to them to choose. (Edwin, church association coordinator)

This is also fairly different from many interventions, both in the West and in Malawi, which consider that parents should decide what information is best for their child to know. Indeed, what Edwin is saying here is that they trust the children more than they trust the parents, a serious reversal in a country where parental authority is very strict.

The moral authority of church and FBO workers means that they are able to raise and discuss topics which others will not touch, for fear of being seen as immoral. The fact that the information is often presented in two moments – first a fairly complete overview of prevention options, then a discussion of the spiritual and moral aspects of sexuality – might seem problematic. Will the second part invalidate the options presented by dismissing some of them as immoral? Or could it help young people separate the options that are available from the personal choices they have to make with regard to their own sexuality? In any case, the very fact that a faith-based initiative does not restrict the information that is made available shows young people that they can be trusted to make their own choices – a respect that young Malawians don't get that often.

The limits to faith-based sex education

Although some initiatives were remarkable for their open communications, their sex-positive approach and the complete information they provided for youth, faith-based prevention is not a panacea.

First, not all churches and FBOs were bastions of tolerance and enlightenment; indeed, there were also typical moralist approaches, which sometimes bordered on bigotry. For example, one stalwart declared that 'condoms were sent by the devil to promote promiscuity', and that youth did not need to be told about them at all (Penny, church worker). At a youth conference on abstinence, when young participants were asked what was the best concrete tool to help their peers with abstinence, one group answered that increasing young people's fear of God was key.

Many religious groups have an ambiguous relation to the secular world. On the one hand, they easily blame the secular world, often connected to Westernization, for social problems, divorce, promiscuity and diminishing religiosity. On the other hand, that very same secular world is used as a reason to justify giving youths complete prevention information.

> We [tell the parents], 'Look here, we don't want to teach them everything, but we need to teach them some basics about issues of condoms because if we don't, the world out there will take advantage of them and spoil them. They need to have information. We don't promote condoms! But we need to teach them what the world teaches.' (Clifford, FBO coordinator)

Sexual diversity is, of course, the weak point of even the most tolerant religious groups in Africa. Churches and FBOs do not talk of sexual orientation, and from a rights-based perspective this discriminates against youth who do not identify as heterosexual. This is not, however, unique to the religious sector in Malawi, where homosexuality is criminalized and heavily stigmatized, and where people who have homosexual practices are almost systematically married to someone of the opposite sex (Muula 2007; Baral *et al.* 2009). While this is a real and serious human rights issue, I think other sectors of society will have to advance sexual diversity before the faith sector can be expected to open up the topic.

Just as in the secular world, the gap between design and implementation, between national leaders and local workers, is difficult to bridge. My research was done mostly at the national and regional level, with well-travelled, well-educated professionals who had mastered development jargon and conventions. The pastors and workers who deal directly with youth, however, may not hold the same opinions as their representatives, especially among Evangelicals, where every church is autonomous.

> One of the major problems that we have is that most of our pastors are not literate.... Possibly they can read, but they are not well-educated. They just manage to read their Bibles, and that is all. Their ability to articulate some issues is limited. Some issues are just above their capacity to engage in a conversation. I'm able to engage with you because of your education and your exposure. But if you were a Malawian pastor coming from a rural area, with a Standard Five education, you may not be able to engage with me at that level. So issues like condoms, it's a bit of a problem for them to engage

constructively and expect them to be able to contribute meaningfully to that. (Clifford, FBO coordinator)

Just as they do with the parents, some FBOs end up giving local congregations half-truths about the programmes they run in order to provide young people with complete information. This, in turn, means that the situation I encountered was highly dependent on a few progressive national leaders, who balanced the right of youth to complete and correct information with their spiritual convictions, and manage to translate this into programmes. If these people were replaced by conservative leaders, Malawian faith-based sex education could become more like the abstinence-only sex education which is found in the USA – characterized by misinformation and the promotion of ignorance (Waxman 2004).

Conclusion: possible alliances?

So what conclusions can one draw from this? Should Christian and other faith-based approaches to sex education be prioritized over secular ones? Can religious approaches to sexuality be made compatible with rights-based and even pleasure-based views? To what extent, and over what grounds, can partnerships be made to help young people grow up comfortably with their sexuality? The American Christian cultural industry has certainly shown that pleasure is a popular Christian theme, but only when it is confined to monogamous, heterosexual relations. It quickly reaches its limits in terms of human rights and inclusion of all sexualities, and it has an agenda of its own that should not be underestimated in the context of the rapid growth of Pentecostal Christianity all over the world. Providing information about sexuality and relationship is a sure way to attract young believers in a context where competition between churches is fierce.

But the examples discussed in this chapter show that if, as the introduction to this book suggests, 'arenas where one might expect an alternative perspective instead reproduce this negativity around sex', so is it possible to find unlikely allies with whom to share common ground regarding a holistic, sex-positive way to talk about sex with young people. We can agree that good sex education should include spiritual dimensions of sexuality, and that good spiritual guidance should take sexuality into account. Is this enough? Clashes on other issues related to sexuality and sexual rights, of which contraception, abortion and sexual orientation are only the most obvious ones, are inevitable. But maybe, just maybe, enough common ground could be found to work together to prevent unnecessary suffering caused by STIs and unwanted pregnancies, and to help young people embrace a sexuality that is joyful and coherent with their values, whatever those values are.

I learned a lot from my Christian informants and friends, despite some fundamental disagreements between us. The loving and supportive way they talked with adolescents and young adults was markedly different from the moralizing tone of most adults, an attitude that I know springs from the message of the New Testament. In a country where the vast majority of young people identify with either Christianity or Islam, I could see that their guidance was welcomed by young people. My ongoing research suggests that young Malawians are not as anxious about the religious implications of sex as one might believe from listening to their elders, but that they do long for sources of information and advice that are both empathetic and reliable. Digital media is opening up new spaces for discussion,[9] but it is only available to those with the means to buy a mobile device, charge its battery and pay for data to surf the internet. For the majority who don't, there is a dearth of information and advice that goes beyond HIV prevention orthodoxy to address the complexities of sex in real life – embedded in material circumstances, communities and emotions. This should remind us of a point that has been made many times before (see, for example, Kvalem and Træen 2000; Tepper 2000; Warr 2001; Philpott *et al.* 2006; Tavory and Swidler 2009), but that remains almost entirely unrealized: that no matter how uncomfortable adults are with adolescent sexuality, HIV prevention must acknowledge the pleasures, some of which are sexual but many of which are not, that young people find in their relationships.

Acknowledgements

My heartfelt thanks goes to Dr Marie-Nathalie LeBlanc and to the Fonds Québécois de Recherche sur la Société et la Culture (FQRSC), whose support made this research possible. Merci!

Notes

1 Unless otherwise specified, the information from this section comes from interviews with Gerald, Takondwa, Charlton and Stephen, who work in education in the public sector.

2 The Malawian school system consists of eight years of free primary education (Standard 1 to 8), followed by four years of secondary school (Form 1 to 4), for which there are school fees. Primary education was made free in 1994, which has improved access but created problems of quality, as the system struggles to serve the large number of pupils. For more on public education in Malawi, see Englund 2004; Al-Samarrai and Zaman 2007; Chimombo 2009.

3 A belief that is shared by just under a third of young people (Wittenberg *et al.* 2007: 20).

4 It must be said that this phenomenon, typical of neoliberalism, is far from exclusive to developing countries. For an analysis of the 'non-profit industrial complex' in the US, see Incite! Women of Color Against Violence (2009).

5 The acronym ABC refers to what has now become prevention orthodoxy, which is that HIV and other sexually transmitted infections (STIs) can be prevented through abstinence (A), being faithful to one partner (B) or using condoms (C).

6 Mainline denominations (Anglican, Catholic, Presbyterian) are older churches that first came to African countries as missionaries under colonial rule; they tend to have fairly rigid hierarchies and extensive health and education infrastructures. Evangelical churches usually date back to the late twentieth century, are atomized in individual churches rather than organized in large denominations (with some exceptions, such as Assemblies of God), and are less involved in

social services. In Malawi, mainline Protestant denominations are grouped under the Malawi Council of Churches, the Evangelicals are grouped under the Evangelical Association of Malawi, while the Catholic Church is on its own. With the popularity of Pentecostal and charismatic forms of Christianity, the line between these categories can become blurry (Jenkins 2006; Marshall 2009).

7 By no means do we imply here essentialist ideas about the 'natural' time of sexual debut, which is obviously socially and culturally constructed, and varies from one person to another. However, some studies do show that both very early and very late sexual debut is linked to later sexual problems; see, for example, Sandfort *et al.* 2007.

8 Condom activities can be placed along an 'encouragement' continuum which goes from information to demonstration, promotion and distribution.

9 See, for example, the Facebook groups 'Malawi breaking news and gossip' or 'Sex in Malawi', which regularly contains messages from subscribers asking readers for advice about sex and relationships, including questions about oral sex, anal sex, HIV testing, multiple partners, porn, abortion and virginity, among others.

References

Al-Samarrai, S. and H. Zaman (2007) 'Abolishing School Fees in Malawi: the Impact on Education Access and Equity', *Education Economics,* Vol. 15, No. 3, p. 359.

Baral, S., G. Trapence, F. Motimedi, E. Umar, S. Iipinge, F. Dausab and C. Beyrer (2009) 'HIV Prevalence, Risks for HIV Infection, and Human Rights among Men Who Have Sex with Men (MSM) in Malawi, Namibia, and Botswana', *PLoS ONE,* Vol. 4, No. 3, p. e4997.

Chandhoke, N. (2007) 'Civil Society', *Development in Practice,* Vol. 17, Nos 4–5, pp. 607–14.

Chimombo, J. (2009) 'Changing Patterns of Access to Basic Education in Malawi: a Story of a Mixed Bag?', *Comparative Education,* Vol. 45, No. 2, pp. 297–312.

Daneel, M. L. (2004) 'African Initiated Churches in Southern Africa: Protest Movements or Mission Churches?', in D. M. Lewis (ed.), *Christianity Reborn: the Global Expansion of Evangelicalism in the Twentieth Century,* Eerdmans Publishing, Grand Rapids, MI.

Englund, H. (2004) *Transnational Governance and the Pacification of Youth: the Contribution of Civic Education to Disempowerment in Malawi*, Centre for Civil Society, University of KwaZulu-Natal, Durban, South Africa.

Freston, P. (2001) *Evangelicals and Politics in Asia, Africa and Latin America*, Cambridge University Press, Cambridge.

Gifford, P. (2004) 'Persistence and Change in Contemporary African Religion', *Social Compass*, Vol. 51, No. 2, pp. 169–76.

Incite! Women of Color Against Violence (2009) *The Revolution Will Not Be Funded: Beyond the Non-Profit Industrial Complex*, South End Press, Cambridge, MA.

Jenkins, P. (2006) *The New Faces of Christianity: Believing the Bible in the Global South*, Oxford University Press, Oxford.

Kvalem, I. L. and B. Træen (2000) 'Self-efficacy, Scripts of Love and Intention to Use Condoms among Norwegian Adolescents', *Journal of Youth and Adolescence*, Vol. 29, No. 3, pp. 337–53.

Marshall, R. (2009) *Political Spiritualities: the Pentecostal Revolution in Nigeria*, University of Chicago Press, Chicago IL.

Muula, A. S. (2007) 'Perceptions about Men Having Sex with Men in a Southern African Country: Case Study of Print Media in Malawi', *Croatian Medical Journal*, Vol. 48, No. 3, pp. 398–404.

National Statistical Office of Malawi (2010) *2008 Population and Housing Census – Education and Literacy Report*, Government of Malawi, Zomba, http://www.nso.malawi.net/images/stories/data_ on_line/ demography/census_2008/Main%20Report/ThematicReports/ Education%20and%20Literacy.pdf (accessed 10 August 2012).

Philpott, A., W. Knerr and V. Boydell (2006) 'Pleasure and Prevention: When Good Sex Is Safer Sex', *Reproductive Health Matters*, Vol. 14, No. 28, pp. 23–31.

Ranger, T. O. (2008) 'Introduction: Evangelical Christianity and Democracy in Africa', in *Evangelical Christianity and Democracy in Africa*, Oxford University Press, Oxford.

Real Reason (2008) *Situation Assessment Brief: Sexuality Education*, Real Reason, Oakland, CA.

Robbins, J. (2004) 'The Globalization of Pentecostal and Charismatic Christianity', *Annual Review of Anthropology*, Vol. 33, pp. 117–43.

Robinson, B. E., W. O. Bockting, S. B. R. Rosser, M. Miner and E. Coleman (2002) 'The Sexual Health Model: Application of a Sexological Approach to HIV Prevention', *Health Education Research*, Vol. 17, No. 1, pp. 43–57.

Sandfort, T., M. Orr, J. S. Hirsch and J. Santelli (2007) 'Long-term Health Correlates of Timing of Sexual Debut: Results from a National US Study', *American Journal of Public Health*, Vol. 98, No. 1, pp. 155–61.

Santelli, J., M. A. Ott, M. Lyon, J. Rogers, D. Summers and R. Schleifer (2006) 'Abstinence and Abstinence-only Education: a Review of US Policies and Programs', *Journal of Adolescent Health*, Vol. 38, No. 1, pp. 72–81.

Tavory, I. and A. Swidler (2009) 'Condom Semiotics: Meaning and Condom use in Rural Malawi', *American Sociological Review*, Vol. 74, No. 2, pp. 171–89.

Tepper, M. S. (2000) 'Sexuality and Disability: the Missing Discourse of Pleasure', *Sexuality and Disability*, Vol. 18, No. 4, pp. 283–90.

Warr, D. J. (2001) 'The Importance of Love and Understanding: Speculation on Romance in Safe Sex Health Promotion', *Women's Studies International Forum*, Vol. 24, No. 2, pp. 241–52.

Waxman, H. A. (2004) 'The Content of Federally Funded Abstinence-Only Education Programs', United States House of Representatives – Committee on Government Reform, Minority Staff Special Investigation Division, Washington, DC.

Wittenberg, J., A. Munthali, A. Moore, E. Zulu, N. Madise, M. Mkandawire, F. Limbani, L. Darabi and S. Konyani (2007) *Protecting the Next Generation in Malawi: New Evidence on Adolescent Sexual and Reproductive Health Needs*, Guttmacher Institute, New York.

9

Why We Need to Think about Sexuality and Sexual Well-Being

Addressing Sexual Violence in Sub-Saharan Africa

Chi-Chi Undie

Sexual violence is a global problem. The scale and implications of this issue have been a focus of increasing attention, resulting in mounting recognition and acknowledgment of its negative impacts on the society at large. Sexual violence is now widely acknowledged as 'a gross human rights violation, a weapon of war and a profound public health issue' (SVRI 2011), not least in the sub-Saharan Africa (SSA) region, where the issue affects substantial proportions of women and transcends the divides of nationality, ethnicity and socio-economic status (Population Council 2008). Survey data from a range of African countries attest to the troubling prevalence of sexual violence among women aged 15 to 49 in the region – 59 per cent in Ethiopia, 15 per cent in Zambia, and 21 per cent in Kenya, for instance (Keesbury and Askew 2011). Among females aged 13 to 24 in Swaziland, 48 per cent had experienced sexual violence (*ibid.*).

Given these realities, several critical international campaigns are currently heavily invested in preventing and responding to sexual violence globally. Notably, the United Nations campaign, UNiTE to End Violence Against Women, is geared toward the achievement of the adoption and implementation of multi-sectoral national plans to address violence against women worldwide by the year 2015. The importance of employing a multi-sectoral (and, hence, presumably 'comprehensive') approach to addressing violence continues to be echoed by a myriad of other campaigns and research and programming initiatives in the SSA region. This multi-sectoral approach has typically involved attention to the health, police and justice, and social service sectors, each of which overlaps and complements the others. Issues of sexual well-being (including, but not limited to sexual pleasure) are notably absent from this multi-sectoral response model, despite the prominence of the social service/ support sector (which involves long-term psychosocial support, among other services) within this framework.

This chapter therefore does a number of things: (1) it highlights the need to consider sexuality and sexual well-being – even when working on sexual violence; (2) it provides an analysis of the public health, religious and development framings of sexuality and sexual well-being; (3) it calls for a more nuanced understanding of sexual violence and an improvement in service provision, particularly in the area of psychosocial support; and (4) it suggests that there are actually parallels in the way that sexual violence and sexuality (more broadly) are framed, and points out the shortcomings of these framings.

Strange bedfellows? Sexual violence, sexuality, sexual well-being

Discussions about sexuality and sexual well-being in SSA countries are relatively limited in general, and, understandably, all the more so in the context of sexual violence. At first sight, the three constructs of sexual violence, sexuality, and sexual well-being appear to clash severely with each other, and it seems counter-intuitive to situate each of them within the same phrase, not to mention the same conceptual framework. When obliged for the first time to consider these constructs in tandem, one is likely to be struck initially by the paradox that seems to be inherent in the three terms.

In contexts of sexual violence in SSA, therefore, is there any merit in considering 'sexuality' or in giving any attention to 'sexual well-being'? If sexuality 'encompasses the physical capacity for sexual arousal and pleasure (libido) as well as personalized and shared social meanings attached to sexual behaviour and the formation of sexual and gender identities' (Dixon–Mueller 1993: 273), and sexual well-being refers to 'the emotional and physical satisfaction of sexual relationships, satisfaction with sexual health or function, and the importance of sex in one's life' (Laumann *et al.* 2006: 145), dare we even consider sexuality and sexual well-being in the aftermath of sexual violence? Or does doing so appear as an insensitive (not to mention frivolous) ploy that makes a mockery of the experiences of actual survivors of sexual violence?

Both are legitimate questions which will be attended to later in this chapter. First, however, the chapter will delve into the subject of sexuality in particular, and how views of this construct are shaped in African contexts. To facilitate this exploration, the starting point will be a brief overview of three key sets of discourses that have been known to inform notions of sexuality, namely: biomedical/public health discourses; religious discourses; and development discourses. As much of what we know about sexuality, sexual well-being and sexual violence is constructed by these discourses, it is important to begin here.

Discourses and their discontents

Referring to biomedical/public health model discourses of sexuality, Maina–Ahlberg and her colleagues explain that the main concern of these discourses are:

> the application of technological solutions, coupled with the dissemination of information, to help individuals prevent transmitting a disease to a sexual partner and through that, to the general population (Levine 1991; Baldwin 2005). Even though it is referred to as technical, because of its appeal to the individual as a moral agent, a type of tapping on the moral sensitivity by which people are believed to perceive right and wrong and to have concern for others, it can in this context be understood in moral and ethical terms. It is a type of moral appeal to the individual to use scientific knowledge to avert disease for the self and others. (Maina–Ahlberg *et al.* 2007: 4)

Citing Tolman's (2002) US-based study, Jolly gives a vivid example of some of the limitations of the biomedical/public health discourse, with its emphasis on disease, reproduction and violence, when it is not tempered by deeper and more nuanced discussions of sexuality and sexual well-being. In her words:

A study of adolescent girls (Tolman 2002) found that some were paralysed with fear of the dangers of having sex, both in terms of their reputation, and in relation to the risks of pregnancy and disease. One such girl explained that she did end up having sex with her boyfriend because he wanted it, although she felt no desire. When she discussed it with him afterwards, he insisted that she had wanted sex. She was confused, and agreed that maybe she had, maybe he knew better than she herself did. In contrast, girls with a more positive view of sexuality were more assertive. One girl who had had and enjoyed sex, encountered a boy from her school who tried to pressure her to sleep with him. She forcefully resisted and succeeded in deterring him. She was quite clear that she didn't want sex, because she knew what it felt like to want sex. If you are not allowed to imagine or discover what it feels like to want sex, how do you know if you don't want it? Does consent have any meaning if you are only allowed to say 'no'? If you are only allowed to say 'no', you have to say 'no', even when you mean 'yes'. (Jolly 2007: 21)

This study illustrates the complexities of decision making around sex, and of responses to health risks, pressure and coercion. The scientific knowledge of how to avoid risk, promoted by the biomedical/public health model, is not necessarily enough to change behaviour. Powerful case studies such as these underscore the need for more complex investigations of sexuality, and a more critical understanding of sexual well-being. The fact that there may sometimes be interconnections between sexual coercion/violence and a lack of engagement with sexuality is also made apparent here.

Religious discourses on sexuality have some parallels with biomedical/public health discourses in terms of the prohibitions that frame them. One of the more visible religions in the SSA context when it comes to public contestations around sexuality is Christianity. The Christian context (as evidenced by texts such as the Bible) provides for the expression of sexuality and for the pursuit of sexual pleasure and fulfilment within the framework of marriage. Warning against extra-marital sex, for instance, the Bible gives the following symbolic injunction to men in particular:

> Drink water from your own cistern, running water from your own well. Should your springs overflow in the streets, your streams of water in the public squares? Let them be yours alone, never to be shared with strangers. May your fountain be blessed, and may you rejoice in the wife of your youth. A loving doe, a graceful deer – may her breasts satisfy you always, may you ever be captivated by her love. (Proverbs 5: 15–19, NIV)

The following is also one of many conversations in the Bible between heterosexual lovers whose journey from courtship to marriage consummation is depicted:

> *He*: How beautiful you are and how pleasing, my love, with your delights! Your stature is like that of the palm, and your breasts like clusters of fruit. I said, 'I will climb the palm tree; I will take hold of its fruit. May your breasts be like clusters of grapes on the vine, the fragrance of your breath like apples, and your mouth like the best wine'. *She*: May the wine go straight to my beloved, flowing gently over lips and teeth. I belong to my beloved, and his desire is for me. (Song of Solomon 7: 6–10, NIV)

Depending on the Christian denomination, however, the use of condoms and other forms of contraception within marriage may be prohibited. A corollary to this is the many heated debates around comprehensive sexuality education in African settings and whether it should be offered to young people or not – the thorny issue of whether providing young people with skills and enlightening them with knowledge is nothing but an endorsement of behaviour regarded as sinful in religious contexts – namely, pre-marital sex.

Like public health discourses, religious discourses are extremely powerful. Religion is typically of profound significance to those who identify with it. For this reason, when it comes to sexuality and sexual well-being, there is a need to find effective ways of working within religious frameworks. For, despite our religious fervour as a continent, young people aged 15–24 years old account for about half of all new HIV infections in the region – a region that currently contends with nearly 70 per cent of all HIV and AIDS cases worldwide (UNAIDS 2006). Should there really still be a question in African countries about the need for comprehensive sexuality and relationship education? Further, marriage is increasingly seen as a risky context in terms of potential HIV-infection (Parikh 2007). Marital sex, in the public health consciousness, has morphed into risky sex in SSA. In the words of Maina-Ahlberg *et al.* (2009: 113), the challenge when trying to figure out how to transform 'wellness' or 'well-being' from a mere concept into action has to do with 'the tension between public pronouncements and performance, and the private realm of individual actors manifested in prohibitive silence' – or, in simpler terms: what people say is often different from what they do.

Development discourses have also been accused of privileging three broad, sexuality-related themes, namely, population control, disease, and violence (Jolly 2003; Cornwall *et al.* 2008). Here again, there has typically been a pervasive negative approach to the subject which places an emphasis on the dangers of sex and sexuality. Furthermore, within this discourse, as Jolly (2007) notes, there is a 'women-as-victim' narrative in which women – particularly 'Third World' women – are homogenized and portrayed exclusively as utterly powerless in their sexual encounters. A complement to this image is the 'men-as-predator' narrative, in which the same homogenizing process occurs, and sweeping assumptions are made with regard to heterosexuality where both men and women are concerned.

The fixation of the development industry on these kinds of narratives may seem understandable: men are typically known to be the perpetrators of sexual violence against women. However, women have also been known to perpetrate sexual violence, and men have been survivors as well as perpetrators of sexual violence on a large scale in developing country settings such as the Democratic Republic of Congo (Johnson *et al.* 2010), Afghanistan, Iraq and India (Petchesky 2005). Furthermore, there is evidence that the current gender paradigms make sexual violence against men invisible, thus allowing it be constructed as that which is not supposed to take place at all (Neumann *et al.* 2008; Lawry 2010). In not allowing for a plurality of experiences or accounts, these narratives inadvertently overlook those that do not fit the heterosexual profile, the male/female gender profile, the presumed 'Third World' woman profile, and so on.

Thus, when we stand back from this portrait of sexuality as something to be feared and regulated, a portrait which these prevalent and powerful discourses have painted for us, it becomes apparent why a broader understanding of sexuality and sexual well-being has been under-explored, especially in relation to sexual violence.

Sexuality and sexual well-being: arguments for keeping them in the conversation

To turn back to the question raised at the beginning of this chapter: in contexts of sexual violence in SSA, is there any merit in thinking about sexuality and in giving attention to sexual well-being? The position of this chapter on the subject is that investigating sexuality is an appropriate first step towards trying to make sense of sexual violence, and that the lack of space, or limited contexts, for discussing sexuality can be held partly responsible for some of the sexual violence the African region has witnessed over the years.

A recent and critically important study by Johnson *et al.* (2010) on sexual violence in the Eastern Democratic Republic of Congo highlights the continued and damaging silence around sexuality in African contexts. Indeed, it raises questions around what meanings sex and sexual pleasure (for instance) hold in various African settings, how these meanings are developed, and why. The study challenges the male perpetrator/female victim paradigm as well as the commonly held notion that women are simply incapable of being perpetrators of sexual violence. Fifteen per cent of male survivors in the study in question listed females as the perpetrators, while 40 per cent of female survivors listed another female as the perpetrator (Lawry 2010).

These findings underscore the dangers of silence around sexuality. The 'official' account of sexuality in SSA has long held that same-sex sexual pleasures and relations are non-existent in this context. Open dialogue on sexuality has only recently begun to slowly chip away at this notion, giving voice to more 'unofficial' accounts. Thus, only recently has the need to ask survivors of violence about the sex of the perpetrator been highlighted in African settings. In general, when asking about sexual violence, healthcare providers do not ask for the sex of the perpetrator, as the latter is invariably assumed to be male (Lawry 2010). The silence around these kinds of issues gives birth to uninvestigated assumptions, which in turn renders various forms of sexual violence invisible, providing fertile ground for these forms of violence to flourish.

The rhetoric of sexual violence must necessarily be linked to that of sexual well-being, for when sexual well-being is overlooked, sexual violence survivors are condemned to a life that is completely and perpetually defined by the incidents of violence that they experienced. And so, when we bring together discussions of sexual well-being with discussions of sexual violence, we are essentially saying, 'There is life after sexual violence; there is well-being (in a sexual sense) despite a past experience with sexual violence.' In so doing, we empower survivors to make informed, healthy and positive choices about their sexuality – choices that are neither born of, nor shaped by, the scars of their past experience, but are informed by the knowledge that it is appropriate to move on with life – indeed, that it is expected that one would do so, and that doing so is their entitlement.

Without an emphasis on sexuality and sexual well-being,

perpetrators of sexual violence are inadvertently left with the impression that sexual violence is an acceptable cultural norm – particularly in a context where the police and justice system are one of several weak links in the much-advocated multi-sectoral response model (Seelinger *et al.* 2011), with perpetrators rarely having to face legal consequences for their actions. They thus learn the erroneous lesson that their behaviour is acceptable and are given the power to define their violent behaviour within their own conceptual frameworks. They have no alternative framework within which to consider or reflect upon their actions – such as the reality that giving sexual pleasure (as opposed to pain) to another can often result in the achievement of one's own pleasure. Thus, a focus on sexual well-being (of which pleasure is a part) and sexuality provides an important frame of reference for *both* survivors and perpetrators of violence.

Gear's (2009) analysis of the prison culture among male inmates in South Africa, in which perpetrators normalize sexual violence by erasing its existence from their everyday discourse (and, thus, from their conceptual framings), is instructive here. As Gear puts it, '[P]arties in the violence are conceptually disappeared.' In other words, 'Male victims of prison sexual violence are no longer even acknowledged as men, but are commonly believed to have been turned into "women".' Furthermore, the author describes how 'marriages' are forcefully brought about in these prison settings through rape, with the perpetrator and victim automatically assigned the man and wife role, respectively. As Gear explains, 'Ultimately, "marriages" smooth over the anxiety-provoking issue of violence by disappearing its protagonists: they turn victims into "wives" and perpetrators into "men".' The Department of Correctional Services is noted as also unwittingly contributing to this process by categorizing acts of sexual violence as 'assault', rather than as *sexual* assault. This poignant case study clarifies how what is not talked about is not acted upon. If sexual well-being is not brought to the fore in contexts of violence, it will be achieved neither by the survivor of violence, nor by the perpetrator.

Should we begin to consider sexuality and sexual well-being

seriously in the context of violence work in SSA, the diversity and complexity of African cultures must also be kept in mind. We are talking here about a myriad of ethnic groups, languages and sub-cultures. We are talking about various and varied legacies bequeathed by colonialism, and about cultures that vary in the extent to which they have changed over time, and in the extent to which they have been informed by modernity and globalization. As a result, approaches towards, or perceptions of, sexual violence on the continent may differ depending on where one is located at the time, one's background, one's education, where one was educated, by whom, and so on. This, in turn, suggests that there can be no 'one-size-fits-all' approach to addressing sexual violence and to locating sexuality and sexual well-being.

A concrete example from the rural Igbo communities in south-east Nigeria may provide insight into the various social contexts of sexual violence in African societies:

> The [Igbo] do not see this heinous act [rape] as a crime committed by one individual against another. Rather, it is perceived as a crime committed by one community or lineage against another community or lineage. The rapist's community is viewed as having raped the victim's community. The rapist's entire community is also regarded as being at fault for not providing adequate training to their erring son to ensure that he manages his urges properly and abides by the laws of the land. In this instance, the notion of the 'communal body' is privileged over the body and personhood of the victim. The body and personhood of the victim are important; however, the serious incident is regarded as having affected a larger body than that of the victim alone. The 'communal body', therefore, appears to take preeminence in this matter. The unobtrusive place occupied by the 'individual body' *vis-à-vis* the 'communal body' becomes more evident when it comes to the aftermath of the crime. Rape is regarded as an abominable act which desecrates the entire community. As a result, the rapist as an individual is not looked upon to compensate the victim; rather, his *community* is required to compensate that of the victim. The rape victim is not left without compensation, however. But her compensation is derived directly

> from the communities involved, usually taking the form of a piece
> of land or the supply of farm produce over a period of years, or the
> rapist may be required to relinquish his oil palm-harvesting rights – a
> major economic loss – to the rape victim for a period of years. In
> effect, the community serves as a channel for the realization of the
> victim's rights – rights which may be unattainable on her own. This
> whole process also involves elaborate rituals of appeasement through
> which both communities, the perpetrator and the rape victim are
> cleansed and restored. This, therefore, suggests that the rape victim
> in this sort of a context may not necessarily see herself as the victim,
> but rather may feel that a crime has been committed against her
> community as well. Thus, pursuing justice via existing channels,
> such as the formal legal system, may seem less effective or logical in
> the eyes of the [rape survivor] than relying on her community for
> redress. (Izugbara and Undie 2008: 162)

This construction of rape has implications for the tailoring
of interventions in relation to sexual violence. What kind of
interventions would be necessary in situations where rape
is constructed in this fashion? Does the level of psychological
trauma differ in such a situation, where the main affront is seen as
directed against the community – and, therefore, the community
(rather than the individual) bears or manages the shame, anger,
and disgrace? Although psychological or psychiatric studies
among rural populations in SSA (such as the Igbo) are limited,
Smith and Kelly (2001) note that survivors' experiences may vary
depending on individual perceptions of sexual violence.

How would the situation differ if the violence survivor were
an Igbo woman living in a capital city in Africa, as opposed to
within a rural setting? In such a situation, the rape survivor's
first port of call might be a health facility, and the rules of the
rural community might not apply at all. This demonstrates
that our approach to sexual violence issues, sexual well-being,
and sexuality must attempt to be context-specific, challenging
though this may be. With the introduction of gender-based
violence recovery centres in SSA, and with health facilities and
providers playing an increasingly important role in sexual violence

incidents, operationalizing a tailored response to sexual violence becomes critical.

Tailored or individualized sexual violence interventions must first consider or assess the survivor's construction of the experience, rather than prescribe how survivors should make meaning of their experience. A shift needs to be made from a 'these-are-all-the-horrible-things-that've-happened-to-you-and-this-is-how-you-should-be-feeling-as-a-result' approach,[1] to an 'educate-me-on-what-this-experience-means-to-*you*' approach, so that survivors are efficiently helped through the aftermath of the experience.

Cross-cultural training for service providers is critical in order to facilitate a tailored/individualized response. Service providers must be keenly aware of the diverse repertoire of possible meanings sexual violence may have from the perspective of survivors, and be able to respond accordingly. Post-sexual violence assessments which incorporate multiple perspectives on sexual violence must also be developed in order to screen for understandings of violence that necessitate deeper psychological interventions, or other forms of support.

Final thoughts

There are some parallels between the treatment of sexual violence and of sexuality itself in SSA. Where sexuality is concerned, until fairly recently we have tended to focus on 'the incident' – the sex act (number of sexual partners, type of sexual partners, condom use or non-use, et cetera), with little knowledge of the feelings involved or of the broader dynamics of sexuality (Undie and Benaya 2006). Similarly, where sexual violence is concerned, we are knowledgeable about such matters as the prevalence, the forms, and the populations, but are yet to accord sufficient attention to the *meanings* the experience has for the people involved. As in the case of sexuality, the positive aspects of a serious issue should not be viewed as tangential to addressing the issue in question – nor should the need to highlight positivity take away from ongoing efforts. Rather, each approach must be seen as forming an integral part of the other, and the possibility of even better results when both work in tandem must be recognized. As has been contended elsewhere,

> In our deconstruction of various sexuality concepts, it is critical not to ignore or oversimplify real, concrete problems pertinent to the sub-Saharan African region.... Issues such as gender-based violence (notably an under-researched area (Erulkar 2004)), women's disadvantaged economic position, and reproductive health concerns are very real in different SSA contexts.... That young women in SSA are especially vulnerable to HIV infection seems clear (Jungar and Oinas 2004). That there are manifestations of gender-based violence in the region is apparent (an entire issue of *Sexuality in Africa* magazine was recently (2004) devoted to this issue; see also Tamale 1992; Amoakohene 2004). That strong male involvement in sexual and reproductive health matters would benefit both men and women is logical. Balancing these facts against the more positive realities of sexuality, which are equally a part of the SSA experience, is our challenge. (Undie and Benaya 2006)

Gosine (1998) observes that there seems to be a 'racialization of sex' in both development discourse and Western popular culture, where positive sensual and emotional aspects of sex are represented for white people in the North, but denied for people in the South, where population and disease are taken to be the primary concerns (Jolly 2003: 5). Parallels may be found here as well: psychological issues associated with sexual violence have for a long time been seen as relevant to the global North only, and have been seen as a frivolity in the African context. A return to sexual pleasure and overall sexual well-being for survivors after experiencing sexual violence is also an issue yet to be considered. What Gosine does not highlight is the complicity of Africans themselves in the development of this discourse. There is a need for Africans to focus a more critical analysis on their own settings and realities, and it goes without saying that they are uniquely positioned to do so.

Note

1　Catherine Maternowska, personal communication, 29 September 2008.

References

Amoakohene, M. I. (2004) 'Violence against Women in Ghana: a Look at Women's Perceptions and Review of Policy and Social Responses', *Social Science and Medicine*, Vol. 59, No. 11, pp. 2373–85.

Baldwin, P. (2005) *Disease and Democracy: the Industrialised World Faces AIDS*, University of California Press, Berkeley CA.

Cornwall, A., S. Correa and S. Jolly (2008) *Development with a Body: Perspectives on Sexuality, Rights and Development*, Zed Books, London.

Dixon-Mueller, R. (1993) 'The Sexuality Connection in Reproductive Health', *Studies in Family Planning*, Vol. 24, No. 5, pp. 269–82.

Erulkar, A. S. (2004) 'The Experience of Sexual Coercion among Young People in Kenya', *International Family Planning Perspectives*, Vol. 30, No. 4, pp. 182–9.

Gear, S. (2009) 'Manhood, Violence and Coercive Sexualities in Men's Prisons: Dynamics and Consequences behind Bars and Beyond', *Concerned African Scholars Bulletin*, Vol. 83: Sexual and Gender-Based Violence in Africa, http://concernedafricascholars.org/bulletin/83/gear/ (accessed 20 June 2012).

Gosine, A. (1998) 'All the Wrong Places: Looking for Love in Third World Poverty (Notes on the Racialisation of Sex)', unpublished MPhil thesis, Institute of Development Studies, University of Sussex.

Izugbara, C. and C. Undie (2008) 'Who Owns the Body? Indigenous African Discourses of the Body and Contemporary Sexual Rights Rhetoric', *Reproductive Health Matters*, Vol. 16, No. 31, pp. 159–67.

Johnson, K., J. Scott, B. Rughita, M. Kisielewski, J. Asher, R. Ong and L. Lawry (2010) 'Association of Sexual Violence and Human Rights Violations with Physical and Mental Health in Territories of the Eastern Democratic Republic of the Congo', *Journal of the American Medical Association*, Vol. 304, No. 5, pp. 553–62.

Jolly, S. (2003) 'Development Myths around Sex and Sexualities in the South', paper prepared for the International Workshop 'Gender Myths and Feminist Fables: Repositioning Gender in Development

Policy and Practice', Institute of Development Studies, Brighton, www.siyanda.org/docs/jolly_gendermyth.doc (accessed 20 June 2012).

—— (2007) 'Why the Development Industry Should Get over Its Obsession with Bad Sex and Start to Think about Pleasure', *IDS Working Paper* 283, Institute of Development Studies, Brighton.

Jungar, K. and E. Oinas (2004) 'Preventing HIV? Medical Discourses and Invisible Women', in S. Arnfred (ed.), *Re-thinking Sexualities in Africa*, Nordic Africa Institute, Uppsala.

Keesbury, J. and I. Askew (2011) *Comprehensive Responses to Sexual Violence in East and Southern Africa: Lessons Learned from Implementation*, Population Council, Lusaka, www.popcouncil.org/pdfs/2010RH_CompRespGBV.pdf (accessed 20 June 2012).

Laumann, E. O., A. Paik, D. B. Glasser, J.-H. Kang, T. Wang, B. Levinson, E. D. Moreira Jr., A. Nicolosi and C. Gingell (2006) 'A Cross-National Study of Subjective Sexual Well-Being among Older Women and Men: Findings from the Global Study of Sexual Attitudes and Behaviors', *Archives of Sexual Behavior*, Vol. 35, No. 2, pp. 145–61.

Lawry, L. (2010) 'Association of Sexual Violence and Human Rights Violations with Health and Mental Health in Territories of the Eastern Democratic Republic of the Congo', presentation given at the Interagency Gender Working Group, 10 May, www.igwg.org/igwg_media/sex-violence-in-drc.pdf (accessed 20 June 2012).

Levine, C. (1991) 'AIDS Prevention and Education: Reframing the Message', *AIDS Education and Prevention*, Vol. 3, No. 2, pp. 147–63.

Maina-Ahlberg, B., A. Kamau and F. Maina (2007) 'Multiple Discourses on Sexuality: Implications for Translating Sexual Wellness Concept into Action Strategies in a Kenyan Context', paper presented at the 2007 Sexuality Institute, 30 October–2 November, Mombasa, Kenya.

Maina-Ahlberg, B., A. Kamau, F. Maina and A. Kulane (2009) 'Multiple Discourses on Sexuality: Implications for Translating Sexual Wellness Concept into Action Strategies in a Kenyan Context', *African Sociological Review*, Vol. 13, No. 1, pp. 105–23.

Neumann, D., O. Patrick and A. Chang (2008) *Gender Against Men* (documentary), Refugee Law Project, Faculty of Law, Makerere University, Uganda.

Parikh, S. (2007) 'The Political Economy of Marriage and HIV: the ABC Approach, "Safe" Infidelity, and Managing Moral Risk in

Uganda', *American Journal of Public Health*, Vol. 97, No. 7, pp. 1198–208.

Petchesky, R. (2005) 'Rights of the Body and Perversions of War: Sexual Rights and Wrongs Ten Years Past Beijing', *UNESCO's International Social Science Journal*, Vol. 57, No. 184, pp. 301–18.

Population Council (2008) 'Sexual and Gender-based Violence in Africa: Literature Review', Population Council, New York.

Seelinger, K., H. Silverberg and R. Mejia (2011) 'The Investigation and Prosecution of Sexual Violence', *Sexual Violence and Accountability Project Working Paper Series*, Human Rights Center, University of California, Berkeley CA.

Smith, M. E. and L. M. Kelly (2001) 'The Journey of Recovery after a Rape Experience', *Issues in Mental Health Nursing*, Vol. 22, pp. 337–52.

SVRI (Sexual Violence Research Initiative) (2011), online at www. svri.org/forum2011 (accessed 20 June 2012).

Tamale, S. (1992) 'Rape Law and the Violation of Women in Uganda: a Critical Perspective', *Uganda Law Society Review*, Vol. 1, No. 2, pp. 195–211.

Tolman, D. L. (2002) *Dilemmas of Desire: Teenage Girls Talk about Sexuality*, Harvard University Press, Cambridge MA and London.

UNAIDS (2006) 'Report on the Global AIDS Epidemic: a UNAIDS 10th Anniversary Special', UNAIDS, Geneva.

Undie, C. and K. Benaya (2006) 'The State of Knowledge on Sexuality in Sub-Saharan Africa: a Synthesis of Literature', *JENDA: A Journal of Culture and African Women Studies,* No. 8, http://www. africaknowledgeproject.org/index.php/jenda/article/view/125.

10
Could Watching Porn Increase Our Expectations of (Safe) Pleasure?
An Exploration of Some Promising Harm-Reduction Practices
• •
Anne Philpott and Krissy Ferris

> Pornographers are the enemies of women only because our contemporary ideology of pornography does not encompass the possibility of change, as if we were the slaves of history and not its makers. (Angela Carter 1978: 3)

Pornography is one of the most explicit ways in which people encounter sex. Regardless of the judgements passed on this particular form of media, it is undeniable that porn has a tremendous effect on sex lives around the world and is a key source of information on sexuality. While many types of pornography are exploitative and perpetuate disempowering visions of gender and sexuality, porn also has the potential to be a medium through which we could promote sexual health, question traditional gender roles and create empowering social scripts. In this chapter we will first discuss the prevalence and importance of porn as a conduit for sex education before describing ways in which the pleasure industry is challenging norms to create pornography that is positive.

This is an extension of our previous argument that sex education would benefit from expanding its scope to motivate behaviour change through sex-positive rather than sex-negative messaging (Philpott 2003; Philpott, Knerr and Boydell 2006; Philpott, Knerr and Maher 2006; Knerr and Philpott 2008). The public health response to HIV has been and continues to be overwhelmingly focused on risk, disease and the negative outcomes of sex (Holland *et al.* 1992; Higgens and Hirsch 2007, 2008; Ingham 2005; Jolly 2007) and ignores positive motivations for sex – for example, pleasure, desire and love. In fact, the pursuit of sexual pleasure, when mentioned, has been characterized as destructive (WAS 2008) or as a major contributor to the spread of HIV, and therefore something to be controlled or suppressed (BBC News 2004; Freitas 2002). Although there is increasing advocacy to challenge this traditionally 'sex-negative' approach, primarily by proponents of comprehensive sexuality education and eroticization of safer sex, this advocacy has rarely expanded to highlight the need to incorporate safer sex and sex-positive messages into erotic media.

What is pornography?

The definition of 'pornography' is the subject of debate. In an extremely broad sense some define pornography as any sexual topic subject to censorship and class dominance. According to Williams (1989), 'Pornography is simply whatever representations a particular dominant class or group does not want in the hands of another, less dominant class or group. Those in power construct the definitions of pornography through their power to censor it.' Although defining pornography could be a lifetime's work, for the purpose of this chapter pornography is an explicit, graphic portrayal of a sexual act created with the intention of sexually arousing the person who consumes it. Of course, each viewer will have different levels of arousal or understanding of explicit sexual acts, but this helps us to differentiate between a medical text book and a 'men's top shelf' magazine.

Erotica, often used in distinction to pornography, are works of art that deal substantively with erotically stimulating or sexually arousing descriptions. The term is often used to describe portrayals of sexual acts or sexuality with high-art aspirations to differentiate such work from commercial pornography. But one person's pornography can be another's erotica, since the term erotica is used as a definition of artistic merit or pretensions. The use of the two terms also shows a class bias – erotica are pornographic works watched by more privileged people or, as Preston (1995: 11) says,

'Pornography and erotica are the same thing. The only difference is that erotica is the stuff bought by rich people. Pornography is what the rest of us buy.' For the purpose of this chapter we will use the term pornography throughout to describe any materials with the intention of sexually arousing the audience.

When we use the term 'pleasure industry' we are referring to the people who produce pornography or other media with the intention of sexually arousing their audience. We would like to emphasize that this encompasses a huge range of stakeholders who have diverse motivations. The pleasure industry, as we see it, is constituted by people who produce or create media or events with the primary intention of arousing the public or their consumers. This definition can include anyone from a film maker who is intent on making huge profits at the cost of workers' rights, to people posting pornographic imagery of themselves on www.youporn.com, to a collective that organizes not-for-profit safer sex parties. On the other hand, when we use the term 'public health industry' we are referring to people who are working to improve the health of the population, but again they have varying intentions. This could include anyone from global condom manufacturers to government-funded HIV prevention campaigns.

There is clearly already an overlap between the pleasure and the public health industries. Sometimes, as we will see later in this chapter, people who identify themselves as producers of pornography will make films with the intention of not only arousing the audience, but also encouraging safe sex behaviours. Our central argument is that further blurring these boundaries can lead to improved public health and encourage a move within the pleasure industry towards the intentional production of pornography that challenges harmful social norms.

What if porn is inherently bad?

It is clear that much pornography reflects negative gender norms in society. But as Lust (2010) puts it, 'Porn exploits women. The fashion industry exploits women. The music industry exploits women. Actresses are being abused by producers and agents everyday in the cinema business. We only blame porn because it's an obvious and direct exploitation.' We believe that within erotic media there is an opportunity to reflect different norms and, as a result, change thinking and behaviour. We believe that a harm reduction approach to pornography would allow us to manufacture pornography that sends the right kinds of messages – that shows safer sex, empowerment, diverse body images and alternative gender roles.

The central tenet of the harm reduction approach is that people may engage in activities that are harmful to their health regardless of the support systems and laws surrounding them. It has been primarily used to describe provision of clean injecting equipment to drug users to reduce risks of HIV transmission from shared needles, the aim being not to stop the harmful practice of drug use but to stop some of the risks associated with it (IHRA 2009). Thus the harm reduction approach aims to provide people with the tools they need to minimize the negative health consequences of harmful behaviours. We argue that the same approach should and can be applied to the making and watching of pornography. While we do not wish to argue that pornography is inherently harmful, we would like to acknowledge that some people hold legitimate concerns about the nature of pornography generally, and especially the potential exploitation within the industry today. However, we would like to assert that, even if you believe that pornography is essentially harmful, a harm reduction approach can still be useful in improving the health outcomes of those who do choose to consume pornography.

Pornography is big business

By the beginning of 2010, more than a quarter of the world's population – 1.7 billion people – were internet users, which is twice as many as in 2003 (ITU 2010). While this rate is still disproportionally tilted toward developed countries, 12 per cent of households in the developing world had internet access in 2008 (*ibid.*). Since these statistics only count households with internet access, adding in public venues like internet cafes, schools and libraries increases the number of individuals who have access to the internet.

Pornography is a huge and expanding global industry – and its audience is growing. A simple Google search in April 2012 shows that 'porn' returns 1.8 billion hits – that's more than one page for every adult in China. The single most popular adult site in the world is LiveJasmin.com, a webcam site which gets around 32 million visitors a month, or almost 2.5 per cent of all internet users (Ogas and Gaddam 2012). While one would expect that statistics on internet pornography are easier to come by than those of other forms of pornography, that is not the case. Hitwise, a US-based company that measures internet traffic, indicates that in December 2010, US visits to adult websites accounted for 4.68 per cent of US internet visits, making it the ninth most visited category (personal correspondence, staff member at Hitwise, 3 February 2011). However, this tells us nothing about who those visitors are, how much time they spend on those sites, or what the traffic patterns outside the US are.

The statistics available on the internet are particularly questionable – for instance, the authors found two references in reliable news sources (NPR and the *Atlantic*) that attribute January 2010 statistics about the proportion of internet users who view pornography online to Nielsen, another market research company. However, in corresponding with Nielsen, this company indicated that the figures circulating on the internet had in fact come from a 2007 survey, and that they had subsequently changed their methodology and no longer measured visits to adult sites. Statistics on this topic can also be used for ideological purposes. Claims that a very high proportion of internet use is related to pornography – up to 30 per cent of all downloads – may be based on a very broad definition of pornography to support moral and religious arguments against porn (see Caslon 2010). However, a recent and more systematic study of porn prevalence on the internet and access shows that 4 per cent of the million most-visited websites are pornographic, and that about 13 per cent of web searches from July 2009 to July 2010 were for porn (Ogas and Gaddam 2012).

Offline pornography is also profitable, a still growing industry. Industry growth can be illustrated by the number of pornography videos released in the US, which has increased from 1,300 titles in 1988 to 13,588 in 2005. Statistics about users of offline porn are very hard to come by, however – even more so than internet pornography visitors. It is not known how many people consume porn through DVDs, VHS tapes, books, magazines, comic books, and public x-rated movie theatres.

For this chapter, we contacted a number of groups to try and get clearer statistics on porn access. However, there are very few reliable sources and even industry specialists do not have global data. *Adult Video News*, the trade magazine for the pornography industry, also indicated in correspondence with the authors that they have never collected data on how many women watch porn or on the global reach of the industry.

Another issue that makes measurement a challenge is the rise of free (or illegally copied) internet porn (Raustiala and Sprigman 2010). In the new, 'democratized' porn industry, much of the content is being created by amateur users of websites – anyone with a simple video camera, or indeed a camera phone, can participate. As this is an emerging phenomenon, the numbers of people involved, its reach, and its implications have not yet been researched adequately. In short, we know from experience and anecdotal evidence that there is a lot of porn out there. However, no one seems to know exactly how much, what it depicts, or who is consuming it.

People learn about sexuality from pornography

While pornography is often maligned for reinforcing negative, limiting and harmful gender norms, it is ubiquitous. For better or worse, in every country where porn has been researched, it

Source: xkcd.com

was found to be an important source of sex education. In the UK, *The Guardian* (30 March 2009) cited three in ten pupils as saying that they learn about sex from pornography and spend on average 90 minutes a week looking at pornography. The article also quotes a small study of teenagers in the UK who, when shown a woman revealing unshaven pubic hair, were shocked, as these teenage girls had seen only images of shaven porn actresses and had started to shave as a norm themselves (Campbell 2009). Other studies in the UK have pointed to the 'pornification' of culture and the rise in access to internet porn as a cause of the huge increase in numbers of women seeking labiaplasty to try and make their vulvas look more like the vaginas they see in porn. One study highlighted that that there had been a 70 per cent increase in surgery on the NHS from 2006 to 2007 (Liao and Creighton 2007). Dr Veale from King's University, author of one as yet unpublished study, linked this rise to increased access to pornographic images: 'We haven't completed the research, but there is suspicion that this is related to much greater access to porn, so it is easier for women to compare themselves to actresses who may have had it done' (Davies 2011).

In their recent publication Ogas and Gaddam (2012) point out the huge jump humans have made in the last decade in terms of global access to pornography from the internet, with growing numbers of people routinely using their computers for sexual gratification.

> It's hard to imagine a more revolutionary development in the history of human sexuality. With a visit to an adult video site like PornHub

you can see more naked female bodies in a single minute than the most promiscuous Victorian would have seen in an entire lifetime. But there is an even more dramatic change. We don't have to interact with *anyone* to obtain erotica.

In low-income countries, too, porn has been found to be an important source of information about sex. In a recent Population Council Study of 100,000 young people in Andhra Pradesh, India, which asked young people where they learn about sex, 5 per cent of young men said it was internet pornography (Population Council India 2007). In China, Ling Li and colleagues (2009) found that pornography was an important source of information about sex for adolescents in Beijing; it ranked as the fourth most-mentioned source for boys, and the ninth for girls. In Ethiopia, Tadele (2006) found that pornography viewed at public movie houses was usually the only source of information about sex for street boys. In this volume, Rashid details how pornography is now one of the main sources of information and misinformation about sex for poor men living in Dhaka, Bangladesh. It is changing their expectations of themselves and their sexual partners, including wanting 'foreign sexual positions', needing to be a 'real man' by having a large penis and having sex regularly with many women.

Another study from Bangladesh on condom use illustrates the impact that depictions of sex in pornography can have on people's sexual health practices. The study found that men contrasted men in Western pornography having unprotected sex – who were presented as virile, strong and masculine – with men in safer sex and sexual health messaging: 'Men sought to preserve a "good" man's image by avoiding condoms, which symbolized promiscuous men in acquired immune deficiency syndrome educational messages' (Khan *et al.* 2004: 217). On the one hand, this study shows the strength of the alluring and sometimes negative image of sexuality or gender norms that pornography presents, and how persuasive it can be in asserting that the images it shows are ideals or even norms. It also illustrates how an oversight in health education messages – here, associating condom use with promiscuity – can undermine safe sex messaging.

Hooking into the power of pleasure

A harm reduction approach to pornography

Public health research has tended to focus on the damage pornography can cause – how it can create damaging psychological expectations of sex, reinforce negative gender norms which disempower women, and create an environment in which violent or coercive sex is more acceptable. A review of public health literature revealed little research on whether pornography encourages a norm or environment of unsafe sex, and no research on how we might use the communication channel of pornography to encourage safer sex, improve self-esteem, enhance body image, challenge gender norms or empower the viewer (Knerr and Philpott 2012).

We found a small range of studies that showed a positive impact on behaviour when people were instructed to use condoms using erotic methods or through explicit films (Kyes *et al.* 1991; Tanner and Pollack 1988; Scott-Sheldon *et al.* 2006). A meta-analysis by Scott-Sheldon and Johnson (2005), which examined the effectiveness of sexual risk-reduction interventions that integrated a safer-sex eroticization component, is the most rigorous piece of evidence to date to show that some amount of eroticization of safer-sex education is successful in reducing sexual risk behaviour. In the 21 experimental studies – which were either randomized control trials or had a quasi-experimental design with an adequate control group – three methods for eroticizing safer sex were used: a visual erotic component, such as a video, erotic poster or brochure; an activity, such as creating erotic ways to use condoms, have safer sex or writing a sexual fantasy; and reading erotic short stories. Participants in eroticized safer-sex interventions showed significant risk-reduction behaviour compared to control groups, and the study concluded that eroticizing safer sex leads to more risk-preventive attitudes, which in turn facilitates less risky sexual behaviour and an increase in condom use (Scott-Sheldon and Johnson 2005; Scott-Sheldon *et al.* 2006; Knerr and Philpott 2012).

There is also anecdotal evidence from a wide range of countries to suggest that safer sex, including condom use, can be eroticized and made pleasurable (Philpott, Knerr and Boydell 2006; Knerr and Philpott 2008; Abramson and Pinkerton 2002). Indeed, researchers and sexual health practitioners working within a wide range of contexts and cultures have been calling for a more pleasure-focused approach to sexual health, in part so that audiences will be more receptive to safer sex messages and recognize them as relevant to their own sex lives (see Banerjee 2006; Calsyn 2002; Chann et al. 2004; Ntahompagaze 2002; Widdice et al. 2006; Abramson and Pinkerton 2002). In a qualitative study with young women in Zimbabwe, Masvawure (2008) posed the question, 'Shouldn't public health practitioners be programming for pleasure, as it is primarily within these contexts of pleasure, rather than of danger, that many young women are probably at greater risk of picking up infection?' Moreover, the World Health Organization (WHO 2004), The International Planned Parenthood Federation (2008) and the World Association for Sexual Health (WAS 2008) now recognize sexual pleasure as a key component of sexual health.

The few studies undertaken in the area of sexual skill as it relates to safer sex show that people become more comfortable and satisfied, and often experience more pleasure, the more they use a safer-sex technology, such as male and female condoms (Kelly et al. 1990; UNAIDS 1999). Rosser et al. (2002) cite evidence that men who have gained 'condom skills' have more positive attitudes towards condoms. While it may not yet have been explicitly tested in an academic study, it is logical to think that a pornographic film that shows a man putting a condom on would help develop more practical condom skills than the typical public health demonstration on a banana or broomstick.

Pornography that blurs the boundary with public health

The Global Mapping of Pleasure was produced by the Pleasure Project, and is a directory of case studies from around the world of organizations, programmes, media and people who work to integrate pleasure into their sex education work, or safety into their pleasure work (Knerr and Philpott 2008). The Pleasure Project began in 2004 as a campaign to encourage a more honest and realistic approach to sexual health, particularly in the context of global health and international development. The Project's aim is to increase the proportion of safe sexual acts around the world, and for pleasure, desire and eroticism to become 'quality markers' for sexuality education and sexual health interventions. For this to occur, there is a need to change the way sexuality education and sexual health interventions are viewed by public health practitioners – from a focus on disease prevention and risk to pleasure and health.

The following section includes a few examples of case studies from the *Global Mapping* that highlight best practice for making pornography safer. They are mainly examples of people making porn and promoting safer sex, but some are also challenging other norms, such as by making porn for a female audience and subverting traditional power norms in their films. Unless otherwise noted, quotations in this section come from published and unpublished interviews from the *Global Mapping of Pleasure* material. The examples were chosen to give an indication of the range of ways pornography can deliver a sexual health message whilst arousing its audience. The mapping directory also includes examples of organizations that aim to increase safer sex by inclusion of discussions of pleasure and desire as sexual motivations. They are therefore examples of practitioners challenging the mainstream pleasure industry norms.

We recognize the enormity of the porn industry and the range of political views within the industry from independent feminist and queer film makers to large mainstream production houses. We also recognize the range of employment conditions of actors: some have the ability to negotiate contracts independently, while others face isolation and exploitation, as in other industries. Erica Lust sums up her motivations and experience well, in ways which reflect the overall sentiments of the professionals we interviewed for the global mapping, when she says:

Porn isn't just porn. It's a way of talking about sex and understanding masculinity and femininity. Right now, this discourse, and the theory behind it is almost entirely male, and often sexist as well. There are almost no women's voices in this discourse, just as there was a time when there were no women's voices in the worlds of politics and big business. I believe that women have the right to enjoy adult films, and we have to do so by demanding our share of discourse as screenwriters, producers and directors. (Lust 2010)

Integrating condom use into pornographic films: Modern Loving

Modern Loving I and *II* are erotic instructional videos for hetero-sexual couples that feature sexy safer sex. They show real couples trying out different sexual techniques and positions as a way to help viewers improve their sex lives (Schaffer 2004). The Pleasure Project provided condom consultancy on set to ensure that the sex is always safe, but the film is still sexy. Scenes include a woman masturbating with a female condom; a man using a female condom for anal sex with his female partner; a man going down on his partner using a dental dam; various examples of the use of male condoms and lube; and a multitude of non-penetrative, super-sexy techniques. We were keen that the entire film was safer sex, but without making this a 'safer sex' film or making the case for safer sex in a separate section of the film. Instead our hope was that the viewer would get turned on by the action which happened to be all safe. In order to do this we supported the script writer to include sexy tips on condom use within the entire dialogue and not just in the usual 'condom section'. Anne Philpott was on set through the entire filming and worked backstage with the actors and actresses to help them feel comfortable using male and female condoms correctly. The actors were obviously keen to look sexy and make condom use look good whilst they performed. This was a new skill for many of them as they are usually not required to use condoms. There was pressure in being filmed in front of a large audience whilst managing the sometimes tricky art of condom use.

The atmosphere on set was like any busy workplace, and as the studio time is expensive there was pressure to get it right on the first take. As the scene was being filmed, Anne would speak to the next performers backstage as they got ready, got erections and focused on how they would act. The actors and actresses were encouraged to innovate by the director, or suggest scenes. There seemed to be significant respect in the team for all the skills required to make the film. The actors were seen as experts on positions and comfortable condom use, and the director was responsible for overseeing the 'look' through the camera. There was also a large amount of mutual problem solving (how to put on a condom with a mouth, how to make condom use in anal sex comfortable, etc.) which could prove useful to a much wider audience. The *Modern Loving* films also feature interviews with the actors in which they describe their experiences while shooting. This system of debriefing reinforces the message that the partners are equals in the sexual act, and that the pleasure of both of them is equally important.

In *Modern Loving I*, the film's narrator instructs, 'If you fancy trying the female condom, ask your man to give you a hand.... The outer ring stays on the outside and rubs against the clitoris for extra impact. Your man also gets off by feeling the inner ring rub against the head of his penis.' A scene featuring the male condom suggests, 'Slowly and carefully tear open the packet. Learn to love the sound of the tear.' The safer sex in the films sends a subliminal message that safer sex is sexy. *Modern Loving I* and *II* don't talk about sexually transmitted infections or HIV; instead they show safer sex as the norm and as a turn-on.

There are also candid comments from the actors and actresses, with their respective partners, including an extended spontaneous monologue of enthusiasm from one of the actors for female condoms, which he had never used before. He said, 'I enjoyed everything today. For me it was a first with Femidom [the female condom] ... it was great. I mean, at least I've got an idea of what it looks like and feels like.'

Condom use in pornographic films

Easy on the eye

Anna Span started shooting porn films after graduating from art school in 1998. It was there that she wrote her dissertation 'Towards a New Pornography', in which she considered what a female perspective on porn would look like. As she put it 'It's like putting sex into soap opera' (Span 2005). She believes that female viewers are poorly served by pornography and want more depth to the characters and a slower build-up to sex, which is usually missing in other films. She sees pornography as one of the last unexplored areas in film. Although other women (like Candida Royalle) have directed films, Anna is the first female porn director in the UK.

The films highlight women enjoying heterosexual and lesbian sex. There is also a focus on 'reality' in script and actor performances, as well as more focus on the male actors than in other pornographic films. Span terms this 'female point of view' shots. Other themes include everyday objects (such as a chocolate bar or orange) being used as sex aids, threesomes, and group sex.

Since 1998, Span has run her own production company, Easy on the Eye Productions,[1] which also releases work of other female porn directors that she has trained. Span's films also break the norm by not only including, but featuring, male and female condoms in some of her films, for example in *Uniform Behaviour*, *A & O Department*, and *Do the Business*. 'I put condoms in films when people [actors and actresses] ask to use them, and also if the story requires it, like a 1950s set piece or medical piece,' said Span. But unlike *Modern Loving*, which is 100 per cent safer sex, Anna's films probably have condoms in '30 per cent of the shots' (her estimate, personal communication). Span admits it is not always easy: there are challenges with distributors who are not keen on condoms in films and see them as less marketable, and some actors don't want to lose their erections by using condoms. She has to balance commercial interests with the intention to include condoms.

This is a point echoed by Hirsch, the CEO of Vivid Entertainment, one of the world's largest producers of porn. He said that Vivid Entertainment had a compulsory condom policy for nearly seven years and 'When we became a mandatory-condom company, we saw sales drop by about 20 per cent' (Cohen 2010). Vivid have since changed this policy back to condom–optional.

The Pleasure Project advised Anna on use of the female condom in her films. Span describes the challenge of integrating condom use into her films:

> Using the female condom is very difficult in films. In *A & O Department* and *Uniform Behaviour*, none of the models or crew could follow the instructions on the back of the pack, regardless of our joint experiences in the world of sex. It just kept coming off on the guy's dick – so we just carried on using it like it was a normal condom. Interestingly, the condom almost fitted one guy – just goes to show how big these guys are!
>
> As for male condoms, some guys lose their hard-ons when they put a condom on, which means they have to rip it off in order to masturbate and then start using a new one. Some scenes they get through seven or eight of them and it makes the day much longer. Male porn stars become a little desensitized in their penis, because they use it so much and because the thrill lessens in time, so using condoms can make this worse. This is the main problem with condoms in porn films for me. It means that I have to be careful what guys I use, which ultimately ends up with less choice of men for women to view. This is why I sit on the fence and say that I will include condoms in a scene if one of the models wants to use them – or if the story requires them – rather than include them in all films. I have to balance making porn for women and being a responsible producer. (Knerr and Philpott 2008)

Compulsory condom use model: wrap it up and stop barebacking

Chi Chi LaRue is a film director who insists on making all of her gay, bisexual and straight films with condoms. She is considered one of the gay adult industry's most successful directors, and also directs straight and bisexual erotic films. A long-time advocate for condom use in gay porn, LaRue announced she would no longer produce films for Vivid Video in 2006 because they adopted a condom-optional policy. She set out on her own and created a production company which requires actors and actresses to use condoms in all of its films.

In response to reports of an increase of 'barebacking' (anal sex without condoms) in porn, LaRue created a four-minute video public service announcement explaining the risks of barebacking porn, and the responsibility of porn consumers to avoid barebacking porn in order to protect the health and lives of porn actors. The video features gay porn video clips run in the background (LaRue 2008). This film has been shown on gay porn sites and blogs and received support from public health organizations such as the US Center for Disease Control and the *Journal of the American Medical Association*. It has been covered by the media, including the *New York Times* and the BBC (Newsnight, 5 March 2008; *New York Times*, 14 January 2008).

LaRue said of her decision to make the public service announcement:

> When I moved to LA in 1987 and took a job in promotions at Catalina Video, the AIDS crisis was in full swing. I lobbied hard to ... get condoms on the models. I would like to think that some of my persuasion helped make condom movies a reality. Since then, gay porn has helped lead the way in showing gay men how to use condoms, how to have safer sex and removed some of the stigma that was associated with condoms at the time.
>
> When I first started seeing barebacking titles appear, of course I was disappointed and very outspoken. The fact is that it was pretty obvious to most that the models 'appeared' to be HIV+ and were having unsafe sex with what 'appeared' to be other HIV+ models. Again not something I have ever heard was recommended, but in any case, it is something that does seem to be more readily practised in the gay community. What we are seeing now is drastically different. We are seeing movies with 18-year-old twinks being gang banged without condoms. We are seeing ... 20-year-olds in the UK who have reportedly become HIV+ after making their first porn. (Knerr and Philpott 2008)

LaRue makes an interesting distinction between pre-condom (pre-AIDS) porn, that she will distribute, and the new range of bare-backing titles. She explains that she puts condoms in all her films because even though viewers might be able to watch non-condom porn and still wear condoms, she thinks that younger gay men have missed the HIV message:

> I guess I don't equate pre-condom titles as 'bareback'. That term didn't exist when these porn classics were created. There was no serious reason for gay men to wear condoms. My critics also accuse me of not giving gay men the credit to distinguish between fantasy and reality. That younger gay guys who didn't have all their friends die, who didn't see deathly ill gay men at the grocery store, and aren't bombarded with AIDS messages on the news daily can watch barebacking porn and it doesn't affect their behaviour. Like I said in my PSA [public service announcement] I think that is true for some people. I also say if that is your argument then you certainly can't claim that viewers can't realize that pre-condom titles were filmed in another era before HIV.

LaRue provides an example of how porn directors can take the initiative to attempt to change norms in society. By expressing a deep respect for the actors and actresses in her films, LaRue sets an example for other directors, and sends a strong message that actors in porn films are people with rights, and whose employers have an obligation to keep them safe and healthy at the workplace.

Adult industry supporting workers' rights

The AIDS Healthcare Foundation of Los Angeles in the USA has taken lawsuits to California courts to try and ensure that the city's public health officials make condom use compulsory in porn films produced there. They were prompted to take this course of action after 22 actors contracted HIV in five years (Fox News, October 2010; BBC News, October 2010). This followed a number of HIV infections in 2005, with a similar level of media dialogue about the need for workers to be able to protect themselves (Romero 2011a; The Pleasure Project 2010). However, to date only a few companies make it compulsory and the ruling has been controversial, with porn film actors and their representative bodies (Romero 2010). The Adult Industry Medical Healthcare Foundation (now AIM Medical Associates PC), which offers sexually transmitted infection services to adult industry workers, tests approximately 1,200 workers every month, and keeps a record of positive STI results with the aim of protecting adult industry workers through self-regulation, was a vocal critic. However the AIDS Healthcare Foundation argues that condom use on set is the only way to be safe and protect workers. Industry insiders say that compulsory condom use reduces sales and would increase filming outside of the US in Mexico (Romero 2011b).

However this debate remains dormant elsewhere, with most heterosexual porn rarely featuring condoms and adult industry workers finding it hard to get regular testing or obtain information on their sexual partner's HIV status.

Pornography that highlights what the mainstream overlooks

Feminist erotic films or porn made for women

Fatale Media produces and markets lesbian erotica, including *Safe Is Desire*, a safer-sex lesbian film described as 'raw lust and passion with a heart'. According to the president of Fatale, Nan Kinney, 'although times have changed since the porn-less lesbian days of the mid-1980s there is still a need to portray images of sexuality that mainstream adult producers overlook, so exploring and eroticizing safer sex for women fit perfectly with that goal'.

When Fatale started, Kinney claims, 'porn was a dirty word' and there was no such things as porn made by and for women, but she has been driven over the past 20 years to set standards for the industry and encourage other women to make their own porn. Part of Kinney's motivation is also to highlight the importance of safer sex for lesbians: 'Although the transmission of HIV between women is low in numbers, we knew there were other ways for HIV to affect women; for example, some lesbians have sex with men, or use needles. And safer-sex techniques are important not just in preventing HIV but all the other STDs as well.'[2]

Kinney said that Fatale wanted to show that safer sex techniques don't have to be a turn-off; they could be a turn-on. For example, instead of using the thick dental dams that were recommended for oral sex, why not have fun with wrapping your partner up in plastic cling film? Or, practise changing the condom on your strap-on to make it easier to switch from anal sex to vaginal sex and barely miss a beat? According to Kinney, 'These sorts of sexy tricks can really change people's attitudes around safer sex.'

Other examples of porn makers who are thinking about the female market or are making feminist porn are Anna Brownfield, Shine Houston and Paris Ovidie. At the Berlin Porn festival in 2009 a discussion between six female porn makers centred on how to make feminist porn and meet the commercial and distribution challenges involved (Berlin Porn Festival 2009; The Pleasure Project 2009). Brownfield says 'I'm a feminist erotic filmmaker who makes film about sex and craft!' and talked about how she uses exciting narrative and characterization and then ensures that the sex stays in. Her film *The Band*, for example, covers a band's tour as well as the subsequent sex. As a director, she enjoys the creativity and realism of including safer sex. When asked in an interview how having a woman behind the camera shifts the paradigm that 'the same old porn' has been locked into, Brownfield said, 'I think it's important when shooting erotica to create your own language and challenge the clichés of the adult film genre and focus on women's fantasies.... I like to objectify the male body, whereas most adult films objectify the female body' (Santos 2010).

Brownfield also says that condoms are compulsory in her films:

> This generation thinks you should use condoms for contraception only and don't think about it also protecting them from sexually transmitted diseases. Hence, I see one of my roles as an erotic film maker is also to educate the audience about safe sex. As most of the sex scenes in *The Band* are one-night stands, where the characters don't know each other's sexual history, it was important to show

condom use. Not only just during the sex scenes, but also the condoms being put on, rather than just appearing.... I feel that the sex scenes are so erotic that it doesn't matter if they use condoms. Also I really don't care as it was one thing I am not prepared to compromise on.

Girls who like porno: making our own

'Girls who like porno' is a group started in 2004 that supports women to make their own porn, subverting the usual stereotypes and power dynamics. Their manifesto states:

> Pornography constructed by its actors and actresses, pornography that does not negate any body type or any practice that emerges from consensus, that visualizes the delicious reality in which HIV-positive people continue living and fucking, that generates new visual references which inspire some and make others melt, pornography which empowers us, surpassing juvenile titters and easy jokes or insults, pornography which dares to speak about sex and our sexualities from a position of power which we have not traditionally had. And all of this without ever forgetting a sense of humour. (GWLP 2005)

Girls who like porno hold workshops to support actors and actresses to make porn and then make the films available online. Their films include *Love on the Beach*, *Porno Terror* and *Suspenders*. They have also curated many art shows, including one specially dealing with safer sex (*ibid.*). Their mission is to take back control of the means of porn production for women. Although this is not necessarily an example of constant inclusion of safer sex in porn, it does show the potential for new production methods such as self-made porn. In similar ways, in the emerging 'democratized' porn industry, home-made content may result in more alternative visions of sex in pornography – a diversification in which the seeds of empowering pornography can flourish. However, it could also go the other way and continue to reproduce stereotypical practices and gender roles. This is a phenomenon that both the pleasure and public health industries will need to grapple with in the future.

Putting safe good sex into women's magazines for women who 'get it'

Scarlet is a UK national women's erotic lifestyle magazine that incorporates fiction – which aims to promote a safe and full sex life for women – in a package that also offers fashion, beauty, celebrity and political features. The Cliterature section prints readers' sexy confessions, erotica extracts and original erotic fiction from the world's leading writers. The magazine also features sex toy reviews, 'sexpertise' (sex tips) from leading sex educators, and profiles of iconic female sexual adventurers, such as Anaïs Nin and Germaine Greer.

Its editor, Sarah Hedley, says of their safer sex policy,

> From the very start, *Scarlet* has promoted safe sex through a policy of eroticizing condom use. We do not feel that lecturing people about what they already know, or scaring them with STI statistics is effective in changing the way people view safe sex…. As house policy all erotic fiction stories feature condom use. It's referred to in an evocative language that invites the reader to be aroused when they hear the crisp, enticing tear of the condom packet, the naughty, sharp twang of rubber…. We don't gloss over it – we enjoy it. We indulge in it. By eroticizing condom use, the presence of condoms becomes part of sex play, rather than a problem. (Knerr and Philpott 2008)

Hedley explained that the magazine had a mixed response in the beginning. 'At first, magazine sellers said that a magazine catering to female sexuality would not sell because "women just aren't interested in sex" – an utterly laughable notion.' It was launched in 2004 and circulation continued to grow; soon it was being carried in major mainstream bookshops and supermarket and pharmacy chains. According to Hedley:

> If gender stereotyping was to be used to promote safe sex, then the following angle could be taken: if men were made to feel that using condoms made them better in bed (because women can let go and enjoy themselves without fear of pregnancy and STIs), then they would be more inclined to use them; if women knew that men were more likely to respect a woman who insisted on condom use, then they may be more inclined to make condom use mandatory.

Scarlet may prove that women *are* into sex. Although the print version went into liquidation in June 2010, it is now an internet-based magazine, and their experience may suggest an untapped potential in the market for erotic media; women want to hear about sex from a positive, empowering perspective, which in turn reinforces their own experiences.

Erotic blogging on kinkier safer sex: sex in the city

Selina Fire is a New York-based sex blogger and writer with a difference – she writes hot, outrageous, filthy stories about her life, and knows how to make safer sex hot without it being a big deal. In her sex blog 'Sex in the City – The Real Version,' she says:

> I am an unashamed sex goddess, intellectual and native New Yorker. I write to show the world that 50-year-old women, or women of any age, for that matter, are sexual; that all women's sexual fantasies are not about riding a white horse on a beach at sunset. Some of us like it down and dirty, and God doesn't judge us for doing so.

She also writes a column for *Penthouse Forum* magazine, and once dedicated a whole column (April 2007) to ideas for kinkier safer sex, including mutual masturbation, mammary intercourse, fisting, getting her partner to come on her face, and exhibitionism. Fire writes about safer sex in an arousing way that shows how much she enjoys it, for example in this recent post:

> 'I want to fuck you like you want to be fucked.' I got up, fumbled in a drawer and then a small case by the bed, searching for the right equipment. It was late. I was tired. I was going to have to do it the easy way. I found the lube I like, and snapped on a pair of our disposable black latex gloves. I lubed up and caressed his balls and asshole with the gloved fingers of my left hand. With the other hand I reached around to tug gently on his dick. He groaned, sleepily, and his dick hardened. 'Yeah, this is the way I'm gonna fuck you.' (Fire, June 2010)

A future research agenda?

We believe that there needs to be more research on, and knowledge of, the porn industry by sex education organizations and academics. There should be mutual learning and respect across the public health and pleasure industries, and awareness of the advantages that they bring to each other's work. In order to harness the huge audience that pornography has been able to capture, public health could know more about:

- The incentives and structural drivers that could increase safer sex, challenge normative depictions of gender, and encourage fair working practices and conditions within different parts of the pornography industry;

- How sex education and porn access is changing in low-income countries in Asia and Africa, with increased access to mobile phones and the internet;

- What type of safer sex in porn would have the biggest behaviour change impact? For whom? Whether a pornography with love and romance could have transformative potential;

- Whether tax breaks in countries where making porn is legal might help to incentivize positive porn;

- Whether decriminalization in countries where pornography is illegal would help actors ask for protection under labour or health legislation;

- Whether unionization of pleasure industry staff enables them to demand improved health and safety standards and other labour rights.

Conclusion: bridging the pleasure divide

The world of pornography is more complex than usually portrayed in the mainstream media or by public health professionals. There are pornographers challenging the usual rules of unsafe sex, sexist scenes and the male gaze. These examples show that it is possible to make sexy safer-sex pornography that can challenge the traditional norms of the industry. They also illustrate the creativity and wonderful range of media being used to promote safer and less traditional forms of porn and erotic media.

But the case studies also show that there are often difficult trade-offs to be made. *Modern Loving*'s actors and those in other films talk of the difficulty of sustaining condom use over long periods of filming. Span has had to make the choice between distribution deals or more condoms. Hedley struggled with the promotion of traditional masculine roles to get men to wear condoms versus challenging gender stereotypes.

Public health organizations and practitioners need to look for new ways to communicate about health and HIV prevention. Rapidly increasing global access to the internet means that more people are learning about sex not in school or from families, but online. This is an opportunity to increase safer, sexy practices and deliver safer-sex messages and techniques to diverse audiences in various contexts. Self-censorship, pre-conceptions and discomfort with issues related to sex, pleasure and explicit representations of sex among public health professionals are common barriers to innovation in health promotion, especially when it comes to broaching the subject of pornography.

The pleasure industry has a wealth of skills and experience that public health practitioners could draw on to increase their effectiveness when it comes to delivering safer-sex messages. The industry needs to accept more corporate responsibility for the lack of safer sex in their films and the risks actors take when making unsafe films. While there are still many parts of the industry that produce porn that perpetuates harmful norms, the public health world could support those who include hot, fun, safer-sexy messages in pornography, to enhance actors' health and well-being and the health of viewers. By combining a range of expertise – from the ability to conduct rigorous experimental trials to the ability to put on condoms sexily whilst being filmed – we can bridge the pleasure divide, enhance global health and continue to have more and more pleasurable safer sex.

Notes

1 http://www.easyote.co.uk/.
2 http://www.fatalemedia.com/about.html.

References

Abramson, P. R. and S. D. Pinkerton (2002) *With Pleasure: Thoughts on the Nature of Human Sexuality*, Oxford University Press, New York.

Banerjee, A. (2006) 'Prevalence of Unprotected Anal Sex and Use of Condoms and Lubricants among Men Who Have Sex with Men (MSM) in Andhra Pradesh, India', paper presented at 16th International AIDS Conference, 13–18 August, Toronto, Canada.

BBC News (2004) 'Promiscuity "Fuelling HIV Spread"', BBC News Online, 8 April, http://news.bbc.co.uk/1/hi/health/3610487.stm (accessed 3 March 2011).

—— (2010) 'Two Porn Companies Postpone Filming over HIV Test', http://www.bbc.co.uk/news/entertainment-arts-11531325 (accessed 3 March 2011).

Berlin Porn Festival (2009) 'Panel "Chicks with Guts"' http://www.pornfilmfestivalberlin.de/pff_e/?page_id=439 (accessed 4 March 2011).

Calsyn, D. A. (2002) 'Beliefs about Condom Use Differ for Men and Women Injection Drug Users', XIV International AIDS Conference, 7–12 July, Barcelona, Spain.

Campbell, D. (2009) 'Porn the New Sex Education', *The Guardian*, March, http://www.guardian.co.uk/society/joepublic/2009/mar/30/teenagers-porn-sex-education (accessed 3 March 2011).

Carter, A. (1978) *The Sadeian Woman and the Ideology of Pornography*, Pantheon Books, New York.

Caslon (2010) 'How Big Is the Web (HBW), Accessibility and Distribution of Information on the Web (ADIW)', in *Caslon*

Analytics Guide: Censorship and Free Speech, http://www.caslon. com.au/censorshipguide2.htm (accessed 3 March 2011).

Chann, B., J. Makin, K. Richter and K. Longfield (2004) 'Targeting HIV/AIDS Risk Behavior in Cambodia: Results from a National KAP survey', 15th International AIDS Conference, 11–16 July, Bangkok, Thailand.

Cohen, N. (2010) 'In Porn Industry Many Balk at Condom Proposal', National Public Radio, USA, http://www.npr.org/templates/ story/story.php?storyId=126289177 (accessed 1 March 2011).

Davies, R. (2011) 'Labiaplasty Surgery Increase Blamed on Pornography', *The Guardian*, 27 February, http://www.guardian.co.uk/ lifeandstyle/2011/feb/27/labiaplasty-surgery-labia-vagina-pornogr aphy?INTCMP=ILCNETTXT3487 (accessed 2 March 2010).

Fire, S. (2010) 'Sex in the City: The Real Version', http://selinafire. blogspot.com/ (accessed 2 March 2010).

Fox News (2010) 'One HIV Positive Star Shuts Down Industry', October, http://www.foxnews.com/entertainment/2010/10/13/ hiv-positive-porn-star-shuts-industry/ (accessed 2 March 2010).

Freitas, M. I. F. (2002) 'Teenagers' Representations about AIDS', 14th International AIDS Conference, 7–12 July, Barcelona, Spain.

Girls who like porno (GWLP) (2005) 'Condoms, Pills and What the Hell Is Safe Sex', part of 'Let's Talk about It', curated by Peter Cramer and Jack Waters, World Aids Day, CCCB, Barcelona, http://girlswholikeporno.com (accessed 4 March 2011).

Higgens, J. A. and J. S. Hirsch (2007) 'The Pleasure Deficit: Revisiting the Sexuality Connection in Reproductive Health', *International Family Planning Perspectives*, Vol. 33, No. 3, pp. 133–9.

—— (2008) 'Pleasure, Power, and Inequality: Incorporating Sexuality into Research on Contraceptive Use', *American Journal of Public Health*, Vol. 98, No. 10, pp. 1803–13.

Holland, J., C. Ramazanoglu, and S. Scott (1992) 'Risk, Power and Possibility of Pleasure: Young Women and Safer Sex', *AIDS Care*, No. 4, pp. 273–83.

IHRA (International Harm Reduction Association) (2009) 'Position Statement: What is Harm Reduction', September, http://www. ihra.net/files/2010/08/10/Briefing_What_is_HR_English.pdf (accessed 3 March 2012).

Ingham, R. (2005) '"We Didn't Cover That at School": Education against Pleasure or Education for Pleasure?', *Sex Education*, Vol. 5, No. 4, pp. 375–88.

International Planned Parenthood Federation (2008) 'Sexual Rights: an IPPF declaration', May, www.ippf.org/NR/rdonlyres/.../

SexualRightsIPPFdeclaration.pdf (accessed 3 March 2011).

ITU (International Telecommunications Union) (2010) 'World Telecommunication/ICT Development Report 2010 – Monitoring the WSIS targets: Executive Summary', International Telecommunications Union, Geneva.

Jolly, S. (2007) 'Why the Development Industry Should Get over Its Obsession with Bad Sex and Start to Think about Pleasure', *IDS Working Paper* 283, Institute of Development Studies, Brighton.

Kelly, J. A., J. S. St Lawrence and T. L.Brasfield (1990) 'Psychological Factors That Predict AIDS High-Risk and AIDS Precautionary Behaviour', *Journal of Consulting and Clinical Psychology*, Vol. 58, pp. 117–20.

Khan, S. I., N. Hudson-Rodd, S. Saggers, M. I. Bhuiyan and A. Bhuiya (2004) 'Safer Sex or Pleasurable Sex? Rethinking Condom Use in the AIDS Era', *Sexual Health*, Vol. 1, No. 4, pp. 217–25.

Knerr, W. and A. Philpott (2008) *The Global Mapping of Pleasure: A Directory of Organizations, Media and People Who Eroticize Safer Sex* (2nd Edition), The Pleasure Project/Taking Action for Sexual Health, Oxford/Delhi.

—— (2012) 'Everything You Wanted to Know about Pleasurable Safer Sex but Were Afraid to Ask: Promoting Sexual Health and Rights through Pleasure: a Literature Review', The Pleasure Project, Oxford/Delhi.

Kyes, K. B., I. S. Brown and R. H. Pollack (1991) 'The Effect of Exposure to a Condom Script on Attitudes toward Condoms', *Journal of Psychology and Human Sexuality*, Vol. 4, No. 1, pp. 21–36.

La Rue, C. (2008) 'When Safe Sex is Hot Sex', www.safesexishotsex. com (accessed 3 March 2011).

Liao, L. and S. M. Creighton (2007) 'Requests for Cosmetic Genitoplasty: How Should Healthcare Providers Respond?', *British Medical Journal*, Vol. 334, 26 May, pp. 1090–2.

Ling, L., M. King and S. Winter (2009) 'Sexuality Education in China: the Conflict between Reality and Ideology', *Asia Pacific Journal of Education*, Vol. 29, No. 4, pp. 469–80.

Lust, E. (2010) *Good Porn: A Woman's Guide*, Seal Press, California.

Masvawure, T. B. (2008) '"Low-risk Youth?": Students, Campus Life and HIV at a Zimbabwean University', unpublished doctoral thesis, University of Pretoria, Pretoria.

Ntahompagaze, T. (2002) 'Using and Access to Condoms for Sex Workers in Bujumbura Township', 16th International AIDS Conference, 13–18 August 2006, Toronto, Canada.

Ogas, O. and S. Gaddam (2012) *A Billion Wicked Thoughts: What the*

Internet Tells Us about Sexual Relationship, Plume, New York.

Philpott, A. (2003) 'Eroticising the Female Condom, How to Increase Usage', presentation at the 13th International Conference on AIDS and STIs in Africa, September, Nairobi, Kenya.

Philpott, A., W. Knerr and V. Boydell (2006) 'Pleasure and Prevention: When Good Sex Is Safer Sex', *Reproductive Health Matters*, Vol. 14, No. 28, pp. 23–31.

Philpott, A., W. Knerr and D. Maher (2006) 'Promoting Protection and Pleasure: Amplifying the Effectiveness of Barriers against Sexually Transmitted Infections and Pregnancy', *Lancet*, Vol. 368, No. 1, pp. 2028–31.

Population Council (2007) 'Youth in India: Situation and Needs 2006–7', Population Council, Delhi, India.

Preston, J. (1995) *Flesh and the Word 3*, Plume/Penguin, New York.

Raustiala, K. and C. Sprigman (2010) 'Copyright Infringements in the Porn Industry', *New York Times*, Freakonomics Blog, 5 May, http://freakonomics.blogs.nytimes.com/2010/05/05/copyrighting-porn-a-guest-post/ (accessed 2 March 2011).

Romero, D. (2010) 'Porn Star Justin Long Vows Boycott of AIDS Healthcare Foundation over Its Attempt to Force Condoms on Porn', LA Weekly blog, 13 December, http://blogs.laweekly.com/informer/2010/12/porn_star_ahf_boycott.php (accessed 2 March 2011).

—— (2011a) 'Porn Industry Clinic Shut Down, but Anti-Porn Group Says It's Still Operating: LA County Leaders Pressed for Action against Condom-Free Adult Films', LA Weekly blog, 25 January, http://blogs.laweekly.com/informer/2011/01/porn_clinic_license_aim_ahf.php (accessed 2 March 2011).

—— (2011b) 'Porn Industry Testing Clinic in the Valley Reopens after Being Shut Down by County, State', LA Weekly blog, 8 February, http://blogs.laweekly.com/informer/2011/02/porn_industry_clinic_open.php (accessed 2 March 2011).

Rosser, B. R. S., W. O. Bockting and D. L. Rugg (2002) 'A Randomized Controlled Intervention Trial of a Sexual Health Approach to Long-term HIV Risk Reduction for Men Who Have Sex with Men: Effects of the Intervention on Unsafe Sexual Behaviour', *AIDS Education and Prevention*, Vol. 14, Supplement A, pp. 59–71.

Santos, A. (2010) 'Women Behind the Camera of Erotica', Playboy Phillipines, February, http://anasantoswrites.com/?p=1192 (accessed 3 March 2011).

Schaffer, B. (2004) 'Modern Loving – The Ultimate Guide To Sexual Pleasure' (DVD), Modern Loving.

Scott-Sheldon, L. and B. T. Johnson (2005) 'Eroticizing Creates Safer Sex: a Research Synthesis', *Journal of Primary Prevention*, Vol. 27, pp. 619–40.

Scott-Sheldon, L., K. L. Marsh, B. T. Johnson and D. E. Glasford (2006) 'Condoms + Pleasure = Safer Sex? A Missing Addend in the Safer Sex Message', *AIDS Care*, Vol. 18, No. 7, pp. 750–4.

Span, A. (2005) in conversation with Anne Philpott, July, UK.

Tadele, G. (2006) 'Bleak Prospects: Young Men, Sexuality, and HIV/ AIDS in an Ethiopian Town', African Studies Centre, Leiden.

Tanner, W. M. and R. H. Pollack (1988) 'The Effect of Condom Use and Erotic Instructions on Attitudes towards Condoms', *The Journal of Sex Research*, Vol. 25, pp. 537–41.

The Pleasure Project (2009) http://thepleasureproject.org/word press/2009/10/28/chicks-with-guts-and-morals-live-from-berlin-porn-festival/ (accessed 2 March 2011).

—— (2010) 'Why Aren't Condoms in Porn Compulsory?', October, http://thepleasureproject.org/wordpress/2010/10/15/condoms-in-porn-why-arent-they-compulsory/ (accessed 2 March 2011).

UNAIDS (1999) 'Sex and Youth: Contextual Factors Affecting Risk for HIV/AIDS: a Comparative Analysis of Multi-Site Studies in Developing Countries', UNAIDS, http://library.unesco-iicba. org/English/HIV_AIDS/cdrom%20materials/PDFfiles/99sandy1. pdf (accessed 2 March 2011).

WAS (World Association for Sexual Health) (2008) 'Sexual Health for the Millennium: a Declaration and Technical Document', WAS, Mexico City.

WHO (World Health Organization) (2004) 'Sexual Health – A New Focus for WHO', *Progress in Reproductive Health Research* 67, http:// www.who.int/reproductive-health/hrp/progress/67.pdf (accessed 2 March 2011).

Widdice, L. E., J. L. Cornell, W. Liang, and B. L. Halpern-Felsher (2006) 'Having Sex and Condom Use: Potential Risks and Benefits Reported by Young, Sexually Inexperienced Adolescents', *Journal of Adolescent Health*, Vol. 39, No. 4, pp. 588–95.

Williams, L. (1989) *Hard Core: Power, Pleasure and the 'Frenzy of the Visible'*, University of California Press, Berkeley CA.

11
Challenging Clitoraid

• •

Petra Boynton

In the spring of 2010 there was a flurry of activity across social media with invitations to 'End Female Genital Mutilation' by supporting the 'Adopt a Clitoris' campaign[1] run by an organization called Clitoraid,[2] which promised to restore pleasure to women who had undergone genital cutting. With these donations, Clitoraid planned to build a 'Pleasure Hospital' in Bobo Dioulasso, Burkina Faso, offering reparative surgery for women who have undergone female genital mutilation/cutting (FGM/C) (see also Jirovsky 2010). At first this sounded wonderful. Donors were asked to 'adopt a clitoris', 'give someone you never met a gift they will never forget', and 'support our sisters'. What could be problematic about a campaign to reverse female genital cutting and help women experience pleasure? Unsurprisingly many academics, therapists, and others from the science and sex education and therapy communities eagerly forwarded calls to build this 'pleasure hospital'.

Closer examination of the Clitoraid campaign revealed several core problems. Clitoraid is a project overseen by the Raelians.[3] Depending on perspective, they can be described as a religion or a cult.[4] Formed by Claude Vorilhon (aka Rael) in 1974, it is generally described as a 'UFO Religion' and has gained notoriety due to its belief in intelligent design – that humans were scientifically created by extra-terrestrials; and unsubstantiated claims to have cloned a human baby.

Faith-based/cult groups have a track record of funding health ventures in developing countries (DeHaven *et al.* 2004), so the involvement of the Raelians is not unique.[5] However, any organization offering health interventions requires careful assessment, regardless of the beliefs underpinning it, to establish whether what is offered is effective, and whether it has been imposed on a culture or developed within a community. Is the organization involved there to do good, or to promote itself – or even operate a scam? When those questions were asked publicly they revealed problems with Clitoraid and the 'pleasure hospital' – leading to hostile responses from the Raelians and some high-profile 'sex-positive' individuals supporting them, along with strong counter-challenges from those working in the fields of health and development.

This chapter uses rhetorical analysis to analyse the Clitoraid campaign, one that has played out in the public domain of websites, blogs and forums. The Clitoraid story provides fascinating insights into how arguments are used to persuade people to support particular health initiatives, serves as a case example of how international practice can be imposed on communities, and indicates where further questions still need asking about the 'pleasure hospital'. A series of wider issues are raised relating to global practice, sex positivity and social media.

Reparative surgery for FGM/C: does it exist?

Reparative surgery for FGM/C has been developed by Pierre Foldes and colleagues over the past 20 years, originally in Burkina Faso but more recently in France (Foldes 2007; Prolongeau 2011). Due to numerous factors, the demand for surgery exceeds supply – there are not enough trained surgeons, and patients lack the finances to afford reparative surgery (Foldes *et al.* 2012). Women seek surgery for many reasons, including pain reduction, an increase in sexual pleasure or clitoral sensation, and a desire to have a 'whole' body/'normal' genitalia (*ibid.*; Villani 2009).

The procedure involves restoring clitoral anatomy and

function to women who have had Type II FGM/C (partial or total removal of the clitoris glans, labia minora and possibly the labia majora) or Type III FGM/C (with infibulation – cutting and sealing the labia majora, and/or excision of the clitoris) (Foldes *et al.* 2012). As the clitoris is a much larger organ (much of which is hidden inside the body) than simply the tip that is (usually) visible (O'Connell *et al.* 2005), Foldes's technique involves cutting back tissue around where the clitoris has been excised and re-exposing the tip. An audit of the procedure with a follow-up survey of women in a French hospital indicates good rates of reducing pain, restoring confidence and improving clitoral sensation. Around 51 per cent of women report experiencing orgasm in the year after surgery, although more indicate an increase in pleasurable clitoral sensation (Foldes *et al.* 2012). Foldes's work suggests women who undergo the procedure may benefit from greater body confidence or a feeling of 'wholeness' that may enable them to experience pleasure without orgasm, or orgasm from physical stimulation other than clitoral. It is worth noting that the trauma of FGM/C or associated problems (such as with menstruation, birth or relationships) may continue to be a barrier to arousal.

While clitoral pleasure is undoubtedly important to many women, one of the major criticisms of sex-positive approaches is the focus on clitoral pleasure as integral to all women's arousal and orgasm. While well-intentioned, this may have the additional effect of suggesting women who do not experience pleasure (or orgasm) through clitoral stimulation are 'abnormal'. It may also overlook women who enjoy vaginal, anal, or breast play; or locate sexual pleasure in other areas of their bodies. For women who have undergone FGM/C this provides additional stigmatization: they may feel set apart as having no possibility of clitoral and/or vaginal stimulation; judged, excluded or abnormal for having undergone FGM/C; or diminished by a limited range of possibilities of what they might enjoy. Women who have undergone FGM/C are, through a sex-positive discourse, not expected to enjoy pleasure or experience orgasm.

It could be argued that a focus on 'adopting' a clitoris taps into familiar discussions of pleasure for Western women, but may also rehearse narratives of abnormality to those who have undergone FGM/C (see also Fahs 2003). Approaches to discussing this issue sensitively remain unresolved as undoubtedly discussing pleasure is important (Jolly 2007), as is exploring the many ways women might experience desire, arousal and orgasm. Overemphasizing clitoral or vaginal orgasm may exclude many, while allowing dominant discourses of aspirational, commercialized and performative sex to go unchallenged. However, questioning both the practices of FGM/C *and* the way Western models of sexual functioning locate female orgasm can lead to being perceived as either condoning FGM/C or discrediting initiatives that seek to think critically about sexual pleasure and the body.

Moreover, 'success' in this area is far more than a surgical intervention, and contemporary research (Villani 2009) suggests restorative procedures are ineffective without considering wider social and cultural factors that result in FGM/C being practised and how challenges to it or reparative surgery may be opposed. Reporting in *The Lancet* in response to the work of Foldes *et al.* (2012), Abdulcadir *et al.* (2012) state:

> [G]rowing up in developed countries, conflict between two cultures, and violent messages against FGM/C can cause a negative perception of genital self-image and negative expectations regarding social acceptance and sexuality. Young women can imagine that their genitalia have been cut away without any possibility of sexual pleasure or, when sexual pleasure is present, assume that they have a less satisfying sexual life than do uncut women.

Throughout the promotional materials for Clitoraid, Pierre Foldes is consistently mentioned. This creates an impression that Foldes's pioneering surgery was created in partnership with the Raelians and that he is a supporter of Clitoraid and supervises the training of their surgical staff. In fact, Foldes distances himself from Clitoraid and is highly critical of the organization. In an interview with *Jeune Afrique* (6 August 2009)[6] he explains that he is considering legal action against the organization for claiming he is endorsing their activities or training their staff.

Investigating Clitoraid

Clitoraid is run as a charity based in Nevada, and asks for financial donations to build and stock a 'pleasure hospital'.[7] It is unclear what additional funding comes from the Raelian organization. Records from 2011 indicate that Clitoraid has a total revenue of $58,828 and total assets of $8,799. In April 2010 international development consultant Matthew Greenall requested information about the funding and surgical activities of Clitoraid from the organization's 'Patient Care and Operation Manager', Nadine Gary, who replied by email:

> Thank you for your interest in Clitoraid. The FGM reversal surgery has been practised for the last 15 years by Dr Foldes in France, who is the creator of such technique. The safety of such intervention has been proven over and over again (the procedure is not a complicated process, see the description of Dr Bowers attached) and the results are measurable.... The authorities are very supportive of our efforts and all permits have been granted for the hospital. It is due to open this summer. Surgeries at the hospital will be offered free of charge, a contrast with other local FB clinics who charge $500 for such surgery (representing a 2 year salary for a woman there).

Note, within this response, the reference to the history of reversal surgery and citation of a respected surgeon who pioneered it, which serve in place of providing specific details about funds raised, and specific information about how many surgical procedures have been carried out and their success rate. When pressed further by Greenall about whether any audit or other research had taken place on surgical activity the reply was, 'No publication yet (we are working on that), just women calling us to report orgasms which is our biggest reward.'

Here, the 'reward' of women reporting orgasm is used in place of any audit of surgical activity, and we are not told how many women have experienced orgasm post-surgery. From a clinical perspective this is not particularly useful as a measure of effectiveness or acceptability. It does not tell us whether all women who underwent the procedure were able to experience orgasm, nor what forms of pleasure were open to them, nor whether this was acceptable to their partner or wider community. It does not tell us whether any adverse events were noted, or complications from surgery. It also bases the measure of 'success' of the repair solely on orgasms, rather than more general pleasurable genital sensations which may be equally important to women. And it does not actually state where the surgery took place, although it implies it happened within Burkina Faso.

Asking for evidence, while not unreasonable, brings with it a set of values and assumptions. Here we can see that what Clitoraid constructs as 'evidence' is not what most health and development practitioners or community activists might perceive as such. 'Evidence-based medicine' remains a well-intentioned but often difficult-to-achieve concept, that has its own set of values, prejudices and problems (see Greenhalgh and Russell 2006). Yet in order for any intervention or programme to work effectively it should be based on some form of evaluative or reflective practice. In a sensitive area like FGM/C this is vital, since communities may well feel judged or resistant to initiatives attempting to change or challenge established practices viewed as culturally significant (Heger Boyle 2002; Shaaban and Harbison 2005).

In the same email exchange Greenall asked Clitoraid how the community was consulted and involved and was told that 'the project is led by Banemanie Traore, a BF (Burkina Faso) citizen who was herself a victim of FGM and who deals with all the local authorities in the building of Clitoraid's hospital'.

Although this reply mentions the words 'building' and 'hospital' it does not explain community consultation or involvement – key issues required for any health initiative to be effective and ethical (Kahssay and Oakley 1999). Projects have failed on countless occasions because of top-down approaches where outsiders have decided what should be done to/for a community (Carney 2006; Campbell 2003), or where people from within a country work on a project but are still not accepted by residents. Indeed fieldwork by Eleana Jirovsky (2010) suggests the presence of the Raelians within Bobo Dioulasso is neither widely accepted nor appreciated by the community.

The idea of a 'leader' working with the authorities does not suggest a collaborative or partnership relationship with communities, vital in any health or educational programme but particularly important when a highly sensitive and complex issue such as FGM/C is being addressed (Simpson *et al.* 2012).

Support for Clitoraid: Betty Dodson and Good Vibrations

As part of the 'Adopt A Clitoris' campaign, Clitoraid gained a commercial partner in the form of Good Vibrations,[8] an American sex store established in 1977. On 24 March 2010 a Good Vibrations press release announced their support of Clitoraid and their donation of vibrators to women who had undergone reconstructive surgery, commenting:

> Good Vibrations, the legendary San Francisco-based retailer that takes pride in providing accurate information on sexuality and toys for grown-ups, is proud to announce its upcoming quarterly partnership with Clitoraid as part of their corporate giving initiative, 'GiVe'.
>
> This summer, Good Vibrations' customers can give the gift of pleasure to women around the world who suffered female genital mutilation (FGM) during childhood. They can do this by making a financial gift to Clitoraid at the time of their Good Vibrations purchase. Clitoraid, a nonprofit humanitarian organization, helps women restore their ability to enjoy sex by offering reconstructive surgery free of charge.
>
> Says Good Vibrations' Chief Operating Officer, Jackie Strano, 'Good Vibrations was founded on the principle that pleasure is a birthright. We support the women on their journey back to reclaiming their bodies, their pleasure, their birthright. We are

confident in the compassion of our customers and we are committed to assisting this humanitarian issue.'

In March 2010 Good Vibrations sent a big box of bath and body treats and vibrators to new patients undergoing reconstructive surgery in Colorado. Patients were from Asia, Canada, the US, Europe, and Africa, and they were eager to discover what they were missing. Good Vibrations has joined forces with Vibratex, the creators of the Magic Wand vibrator, to incorporate high-quality toys into the post-op physical therapy sessions with esteemed sexologist and sex educator Betty Dodson.

Included in the care packages was the 'Pleasure Me Purse' from Good Vibrations, which features the Magic Touch Bullet Mini Vibrator, a small, high-powered vibrator. Among the recipients was a woman who had undergone surgery several months prior, and had yet to experience an orgasm from her reconstructed clitoris. After the women received their gifts and went to bed, the head of patient care got a call at midnight from an ecstatic woman who apologized for waking her but had to share: dismayed by the smallness of her clitoris, she disregarded the larger vibrator in favor of the bullet vibe. Much to her surprise and delight, she had her first orgasm!

Dr Carol Queen, Good Vibrations' staff sexologist and company spokesperson explains, 'No form of physical therapy for a woman with this type of nerve damage is likely to be as successful as vibrator use, so we are thrilled to be able to provide something truly useful to the women served by Clitoraid. With the kind of consistent stimulation a vibrator provides, neural pathways may actually be able to grow, supporting the surgical intervention of Clitoraid's doctors. The clitoris is devoted to carrying pleasurable sensations, and Clitoraid is giving women back their birthright!'

Good Vibrations and core staff supporting Clitoraid, such as Carol Queen and Betty Dodson, have an established reputation within sex-positive work. So it was somewhat surprising that these key figures seemingly backed a venture without sufficiently diligent checks on Clitoraid.

Asking critical questions

As the calls to support Clitoraid grew, critics became alarmed and began asking questions via blogs and on Twitter about the Raelians, procedures offered, wider social and cultural issues, and the involvement of sex-store partners. Reactions to this questioning varied. Some colleagues began investigating themselves. Some drew attention to the uncomfortable issues raised by asking Westerners to 'adopt' African women's genitals. Some thought it was a joke or a scam. Some became hostile, arguing that FGM/C was so abhorrent that any intervention to undo excision should not even be questioned; or that even if the work was funded by the Raelians and hadn't been fully evaluated, it didn't matter as giving women back an orgasm was paramount. A few argued we were racist for questioning Clitoraid, or accused us of endorsing FGM/C. Others felt that if people were aiming to do something that might 'bring pleasure' such sex-positive initiatives should not be questioned – particularly not publicly. A few withdrew from discussions, feeling conflicted at having to question established sex-positive colleagues.

Wanjiru Kamau-Rutenberg from the University of San Francisco used her blog[9] to document her questioning of Good Vibrations about their involvement with Clitoraid. Their response stated the 'request for more scientific evidence that supports Clitoraid was a bad idea', and an admission that they had not spoken to any women from Burkina Faso. They had spoken with Betty Dodson, who is quoted as describing the encounter with 'her' first circumcised African woman: 'Carlin and I were ecstatic. Then my brilliant business partner looked at me and said, "This is an op-ed piece for the *New York Times*." "I'd rather see it as an article in *Vanity Fair*," I replied. At that point we grinned from ear to ear, did a high five and called it a day.'

Wanjiru's detailed accounts of her research into Good Vibrations and Clitoraid illustrate a familiar picture that many involved in development, health and sex-positive working will recognize. Reading up on evidence and working closely with communities at a grassroots level may be sidestepped in favour of talking to representatives who may not originate from, nor know much about the community being supported. Moreover, in the rush to garner personal/organizational publicity and promote sex-positive activities, careful checks and thoughtful practice may be avoided. Requests to provide evidence about working practices can be met with defensive responses that deflect criticism back at those doing the questioning, with requests that they prove 'scientifically' a person or organization is wrong.

Despite the claims that the 'pleasure hospital' in Burkina Faso was a unique venture, Elizabeth Wood from Sex in the Public Square blog discovered a number of hospitals in Burkina already offering reconstructive surgery free of charge (although these institutions struggle through a lack of funds). She wrote:

> One of the problems I want to address is that, while the Raelians are collecting money to build a brand new hospital that they will control, there are already hospitals in Burkina Faso, both public and private, that are performing these surgeries and have been for years. According to IRIN (Integrated Regional Information Networks) nearly 1000 surgeries, funded by the state, to reopen women's vaginas had been performed between 2001 and 2009. In 2006 surgeons began performing clitoral reconstruction surgeries. Over 100 such surgeries have been performed at a cost of roughly $140, well out of reach of many women in Burkina Faso. Still there is a waiting list because not all the women who want the surgery can be accommodated. Given all this work already going on in the country, it puzzles me that the Raelians are choosing to build a new hospital instead of supporting local efforts that are desperately in need of the funds being syphoned into this new initiative.... Why build a whole new hospital, ignoring local cultural issues while doing so, and running into all the troubles that generally accrue to top-down, outsider-focused interventions? Why not donate equipment, help expand the existing surgeries, and donate funds for subsidizing the surgeries for women who can't afford it? There may be reasons that collaboration with institutions in Burkina Faso is problematic but none are mentioned in any of the Clitoraid literature about this.

Digital Journal noted Clitoraid had been asking for funds to build their pleasure hospital since 2006.[10] Conflicting figures about what funding has been collected and the progress of the 'pleasure hospital' can be detected across the press releases, website entries and emails from Clitoraid.

Matthew Greenall discovered that community opposition towards the planned 'pleasure hospital' had been shared in an online forum, but was disregarded by Clitoraid while the Raelians threatened to sue the website hosting these discussions. Clitoraid's newsletter (September 2008) indicated opposition to their use of the term 'pleasure hospital', along with their intention to ignore these concerns:

> The official name of the hospital was another ball game! The name 'Pleasure Hospital' seems to have shocked some people along the administrative trail of the file. One of the women who were to sign for the Health Ministry, retained the file for several months, asserting that she would never sign as long as the word pleasure would not be removed from the official name. After many endless discussions, the women's access to pleasure who were waiting, appeared more important to us than the name itself and the hospital thus became: The 'Kamkasso Hospital' which means in the local language, the women's house. But we will keep for our communications the name 'Pleasure Hospital', no matter how displeased that woman was that we could associate a clitoris and pleasure.

While it may be argued one Health Ministry representative may be no more of a spokesperson for the community than Clitoraid, it is noteworthy this critical voice was overruled. What would have been more appropriate would be for Clitoraid to explore why the term was problematic, what the community felt about the naming of the hospital, and the likely impact on the numerous existing services already documented.

The role of social media

Using social media (particularly blogs and Twitter), people were able to work together to:

- publicly question Clitoraid, investigate the organization and publish their findings
- repeat this process with Good Vibrations and Betty Dodson
- network together to share information
- create a Facebook group[11] and petition against Clitoraid[12]
- encourage other bloggers to raise their concerns about Clitoraid, colonialism and sex positivity.

The involvement of bloggers writing about this issue in terms of gender, politics and race added an important dimension to the discussions around community, culture and health. Drawing these topics together helped a diverse community of writers, activists, community members, health and development professionals, and people who'd simply been asked to pay to 'adopt a clitoris' reflect on what kinds of activities are appropriate – and when.

Despite there being good evidence for the effectiveness of reparative surgery, interrogating the Clitoraid programme indicated it was unclear if it were a genuine activity or a money-making scam. If genuine it was unlikely to be effective without wider social/community support programmes and psychological therapy. Clitoraid representatives would not disclose any evidence for community partnerships or the effectiveness of their surgical programme. Yet after being told of all these shortcomings Good Vibrations did not immediately withdraw their support from Clitoraid, and only when a number of bloggers critiqued them and brought their involvement to the attention of the *San Francisco Chronicle*[13] did they change their position.

Given that this chapter is about community practice, it is fair to say that fast-moving and public debates via social media may be effective in highlighting problematic practice and intransigent responses, but may gloss over the real impact on people's lives and businesses. The focus on staff at Good Vibrations was certainly upsetting to them, and their initial reluctance to accept criticism was undoubtedly a reaction to an unanticipated public confrontation. Their decision not to work with the Raelians could be seen as a 'win' in social media terms, but in community practice terms it may not be so positive. Naming and shaming approaches may well halt an activity but they are unlikely to really encourage people to reflect on why their initial behaviours/activities were problematic – and how to avoid them in the future. This case study may be a teachable moment for those not directly involved, but more reflection and research is needed to unpack what happens when faced with a social media challenge, and if that can change practice for the better. Elizabeth Wood noted how Good Vibrations, because of their association with sex products, would struggle to find charities that would accept their donations. This does not excuse a failure to assess the work of Clitoraid and its problematic approach to community partnership more carefully, but it goes some way to explaining their actions.

The Raelians respond

After Good Vibrations pulled their support for Clitoraid another endorser, Betty Dodson, continued to back the organization. In a statement issued through Clitoraid she explained why she supports the Raelians, her problems with other faiths (particularly Catholics and Muslims) and challenged her critics:

> I knew that a battery operated vibrator would be a great help for African women the same as they have helped my demographic of women. My business partner Carlin and I agreed that Good Vibrations would be a good choice to donate vibrators, so I contacted Carol Queen. In no time there was a shit storm on her end. An African American academic feminist teaching at San Francisco University objected to our interference in a culture that we supposedly know nothing about. Good Vibrations pulled out. The store depends upon the good will of a community that has its share of nit picking academic sex-negative feminists. Since dodsonandross is a website we have all the freedom in the world to do and say what we choose. It's called freedom of speech!

This statement appears to focus specifically on Wanjiru Kamau-Rutenberg, who responded with a post repeating her concerns about Clitoraid and raising questions about how challenges to sex-positive feminism may be rebutted.[14]

It is worth noting that rather than one person complaining about Clitoraid, questions about the organization have been increasing steadily for at least four years and a range of people of different genders, races and political persuasions signed the petition and joined a Facebook group against Clitoraid. Critics questioned why Betty Dodson focused her response solely on one black woman when numerous white UK and US practitioners also raised questions about Clitoraid. They also interrogated the accusation of being 'sex-negative' for opposing the provision of vibrators to women who had undergone reparative surgery.

In the mediated battle that sprang up around this case Betty Dodson's business partner Carlin Ross responded to Wanjiru's questioning of Clitoraid with a reminder of hierarchies of power:

> I'm glad we're having this discussion. Yes, no one will touch Betty because, at this point, she's a legend. If you google her, her history is all there. She's pretty amazing.

Good Vibrations and Dodson both stressed their good intentions and history of sex-positive working, but at the same time their responses suggested they were not open to feedback and wider reflection. Part of international practice means thinking carefully about any criticism. Nobody, no matter what their status, should be above this process. However in a tense situation where arguments are being played out online it is hardly surprising people may not be in a place to listen, and where commercial interests are involved also have to attend to these. Unsurprisingly in a press release on 21 April 2010 and in a more frank statement on their website,[15] Clitoraid argued those who were questioning them were akin to Nazi sympathizers:

> 'Brutal, violent acts like female genital mutilation don't call for sensitivity', she said. 'They demand immediate action, and that's what CLITORAID is doing.' She likened the call for sensitivity toward those in Africa who perpetuate and condone FGM to those who were 'sensitive' toward slave owners or Nazis. 'Slave owners in

the American South thought Northerners were insensitive to their needs,' Gary said. 'And it wasn't considered polite in Nazi Germany to ask what was happening to the Jews. Both situations demanded blunt, effective, immediate opposition, not sensitivity toward the perpetrators and their supporters.'

Their statement continued:

'It's very clear to us at Clitoraid that the criticism we receive is mainly from individuals who don't consider sexual activity important', declared Dr Brigitte Boisselier, head of Clitoraid.

This is an interesting and challenging statement, one that could be recognized as another device to divert attention from criticisms of Clitoraid while casting doubt on their detractors. Among those who criticized the campaign there was no suggestion that the reason for questioning Clitoraid was to deny the importance of sexual activity. Indeed many of the resulting discussions between practitioners have been about reframing and reflecting on female pleasure and the importance of sexual activity within different cultural contexts.

The Raelian Movement, thanks to its pleasure-embracing philosophy, is the only religion working to restore sexual pleasure, and we will continue to do so no matter what opposition stands in our way. We owe it to the 135 million FGM victims who have no other recourse.

This is a bold assertion. It appears Clitoraid claim to be the only organization offering reconstructive surgery or pleasure-focused initiatives with women. This chapter has demonstrated this is not the case. To argue you are the only person offering help and therefore above question is a notable reaction to criticism but a risky strategy in an area where contradictory evidence can be easily produced.

Regarding the lack of scientific data often mentioned by critics, Boisselier said the surgical technique was developed more than 20 years ago by Dr Pierre Foldes in France and published in a peer review journal, and that it is now practised by many other surgeons trained by Foldes. Numerous testimonies from women praise his practice.

As already mentioned, Foldes has found himself co-opted without consent into the media messaging of the Raelians.

Meanwhile in the statement of 19 April 2010 from the Clitoraid website the organization responds:

> This baseless smear campaign is costing genitally mutilated women the valuable support they need to get corrective surgery.
>
> Professor Wanjiru Kamau-Rutenberg, assistant professor of politics at the University of San Francisco, and Caille Millner, a columnist for the *San Francisco Chronicle*, spearheaded what CLITO-RAID representative Nadine Gary called 'a vicious attack of misinformation and distortion of truth'.
>
> 'Their statements, especially in Millner's April 14 article "Wrong Approach to Genital Mutilation", led to an online petition that cost CLITORAID the participation of its fundraising partner,' Gary said, adding that adult toys retailer Good Vibrations of San Francisco 'was bullied into cancelling its summer fundraising campaign on behalf of CLITORAID after receiving a petition signed by over 200 people'.
>
> 'The funds from Good Vibrations would have purchased medical equipment for our new hospital in Burkina Faso,' Gary said. 'Now that won't happen. It's so unfair. The allegations are baseless – and some are just plain stupid.'

This states there is a hospital in Burkina Faso, for which medical equipment would be purchased – contradicting earlier requests for funds to build a hospital and quite different from purchasing medical supplies.

The statement continued:

> 'This is a senseless, horrible act that causes excruciating pain and sexual deprivation for millions,' Gary said. 'While other organizations just discuss and wring their hands, CLITORAID acts. Our first hospital dedicated to clitoral repair surgery will open in Burkina Faso in 2011.'

Previously the statement claimed the withdrawal of Good Vibrations support would result in equipment not being purchased for the hospital, yet here it seems the hospital is not built and won't be for at least another year. This is the same hospital for which funds have been collected since 2006. As we will see by the close of this chapter the hospital did not hit the promised target of a hospital 'dedicated to clitoral repair' being open in 2011. None of these discussions explain why Clitoraid is collecting for medical supplies for a hospital that is nowhere near completion.

> Gary said Larry Ashley, PhD, a University of Nevada, Las Vegas, university professor and sexual trauma counsellor, sees each Clitoraid-sponsored patient, and that renowned sexual therapist Dr Betty Dodson created the post-surgery sexual therapy program that complements the procedure. 'This great team of volunteer professionals is made up of non-Raelians who have chosen to work with Clitoraid,' Gary said. 'I notice our critics neglected to mention them.'

This is not correct. Those supporting Clitoraid were also invited to reflect on their involvement and Betty Dodson's vocal commitment to the organization was clearly noted in blogs and on Twitter.

> Millner and Professor Kamau-Rutenberg say Good Vibrations should have exercised due diligence before associating with Clitoraid, but they didn't do their own. These two women should have known better. They turned the truth about Clitoraid completely upside down out of their own prejudice and a lot of ill-founded assumptions. In the process, they hurt many good people. And those they've hurt most are the FGM victims on our waiting list.

Here we see a powerful use of language to try and make critics of Clitoraid appear to be the problem by using their own rhetoric – calls for evidence – against them. Clitoraid argue that they have been misrepresented and not fully researched. The lengthy and in places highly personal statement from Clitoraid is understandable given that they are seeking to counteract public criticism, but it also forms a smokescreen against the criticisms made against them. Amid this confusion, questions about the creation and evaluation of the content, delivery and effectiveness of the 'post-surgery sexual therapy programme' for women who have undergone FGM/C remain unaddressed.

The Clitoraid story can be read in several ways. It is an example of how social media can be used to promote and fundraise (in the case of Clitoraid); and to network, campaign and question healthcare practices and fundraising (in the case of Clitoraid's critics). It is also an example of how well-intentioned, Western 'sex-positive' practitioners may struggle with or simply avoid sensitive cross-cultural community engagement, and may be poorly placed to respond to resulting criticism. It also indicates how activities need to be built on a thorough search of available evidence, a critical unpacking of said evidence, and close working with communities in sensitive ways. More positively, it shows how a robust and well-referenced debate in the public domain can raise the profile of FGM/C, introducing people who were unaware of the practice to it and increasing opposition and activism. A comprehensive online record of Clitoraid's activities now exists. There have been lone voices asking questions as far back as 2006, but this more centralized record of criticisms will help anyone who is now asked to donate decide what to do. This case serves as an excellent example of questions to ask, and how to undertake due diligence in checking organizations to collaborate with on international projects. For anyone working cross-culturally in health, development and education this is undoubtedly a useful, albeit painful, case to study. It also serves as a script for predictable responses to criticisms and counter-criticisms in health, development and sexuality.

The consequences of challenging Clitoraid have been far-reaching. While Betty Dodson undoubtedly retains a reputation for groundbreaking work on women and sexuality, her association with the Raelians and Clitoraid, and seemingly arrogant dismissal of those asking her to reconsider her position, may have harmed her reputation and detract from her previous portfolio of work. Good Vibrations seems to have fared better in public, although tensions remain among staff involved with the store and those who have criticized them publicly. These relationships may never recover. Pierre Foldes is still pushing to promote reconstructive surgery and distance himself from the Raelians. Clitoraid continues to seek donations.

Catching up on Clitoraid: where are we now? (Summer 2012)

At the time of writing the 'pleasure hospital' has not been finished. Reports from those working in Bobo Dioulasso suggest that in 2009 building work on the hospital was put on hold (Jirovsky 2010). The Clitoraid website includes a short film, apparently made in 2010, that features women singing and dancing and signs of ongoing building work, but no completed hospital. Relating back to the theme of community involvement that runs throughout this chapter, it is concerning to see the final statement on the plans for the hospital:

> Finally the perimeter fence with guard is designed to secure the whole area from thieves and those upset by such cultural change.

Arguably this serves as a metaphor for the Clitoraid story. Those who oppose the actions of the Raelians are blocked out by guards and fences. Questions and criticisms are not listened to; information is not transparently shared; and community opposition is placed on a par with theft.

Due to the lack of transparency in this case it remains unclear whether the requests to sponsor a clitoris are part of a financial scam (so no hospital will ever be built), or whether Clitoraid is genuine but is taking a long time to raise money for a hospital – one that is being imposed on a community that has not been genuinely consulted, and who may well struggle to accept women who have undergone reconstructive surgery. Within a context of existing hospitals already offering reparative surgery that are struggling to meet demand in a resource-poor situation, both of these scenarios are deeply troubling.

Where next?

Following a lot of attention to Clitoraid across social media in 2010 the story seems to have quietly disappeared. Occasional press releases are distributed by Clitoraid but the widespread 'adopt a clitoris' campaign seems to have been ignored. I hope we can keep attention on Clitoraid and the work it is doing. We need answers about what is being undertaken, how much money has been collected, and what it has been used for. Has it really benefited a community?

Those who are interested in this case beyond an account of social media argument may well wish to look further into the activities of the Raelians in Burkina Faso, and more importantly the views and experiences of the communities of Bobo Dioulasso, who have remained silenced and sidelined throughout this process.

Acknowledgements

With grateful thanks to Matthew Greenall and Wanjiru Kamau-Rutenberg for their support and activism in relation to Clitoraid, and to Kylie Sturgess for encouraging greater reflection on this case. This chapter is built upon previously written blog posts of mine that documented the unfolding Clitoraid drama, but has since been subjected to rhetorical analysis.

Notes

(All websites accessed 4 July 2012)
1 Adopt a Clitoris page, http://www.clitoraid.org/page.php?2.
2 Clitoraid home page, http://www.clitoraid.org.
3 Raelians' home page, http://www.rael.org.
4 Wikipedia entry on the Raelians, http://en.wikipedia.org/wiki/Ra%C3%ABlism.
5 Home page for Raelians in Africa, http://raelafrica.org/news.php.
6 *Jeune Afrique* interview with Foldes, http://www.jeuneafrique.com/Article/ARTJAWEB20090806173135.

7 National Centre for Charitable Statistics records for Clitoraid, http://nccsdataweb.urban.org/orgs/profile/204818106?popup=1.
8 Wikipedia entry on Good Vibrations http://en.wikipedia.org/wiki/Good_Vibrations_(business).
9 'No, You Can't Have My Clitoris' (blog post), http://savingafrica.wordpress.com/2010/04/05/no-you-cant-have-my-clitoris.
10 *Digital Journal* on Clitoraid, http://digitaljournal.com/article/290563.
11 Feminists Challenging Clitoraid Facebook group, http://www.facebook.com/pages/Feminists-Challenging-Clitoraid/1030367 29737458?ref=mf.
12 Feminists Challenging Clitoraid Petition, http://www.thepetition site.com/1/feministschallengingclitoraid.
13 'Better Choice for Fighting Genital Mutilation', San Francisco Chronicle, http://www.sfgate.com/cgi-bin/article.cgi?f=/c/a/ 2010/04/14/EDP91CUMEJ.DTL.
14 'Betty Dodson and Audre Lorde: Can I Possibly Use the Master's Tools to Demolish Her House?' (blog post) http://savingafrica.wordpress.com/2010/04/16/betty-dodson-and-audre-lourde-can-i-possibly-use-the-masters-tools-to-demolish-her-house/.
15 Clitoraid responds to their critics, http://www.clitoraid.org/news.php?item.44.2.

References

Abdulcadir, J., M. Boulvain and P. Petignat (2012) 'Reconstructive Surgery for Female Genital Mutilation', *The Lancet*, Eprint (online first).

Campbell, C. (2003) *'Letting Them Die': Why HIV/AIDS Prevention Programmes Fail*, Indiana University Press, Bloomington IN.

Carney, J.K. (2006) *Public Health in Action: Practicing in the Real World*, Jones and Bartlett, Boston MA.

DeHaven, M. J., I. B. Hunter, L. Wilder, J. W. Walton and J. Berry (2004) 'Health Programs in Faith-Based Organizations: Are They Effective?', *American Journal of Public Health*, Vol. 94, No. 6, pp. 1030–6.

Fahs, B. (2003) 'Analytic Dualisms, Stunted Sexualities, and the "Horrified Gaze": Western (Feminist) Discourses about Female Genital Mutilation', *Michigan Feminist Studies: Gender and Globalisms*, Vol. 17, http://hdl.handle.net/2027/spo.ark5583.0017.003.

Foldes, P. (2007) 'Lecture: Surgical Repair of the Clitoris after Ritual Genital Mutilation: Results On 453 Cases', World Association of Sexology Visual.

Foldes, P., B. Cuzin and A. Andro (2012) 'Reconstructive Surgery after Female Genital Mutilation: a Prospective Cohort Study', *The Lancet*, Eprint edition (online first).

Greenhalgh, T. and J. Russell (2006) 'Reframing Evidence Synthesis as Rhetorical Action in the Policy Making Drama', *Healthcare Policy*, Vol. 1, No. 2, pp. 34–42.

Heger Boyle, E. (2002) *Female Genital Cutting: Cultural Conflict in the Global Community*, Johns Hopkins University Press, Baltimore OH.

Jirovsky, E. (2010) 'Views of Women and Men in Bobo-Dioulasso, Burkina Faso, on Three Forms of Female Genital Modification', *Reproductive Health Matters*, Vol. 18, No. 35, pp. 84–93.

Jolly, S. (2007) 'Why the Development Industry Should Get over Its Obsession with Bad Sex and Start to Think about Pleasure', *IDS Working Paper* 283, Institute of Development Studies, Brighton.

Kahssay, H. M. and P. Oakley (1999) 'Community Involvement in Health Development: a Review of the Concept and Practice', *Public Health in Action* 5, World Health Organization, Geneva.

O'Connell, H. E., K. V. Sanjeevan and J. M. Hutson (2005) 'Anatomy of the Clitoris', *Journal of Urology*, Vol. 174 (No. 4, part 1), pp. 1189–95.

Prolongeau, H. (2011) *Undoing FGM: Pierre Foldes, the Surgeon Who Restores the Clitoris*, UnCUT/VOICES Press.

Shaaban, L. M. and S. Harbison (2005) 'Reaching the Tipping Point against Female Genital Mutilation', *The Lancet*, Vol. 366, pp. 347–9.

Simpson, J., K. Robinson, S. Creighton and D. Hodes (2012) 'Female Genital Mutilation: the Role of Health Professionals in Prevention, Assessment, and Management', *British Medical Journal*, Vol. 344, 14 March.

Villani, M. (2009) 'From the "Maturity" of a Woman to Surgery: Conditions for Clitoris Repair', *Sexologies*, Vol. 18, No. 4, pp. 259–61.

12

How Was It for You?

Pleasure and Performance in Sex Work

●●●

Jo Doezema

What does pleasure mean for sex workers? Are they only concerned with their client's pleasure, or does their own desire for sexual pleasure motivate them 'on the job'? These questions are beginning to be seen as increasingly relevant to research, policy and activism around sex work. For example, a recent issue of the journal *Research for Sex Work*, produced by the activist network the Global Network of Sex Work Projects (2009), takes pleasure as its theme. In this issue, we find sex workers reflecting on their own experiences of pleasure at work and in their private lives. Sex workers in India, for example, discuss their relationship to their vagina, describing it in ways that situate it as a place of pleasure and playfulness. Research with sex workers in Spain demonstrates the links between experience of pleasure at work and a happy sex life at home.

This research demonstrates that foregrounding sex workers' experience of pleasure can provide a fresh angle on familiar arguments. This is particularly important in the study of sex work, where ideological conflict and political necessity have tended to harden into fixed positions and inflexible ways of thinking. This chapter follows the lead provided by sex workers themselves in taking pleasure seriously. It highlights the various ways in which sex workers experience and understand pleasure, drawing on published materials and on ethnographic material from interactions with female sex workers and sex worker organizations. It examines the ways in which individual experiences of pleasure are

251

connected to wider societal issues, such as legal regimes, gender relations and work relationships. It suggests that sex workers' understandings of pleasure, derived from their work with clients, may help us reach new, and beneficial, understandings of how and why we experience sexual pleasure.

Giving pleasure

> Your pleasure is my business. (Slogan from Denver Escorts website, http://denver.backpage.com)

The most common way of looking at sex work and pleasure is with the 'pleasure' reserved for the paying customer. In many ways, this is legitimate. For most if not all sex workers, the primary reason for doing this work is economic: it is a way to earn money.

A report by sex worker organization SWING (Service Workers In-Group Foundation) in Thailand agrees that 'the main attraction of sex work is the earnings ... sex work provides most sex workers much greater earnings than they could expect in other occupations' (SWING 2009: 11). This finding is confirmed by the recent pan-India survey of sex workers, which found that – both for those switching to sex work from other occupational groups, and for those in sex work as their first occupation – the prospect of better earnings than in other available options was the job's main drawing power (Sahni and Kalyan Shankar 2011).

Questions that arise about whether sexual pleasure is something that can, or should, be bought or sold often rest on the assumption that the pleasure that is commodified is the pleasure of the client, not of the sex worker. For some feminists, it is this very commodification that lies at the heart of their objection to sex work. In this view, sex is inherently different to commodifiable services, only being legitimate as an adjunct of some sort of intimacy, or what is growing increasingly common, of mutual pleasure. It is because sex workers are supposed to experience no pleasure that the sex is seen as illegitimate. As Carole Pateman writes, 'prostitution is the use of a woman's body by a man for his own satisfaction. There is no desire or satisfaction on the part of the prostitute' (1988: 198). Yet for many sex workers, the commodification of sexuality is both self-evident and unproblematic, as in this quote from Japanese sex worker Momocca Momocco: 'Any pleasure is now a commodity in society, and sexual pleasure can also be seen as a commodity' (Momocca Momocco in Kempadoo and Doezema 1998: 179).

A recent video by the European Women's Lobby (EWL), targeting clients of sex workers, prompted an intriguing discussion about pleasure during the Sex Worker Open University (SWOU, London, 12–16 October 2011), which I attended. The video targets male clients of female sex workers, and is intended to discourage them from paying for sexual services. In the video, an attractive young man is seen opening the door to an elderly woman. Without a word, she puts money on the table, removes her tights and undergarments, lies on the bed and opens her legs. The young man kneels on the bed before her, his face buried between her upraised knees. The video continues to show a succession of encounters with a number of women, each one taking place without a word or a smile exchanged between the client and the sex worker. After each encounter, the camera shows the sex worker vigorously brushing his teeth, and the voice-over asks, 'If I had to have sex with strangers 10 times a day for a living, at what point would I begin to feel sick? From the beginning, surely....'[1]

The SWOU screening was followed by a brainstorming session, in which the audience of sex worker activists developed ideas for a video rejoinder to the EWL perspective. A number of sex worker activists remarked on the ways in which the video exposed the stereotypes and assumptions that many people, including the EWL feminists, held about sex work. Many activists noted the portrayal of the female 'client' as elderly and (thus) sexually unattractive. They shared the ways in which this portrayal differed from their own experience, where young, conventionally attractive clients were common. But the more interesting discussion followed after one sex worker related that she actually reached orgasm more easily with clients that she didn't find attractive. She reasoned that this was because she was able to relax more fully. She felt that in this relaxed state, pleasure came unawares and unbidden. So participants uncovered an even more insidious stereotype, the idea that youth and beauty equate to (possibilities of) sexual pleasure. One participant remarked on the irony of a feminist video propagating this stereotype, as much of feminism has been concerned with challenging the preoccupation with physical appearance. Others suggested that sex workers could, through sharing their experience of sexual pleasure with 'unattractive' people, help explode some damaging myths about sex and pleasure.[2]

This suggests that sex workers could bring an intriguing new perspective to current debates around the 'sexualization of culture'. These debates concern a perceived increase in sexual imagery and sexual merchandizing. There are fears that this sexualization may be harmful to gender relations, as men are believed to be encouraged to perceive women primarily as sexual objects, while women are believed to be accepting this valuation of themselves. This perceived sexualization is seen to be reaching girls, who become worried about their attractiveness from a young age. While this concern has led to some thoughtful work on sexual imagery in the media and marketing, it has also been a platform for more 'sex-negative' tendencies. These favour a closing down, rather than an opening up, of discussions on sexuality and its meaning in society. The voices of sex workers could strengthen the 'sex-positive' chorus, adding experience and analysis of positive sexuality beyond youth and beauty.

Getting pleasure

Recent research validates this anecdotal evidence of sex workers' experience of sexual pleasure on the job. A very interesting paper by Anna Kontula, head of the Finnish sex professionals' organization and a well-known sex worker rights advocate, is entitled 'The Sex Worker and Her Pleasure'. She interviewed sex workers in Finland and found a great variety of types and extents of sexual enjoyment for sex workers. According to Kontula (2008), there is no contradiction between the money-making and the enjoyment aspects of providing sexual services, indeed, these exist hand-in-hand for many sex workers. In my own work with sex workers, it was very common for sex workers to accept sexual pleasure as a work bonus. This is borne out by a Spanish study of 146 sex workers, 81 per cent of whom were women, in which it was found that 70 per cent 'had orgasms *sometimes* or *several times* when they were with clients' (Gonzalez 2009: 9, italics in original). Some of Kontula's respondents even reported that the satisfaction of their own desires was paramount during encounters with clients. Taru said:

> Then I decided to start using [men] just for sexual satisfaction. If I do it anyway and get money from it, then I can also take my pleasure from it. And I succeeded in it so well that I really began to see men only as a walking piece of meat or something. That they can give to woman nothing else but sex. (Kontula 2008: 610)

A study by Susie Jolly reports on a focus group discussion with sex workers in China, in which 'several sex workers said that they had enjoyed orgasms with clients who were cute, clean, polite or "high quality"' (2003: 6).

It is not a straightforward case of all sex workers having un-complicated multiple orgasms time after time at work. As one of Kontula's interviewees stated:

> I have never come with a client and I don't even try to. In a way it's easy but sometimes I'm annoyed by those who want 'forcibly' to give me pleasure. It's exhausting to fake coming time and time again, thinking what would be a suitable and believable interval for coming when useless and unskilled nerds make my clit ache. (2008: 612)

And a sex worker from DANYANA sex worker project in Mali remarks that 'There are clients with whom women find pleasure, but they constitute a minority' (Mollet and Fatoumata 2009: 2). Some sex workers that I have spoken to and worked with felt that having orgasms made you 'less professional'. And while some sex workers may be in it primarily for the sexual pleasure, for a clear majority the financial aspect of the transaction is paramount. This is borne out by Kontula, who found that some sex workers would actively avoid orgasms so as not to get worn out. As Sofia describes her experience:

> I have always (for as long as I can remember) had fantastic orgasms that blow my mind ... with tricks I also try to be – to think something else so that I won't shout and freak out when I come. Anyway, sometimes it happens that I just do come and I can't help that. On occasions I have even ejaculated.... Then I wonder why on earth I'm sometimes totally knackered after two tricks. (2008: 613)

One of her respondents even reported a less-than-enjoyable multi-orgasmic experience:

> They say that prostitution is easy money. So. Once I had a trick who didn't come whatever I did. It took two and half hours of sucking before he came. Well it wasn't so bad, I had three orgasms and got 300 euros, but still. You should suck a dick two and half hours and then come and tell me it is easy money. (2008: 611)

This sexual pleasure at work may have a 'spillover' effect into sex workers' non-working lives. The Spanish study suggests that sex workers' 'sexual satisfaction' outside of work may be higher than that of the general population (Gonzales 2009). Kontula's respondents also reported having very satisfactory private sex lives. And a focus group discussion of sexual practices of sex workers in Kerala, carried out by Jayasree (2009), attests to sex workers' high levels of enjoyment of private sex. For instance, all of the sex workers reported that they 'liked very much' having their breasts sucked. One said that it gives 'shivers of happiness' in the entire body and high arousal. Licking the vagina was said to 'give(s) ultimate satisfaction. "My man" is doing it for me, so this feeling itself gives me great pleasure. We have so much respect and value for our lover, and if he is doing it for me it gives kick and great pleasure.' And they were very positive about the aphrodisiac effects of moonlight.

I had sex in moonlight with my husband; it gave lot of enjoyment and was better than anything else. We put a cot on the terrace – this was the best experience of my life.... (personal communication to Jayasree, 2003)

Pleasure is not just to be found in orgasms. Sex worker experience can help us widen pleasure's ambit beyond the genital and, perhaps surprisingly, beyond the heterosexual. As a young female sex worker from Kerala reports: 'I have a client who is an elderly woman. I enjoy the relation with her. You may not believe. But that is my best relation' (Jayasree 2009: 7). As Kontula writes:

> In [the] light of my material, getting orgasm is just one of many ways to find enjoyment. Sexual pleasure can mean all those sensations, reactions and acts that people conceive as sexual and that produce pleasure on a physical, mental or spiritual level. (2008: 610)

It is possible to view pleasure in the sexual aspect of sex work in a way that is distinct from physical pleasure – a form of sexual pleasure that is not even recognized outside of the sex work context. Sex workers who work in a more avowedly spiritual manner, such as those practising tantra or other sexual-spiritual practices, see the sexual act as an exchange of life energy, a spiritually fulfilling way of connecting with another human and with the divine. 'Conscious Kink' practitioner Ruby May describes what she does as follows:

> [It] is the art of enjoying the full spectrum of our sexuality in all its colourful and varied palates, regardless of whether our turn-ons are things society deems as taboo or politically incorrect. Rather than suppressing or acting out in unconscious ways, we consciously explore our erotic wiring.... Through claiming our deepest desires and allowing ourselves to be truly seen we create a greater self-acceptance and authenticity. Consciously engaging on all levels: physically, emotionally and energetically, we enjoy deeper levels of pleasure, connection and intimacy. Our play becomes a powerful force for self-exploration and discovery, providing endless potential for personal growth and fulfilment, and offering joy in unexpected places along the way. (http://embodimentofbliss.com)

Pleasure and power

Feminists who believe that it is impossible for sex workers to feel pleasure on the job liken the experience of prostitution to that of rape: according to them there is no difference. It is impossible to imagine that a woman would enjoy rape and, for them, just as impossible to imagine that a prostitute would enjoy sex with a client. This impossibility is located in the supposed power imbalance between the man and woman. In this highly binary view of sex work (male and transgender sex workers neither fit in nor impinge on the analysis), it is the man who by virtue of his gender has all the power, and the woman, by virtue of hers, who is powerless. As Kathleen Barry puts it:

> My study of sex as power … inevitably, continually, unrelentingly returns me to prostitution.… [O]ne cannot mobilize against a class condition of oppression unless one knows its fullest dimensions. Thus my work has been to study and expose sexual power in its most severe, global, institutionalized, and crystallized forms.… Prostitution – the cornerstone of all sexual exploitation. (1995: 9)

There are numerous criticisms to be made of this position. The most important one for this chapter is to consider the way in which this feminist interpretation makes it impossible to examine the actual power dynamics in the encounter, and thus denies the possibility of increasing sex workers' power at all. In what follows, I would like to focus on the way in which sex workers' experience of pleasure can give us a radically different interpretation of power, one that can be of actual use to sex workers in their daily or nightly encounters.

I suggest that part of the reason that so many sex workers are able to find sexual satisfaction on the job has to do with a different relationship to their body and their sexuality. In an article on the vagina as a site of strength, sex worker researcher Jayasree reports on how sex workers in Kerala are able to reclaim their vagina as their own.

> They seek pleasure by talking about sex together, using slang and puns to get free from the stressful situations of sex work. But

where they might have felt subjugated when men said these things, now they can derive their own pleasure and construct their own subjectivities with them.... I remember one sex worker singing and acting to describe different qualities of the vagina. (2009: 7)

Some sex workers report that feeling pleasure at work increases their sense of control.

One of the things that I realized was that those orgasms were mine. They didn't belong to anybody else. It was up to me to let them be known or not. But they were really mine in that I was the one creating them. It had nothing to do with who I was with; it wasn't about being so turned on by this guy instead of that one. It was about me. It really challenged the idea that orgasms are something a man 'gives' you. That's part of the traditional belief that women aren't supposed to be in control of sex. Instead, you're supposed to be passive, accepting whatever happens. But, as a prostitute, you really do determine what goes on, you hide the entire experience. (Maryann, in Chapkis 1997: 85)

One of Kontula's most interesting findings was that sexual pleasure at work was related to the amount of control that a woman felt over the situation. She finds two factors that influence the power dynamics of the situation: one could be considered 'external' characteristics of the wider sex market, taking in broad socio-economic factors, and the other relates to the 'individual skills and resources of the two parties' (2008: 617). In Finland, the first factor is seen in the relative over-demand related to supply (a situation very different to other countries). Because clients had to compete to some extent for sex workers, the sex worker could afford to be choosy. Sex worker Tinna said:

And if I have no fun with a client, I'll know it by the second time and say straight to the client that it doesn't work. I just say straight that 'You should look for the service somewhere else because you can't get it from me.' I have had to say this tens of times but it's true. I have as much right to choose my clients as they have to choose me. (2008: 616)

This is a very interesting finding because, according to

anti-sex work feminists, it is the lack of supply that fuels trafficking and thus decreases the power of sex workers. In the Finnish scenario, it is exactly the opposite, with the lack of supply behind sex workers' feelings of increased control.

The second 'external' factor identified by Kontula is the Finnish social welfare system, which provides a good basic income for everyone and so gives sex workers a good fall-back position. Finnish sex workers find it easy to reject an undesirable client, or to take fewer clients, because the social welfare system gives them broad support. For sex workers in other countries, particularly the United States and developing countries, this is not the case. I have identified a third factor (discussed elsewhere by Kontula), and that is the nature of the employment relationship of the sex worker. That is, the more control the woman has, for example, to choose working hours or to choose clients, the more pleasurable her work may prove to be.

In terms of personal resources, a number of things are important and affect the relationship. In Kontula's study, age, experience and migration status emerge as important. Minna tells the story of an incident that happened when she was 16 and new to the work:

> One time – well this isn't really a bad story but it still somehow left a scar. After the sex, the client wanted to take me to a parking lot and called some friends there. I had to get out of the car and turn around so that they could see me properly. Just like a cattle show. (2008: 617)

On the other hand, Wendy, a sex worker from London, feels that her personal attributes, including her longer experience of sex work and her positive view of sexuality, have empowered her in relationships with clients and so enhance her ability to feel pleasure at work (personal communication). Jolly reports that for the Chinese sex workers, it was the ability to negotiate condom use that enhanced sex workers' pleasure, as they no longer had to worry about AIDS or other STDs (Jolly 2003). Zatz identifies stigma as a cause of personal powerlessness (1997).

Sharing pleasure

As 'pleasure professionals', sex workers have valuable skills. Enabling sex workers to share their experiences with each other, and with the public, can provide entry points for a more pleasure-based approach to sexuality education and HIV prevention. There are many positive examples. Those that stand out include the 'wonderful sex' workshops organized by the Hong Kong sex worker organization Zi Teng, to let the public learn more about sexual pleasure. Yan Yuelian, Zi Teng founder, describes the process:

> There were four sessions in each workshop. We taught the partici-pants different things. In the first session, we first guided them to describe their thoughts and feelings over sex and gender. Usually we found that people in Hong Kong were very reluctant to describe their true feelings towards sex. But if they were encouraged, they could then talk more. In the second and third session, we started to tell them how partners could please each other. This included some theories about gender equality and techniques. Usually most participants were very excited in these sessions. They were eager to learn, as if they had never heard of such theories and techniques. In the last session, we would introduce something 'unusual', or what we describe as 'abnormal sex' to the participants. This is to broaden their scope of horizon. There we also had the evaluation. Participants were basically very satisfied, told us that they learnt a lot from the workshops. (Personal communication, Yan Yuelian, 19 December 2007)

The Sex Workers' Forum of Kerala called the annual national sex workers' conference that they organized the 'Festival of Pleasure'. Sex Workers Outreach Project Chicago has begun organizing a monthly 'pleasure salon' for the 'sex-positive community' (http://redlightchicago.wordpress.com).

Seeing sex workers as a 'pleasure resource' for the wider com-munity (and not just for their customers) could be beneficial in a number of ways. Sex worker stigma derives from stigmas around sexual pleasure: involving sex workers in challenging these stigmas situates their empowerment in a broader context, in which all can share in the potential benefits of a less-stigmatized sexuality.

Conclusion

If we are to take seriously sex workers' own reports of feeling pleasure at work, we must question an interpretation of prostitution that would make that very pleasure an impossible experience. We must accept that sex work can be pleasurable. And if we accept that sex work can be pleasurable, we must accept that sex workers have some control over their encounters with clients.

The implications of this for political activism around policy and practice are clear. The trend towards 'demonizing demand', that is, for penalizing clients of sex workers, is one based on the assumption of male power and female powerlessness in prostitution. Male sexuality is cast as active, predatory and exploitative, while female sexuality is passive, injured and exploited. Yet the above stories show us a different version of female sexuality: active, creative, dynamic and, above all, powerful. A powerful female sexuality explodes the binary of exploitative male and exploited female, because the terms of the binary depend on each other for their content. This means that if we are to accept the possibility of a powerful female sexuality at play in sex work, we must also re-think the terms in which we think of the male clients' sexuality.

The solutions then, lie not in criminalizing demand, but in shoring up those structures and strengthening those elements that give women control in the sex work encounter. These include such development goals as broadly targeted, gender-based anti-poverty initiatives, girls' education, and citizenship rights. Important, too, are focused interventions for sex workers such as complementary income-generation programmes and HIV-prevention projects. Measures to combat stigma in the community should be initiated, along with the reform of laws that target sex workers, their associates and their clients. On-the-job training and improved workers' rights would also further empower sex workers.

Pleasure is directly related to, both reflective and constitutive of, the social conditions in which sex work takes place. While sex workers working amidst a great variety of social and legal conditions report experiencing sexual pleasure on the job, it is notable that sexual pleasure is strongest where social stigma and the accompanying restrictions are weakest. This suggests interrelated directions for further work. This might include research into sex workers' experience of sexual pleasure and its relation to social/legal constructs as well as on-the-job 'success'. Projects targeting sex workers could disseminate sex workers' experience and expertise to the wider community, especially to women. They could also encourage sex workers to share and develop pleasure techniques with other sex workers and the wider community.

Sex workers' pleasure often goes unrecognized (by others), or is seen as incidental or trivial. This chapter suggests that we move sex workers' experience of pleasure to the centre of our analysis and practice. In so doing, we can give meaning to the term 'empowerment', by locating its source in sex workers' bodies.

Notes

1 The video can be viewed at www.womenlobby.org.
2 Information about the Sex Worker Open University can be found at www.sexworkeropenuniversity.com.

References

Barry, K. (1995) *The Prostitution of Sexuality: the Global Exploitation of Women,* New York University Press, New York.

Chapkis, W. (1997) *Live Sex Acts: Women Performing Erotic Labour,* Cassell, London.

Global Network of Sex Work Projects (NSWP) (2009) *Research for Sex Work,* No. 11.

Gonzalez, R. P. (2009) 'Sex Work and Sexual Pleasure', *Research for Sex Work,* No. 11, p. 9.

Jayasree, A. K. (2009) 'The Vagina as a Site of Power and Playfulness', *Research for Sex Work,* No. 11, pp. 6–7.

Jolly, S. (2003) 'Development Myths around Sex and Sexualities in the South', paper presented at 'Gender Myths and Feminist Fables: Repositioning Gender in Development Policy and Practice', Institute of Development Studies, University of Sussex, 2–4 July.

Kempadoo, K. and J. Doezema (1998) *Global Sex Workers: Rights, Resistance and Redefinition*, Routledge, New York.

Kontula, A. (2008) 'The Sex Worker and Her Pleasure', *Current Sociology*, Vol. 56, pp. 605–20.

Mollet, S. and Fatoumata (2009) 'Brothels in Bamako Today', *Research for Sex Work*, No. 11, pp. 2–3.

Pateman, C. (1998) *The Sexual Contract*, Polity Press, Cambridge.

Sahni, R. and V. Kalyan Shankar (2011) *The First Pan-India Survey of Sex Workers: a Summary of Preliminary Findings*, mimeo, http://sangram.org/Download/Pan-India-Survey-of-Sex-workers.pdf.

SWING (Service Workers In-Group Foundation) (2009) 'SWING's Research Experience', *Research for Sex Work*, No. 11, p. 19.

Zatz, N. D. (1997) 'Sex Work/Sex Act: Law, Labour and Desire in Constructions of Prostitution', *Signs*, Vol. 22, No. 2, pp. 277–308.

13
Eroticism, Sensuality and 'Women's Secrets' among the Baganda

Sylvia Tamale

Sexuality is intricately linked to practically every aspect of our lives: to pleasure, power, politics and procreation, but also to disease, violence, war, language, social roles, religion, kinship structures, identity, creativity.... The connection and collision between human sexuality, power and politics provide the inspiration for this chapter, which explores the various ways the erotic facility is used, as both an oppressive and empowering resource. In her compelling essay, sub-titled *The Erotic as Power*, Audre Lorde (1984) argues for the construction of the erotic as the basis of women's resistance against oppression. For her, the concept entails much more than the sexual act, connecting meaning and form, infusing the body and the psyche. Before Lorde, Michel Foucault (1977, 1990) demonstrated how the human body is a central component in the operation of power.

In a bid to gain a better understanding of African women's sexuality, this chapter focuses on one particular cultural/sexual initiation institution among the Baganda[1] of Uganda, the *Ssenga*. Talk of *ensonga za Ssenga* (*Ssenga* matters) signifies an institution that has endured through centuries as a tradition of sexual initiation. At the helm is the paternal aunt (or surrogate versions thereof) whose role is to tutor young women in a range of sexual matters, including pre-menarche (first menstruation) practices, pre-marriage preparation, erotics and reproduction. In Uganda's capital, Kampala, the phenomenon of commercial *Ssenga* services has emerged. Print and electronic media have adopted *Ssenga*

265

columns and call-in programmes. *Ssenga* booklets are also on sale in Kampala's streets. The institution is being transformed by modernization and urbanization, as well as capitalist economic practices within the liberalized market economy.

Sexuality is a key site on which women's subordination is maintained and enforced in Africa (McFadden 2003; Pereira 2003). This study of *Ssenga* is set against the backdrop of the institution of patriarchy and the legacy of colonialism. In Uganda, colonialist constructions of Africans as profligate and hypersexual led to the intensified repression and surveillance of African women's sexuality in particular. Colonialists worked hand in hand with African patriarchs to develop inflexible customary laws that evolved into new structures and forms of domination (Schmidt 1991; Mama 1996) and deployed various legal and policy strategies and discourses in the areas of medical health and hygiene. Traditional customs were reconfigured to introduce new sexual mores, taboos and stigmas. Women's sexuality was medicalized and reduced to reproduction (Vaughan 1991; Musisi 2002). Through adopting Christianity, Africans were encouraged to reject their previous beliefs and values and to adopt the 'civilized ways' of the whites. A new script, steeped in the Victorian moralistic, anti-sexual and body shame edict, was inscribed on the bodies of African women and with it an elaborate system of control.

Through all this and into the present, the boundaries of the institution of *Ssenga* have been re-drawn to suit the times (Kisekka 1973; Sengendo and Sekatawa 1999). Yet, as I go on to argue, while *Ssenga* facilitates and reinforces patriarchal power, at the same time it subverts and parodies patriarchy. Judith Butler's (1990) theories of subversion and performativity help tease out the transgressional features of the *Ssenga* institution. Butler's observation that gender is a daily, habitual, learned act – a performance – based on cultural norms of femininity and masculinity draws attention to the ways in which we performatively produce and reproduce gender and sexuality. Through a deconstruction of the arrangement of gender and sexuality as constituted by the institution of *Ssenga*, this chapter investigates constructs of Kiganda sexuality, and of femininity and masculinity within them. How has the evolution of *Ssenga* affected the (re)interpretation of entrenched norms concerning femininity, masculinity and subjectivity? And does it in any way represent any liberating possibilities for women?

Ssenga: past and present

To my knowledge, no scholarly study has analysed the Kiganda institution of *Ssenga* systematically; therefore, most of the historical material in this subsection is based on oral history, tales told to me by *Ssengas*, and popular belief.

Among the father's many sisters one would be selected (based on exemplary behaviour) to play the role of *Ssenga*. Her role was to socialize her nieces in the art of becoming good wives who were subservient and ensured their husband's sexual pleasure. Accorded the same respect as one's father-in-law and widely respected within the family, over the years *Ssenga* grew in status, power and respect among the Baganda. *Ssenga* could freely come and go in her brother's home under the responsibility of instructing the children. She could even take the children to her own home for tutelage. She made sure that young girls became well versed in the appropriate feminine behaviours and roles – details included proper ways a good girl should sit, walk, conduct herself, respect elders, and cook. The young adolescent received her lessons of 'visiting the bush', which, as I go on to discuss, involved a procedure of stretching or elongating her labia minora before she experienced menarche. As soon as she started menstruating, the *Ssenga* would begin preparing the young girl for marriage.

Under the ancient system, marriages were not prearranged but the *Ssenga* played a pivotal role in negotiating her nieces' marriages. The *Ssenga* fulfilled her primary responsibility of grooming her nieces to become good subservient wives or co-wives. A husband who was dissatisfied with his bride's behaviour, particularly bedroom etiquette, would blame it on the laxity of her *Ssenga*; and would return the bride to the *Ssenga* for proper training. However, *Ssenga's* tutelage also included some empowering messages to the young girl. For instance, *Ssenga* encouraged her niece to engage in some home cottage economic ventures (such as weaving or pottery) in order to avoid total dependence on her husband. *Ssenga* also made it clear that a wife did not have to tolerate an abusive spouse. Sexual placation was a key strategy in counteracting domestic violence, and it was the *Ssenga's* responsibility to inculcate in her nieces values and behaviours geared to create maximum pleasure for the husband. Nevertheless, married women had the option of abandoning abusive husbands and returning to their parent's home, a cultural practice known as *okunoba*. Failure to sexually satisfy a wife was another recognized ground for *kunoba*. This points to the fact that traditionally, among the Baganda, women had the right to sexual satisfaction.

Needless to say, sexuality featured prominently in *Ssenga's* tutorials focusing on eroticism, sexual paraphernalia and aids, as well as aphrodisiacs like herbal scents, erotic oils or sexual beads (*obutiti*). Use of vulgar speech was generally not permitted among the Baganda. However, the *Ssenga* was exempted from this taboo. As a result, *Ssengas'* advice to their charges abounds in 'sex talk', masked in metaphors and symbols.

In their bid to eliminate harmful cultural practices and to Westernize the sexual morality of the natives, missionaries and the colonial establishment had a special interest in Baganda women. Nakanyike Musisi observes:

> Through their pedagogy and medicine, missionaries like Cook managed to make sexuality, particularly women's, not only a religious concern but a secular one as well, one that needed to be regulated by the colonial state. To be more explicit, sex became an area that required legislation that would put individuals under colonial surveillance. The medical and sociopolitical project of managing births, children, and mothers' lives required that sexual morality itself be controlled by the state rather than by clan and kinship groups. (Musisi 2002: 101)

A massive moral purity campaign was launched by the colonial administration in the early twentieth century, threatening many of the values within the *Ssenga* institution. Although *Ssenga* represented an ideal establishment through which the British could spread their Christian ethic of sexuality among the Baganda, there is no evidence to show that this was ever tried. This is probably because colonialists dealt mostly with the elite male Baganda chiefs, largely excluding women from governance. All in all, the cultural institution of *Ssenga* remained intact through the colonial era.

As in many other African cultures, marriage and the family (read procreation) were (and in many ways still are) viewed as the basis of society. In this sense, given the crucial role that *Ssenga* played in this sphere, she ceased to be an individual; her role and practice became an institution in and of itself within Kiganda culture. In many ways *Ssenga* as an entity established (and still influences) patterns of expectation for Baganda men and women, ordering the social processes of everyday life (*cf.* Lorber 1994). Hence, contrary to popular belief, the institution of *Ssenga* is not restricted to erotology, nor is it an aphrodite cult of the genre elaborated by Abdoulaye (1999); it extends into every area of Baganda women's lives (*cf.* Tshikala 1999). *Ssenga* as an institution is fraught with contradictions and ambiguities; amid her main theme of subservience are subtexts of defiance, manipulation and control by women.

The institution of *Ssenga* has in many ways exhibited resilience and tenacious adaptability in the wake of widespread socio-political and economic changes in Uganda.[2] The economic and political hardships that dogged Uganda from the early 1970s had a significant impact on the household, and on the ideology of domesticity (Tamale 2001; UWONET 1998). For the average Ugandan, the structural adjustment process meant desperately fighting for basic survival; in real terms, it is women who paid the highest price. In addition to traditional reproduction and production roles in the domestic arena, many women were forced to engage in income-generating activities outside their homes to make ends meet. Poor urban families were the hardest hit.

The emergence of commercial *Ssengas* was one of the creative ways in which women responded to diminished economic opportunities in urban areas. Far from being a simple demand-and-supply response, the traditional role of *Ssenga* metamorphosed into a new, liberalized form; its discourse shifted from the private to the public sphere. A historical institution that served a specific role of initiating young girls for marriage and domesticity suddenly held great potential as a moneymaking venture. The urban setting appears to have provided a ready and willing market, tailor-made from historical realities and the vacuum created by socio-economic and political circumstances pertaining in the country. The withdrawal of public health and educational services, for example, facilitated *Ssenga* as an income-generating activity in an era of income-generating promotion. Thus, *Ssenga* presented an informal source of career opportunity, providing a material base to an ongoing socio-cultural institution.

Men were also quick to cash in on this new career opportunity. Within the new discourse of liberalized sexuality, a male *Ssenga* is referred to as *kojja*.[3] The numerous call-in *Ssenga* programmes that have emerged on the vibrant FM radio stations plus the various *Ssenga* newspaper columns have not only expanded employment opportunities in this area, but have also transferred Kiganda sexuality from the private realm of the home to everyday discourse in a very public way. Listeners who call into *Ssenga* radio programmes or read their columns are usually provided with the personal mobile phone numbers and e-mail addresses of various *Ssengas* to enable them to arrange one-on-one encounters. Similarly, many *Ssengas* today surf the internet for information on sexuality, and then feed this to their audiences.[4]

Today, the *Ssenga* institution is made up of both conservative elements that will not bend from century-old practices and progressive ones that go with the times. Age and education seem to be influencing factors here, with younger, more educated *Ssengas* leaning towards more liberal views than their older uneducated counterparts. Among other contemporary influences are forces such as religion, feminism, HIV/AIDS, increased intermarriage and information technology. Commercial *Ssengas* are self-appointed and do not undergo any formal training or nomination. Most draw their knowledge from their own *Ssengas,* popular literature, mass media and various people knowledgeable in the subject. The institution has itself redefined urban domesticity, even as modernity infringes on it. The ancient and the modern negotiate a delicate coexistence and this is well captured in a common *Ssenga* mantra, *Ssabasajja awangale* (long live the king). As expected, the institution of *Ssenga* is a vital cog in the socio-political wheel of the Buganda kingdom. Not surprisingly, the Minister for Culture and Tradition in the kingdom is a commercial *Ssenga* herself.

While women's sensuality and eroticism are recognized in Uganda, their sexuality is greatly feared. While heteronormativity is promoted at every turn, women are largely denied the expression of their sexuality in the public domain. These contradictions and dilemmas surrounding Ugandan women's sexuality come into bold relief when women's eroticism and pleasure are discussed in public. This was exhibited in full force in February 2005, when four Ugandan women's groups collaborated to stage Eve Ensler's play, *The Vagina Monologues*, in Kampala. Designed to celebrate female sexuality as well as spotlight sexual violence against women, the play promised to break every sexual taboo in Ugandan society. Government, through the Media Council, was quick to slap a ban on the play, arguing that the title was 'offensive to cultural sensibilities' and that the content was 'too obscene' and 'promoted lesbianism in Uganda'.[5] In this way the patriarchal state exposed its undemocratic denial of women's basic freedom of expression, and its fear of women's sexual liberation. The play threatened to disturb the order of gender and sexual politics in Ugandan society.[6]

Beneath the surface of the kind of overt political repression that was evident in this case are women's subversive and counter-hegemonic 'silent struggles'. Behind the public silence about women's sexuality and eroticism is the realm of 'women's secrets'. Only females are privy to such secrets, with the *Ssengas* being the chief custodians of Baganda women's sex secrets archives. In the following sections, I explore the part played by the *Ssengas* in sharing these sex secrets and abetting these 'silent struggles', through the use of metaphor, by creating opportunities for women to talk about sexuality and eroticism and by tutoring their charges in the arts of pleasure.

'Mortar-pestle dialogues': metaphorically speaking

As *Ssenga* grooms, moulds and regulates young girls to turn into good Baganda women, s/he performatively and discursively reinforces the dominant culture (patriarchy, heteronormativity, repronormativity). But parts of the *Ssenga* discourse also destabilize assumptions that underlie the dominant culture, holding potential for gender transgression. Metaphors and symbols play a central role in the *Ssenga* discourse. Referred to as *okwambaza ebigambo* (dressing words), metaphors and symbols provide an acceptable medium of accessing the secret world of unverbalized sexuality, shifting it from the private to the public realm. It also allows for coded communication about sexuality, decipherable by women and other adults but hidden from children. Through sexual metaphors, erotic symbolism and nuanced interpretations of culturally significant ambiguities, *Ssenga* maps Kiganda gender identity.

As cultivating is the primary economic activity of the Baganda, many of the sexual metaphors and symbols in *Ssenga* are couched around this theme. Related activities – ploughing, sowing, watering, weeding, harvesting and eating – are all freely used for encoding knowledge about the sexual lives of Baganda women and men. Hence a man who is impotent is described as 'no longer able to cultivate his farm' (*takyalima nnimiro*); one who is lousy in bed is a 'bad farmer' (*ennima embi*); one who gets premature ejaculations is referred to as 'unable to complete his *lubimbi* (piece of arable land apportioned for the day)'; to 'eat one's dinner' *(okulya eky'ekiro)* or 'digging one's *lubimbi'* both refer to having sex; 'food must be eaten with *ebirungo* (spices)' means to introduce variety in sexual activity. A woman burns the pot *(asiriza entamu)* if she is not adequately lubricated. The sexual symbol of mortar and pestle is universal: thus *omusekuzo* (pestle) is an erect phallus and *okumusekula* (pounding) refers to its motion in sexual intercourse.

Games provide another popular theme. A famous ancient Kiganda board game called *omweso* (mancala), of the 'count and capture' genre of games that involves two players moving seeds *(empiki)* along a wooden board with the objective of capturing the opponent's seeds, provides an example. The terms used in *omweso* are sexually suggestive, for example, 'sowing' (moving the seeds), 'capture' and 'reverse-capture' (taking opponent's seeds). There are various ways that the game may be won, including *ekutema* (literally, to chop), *akakyala* (literally, feminine) and *Emitwe-Ebiri* (literally, two-headed). Hence, *Ssengas* will use suggestive phrases such as *okutebuka, nosinzira empiki n'ozizako emmabega* (to hesitate during the game and move the seeds backwards), *okutambuza empiki z'omweso* (to move the seeds along the board) and *omweso gw'omuddiriŋŋjano* (playing back-to-back *mweso* games), all of which have sexual undertones.

Traditional folklore, lullabies and children's songs also provide metaphorical models to mediate sexuality messages among women. Teaching about sexuality involves many elements for the *Ssenga*, most importantly the ability to impart conceptual understanding and a sense of intellectual excitement about the topic. The creative use of metaphor is vital in that process, facilitating in the construction and consolidation of sexuality by the *Ssenga* institution. Furthermore, it validates gender/power relations among the Baganda as well as helping to create and sustain the discourse of heteronormativity (as in the mortar and pestle metaphor). Hence, through sexuality the subordination, dependency and control of women is guaranteed. Yet, as is the case with all hegemonic ideologies, deviancy discourses exist within the institution of *Ssenga*.

Gender/sexuality non-conformity: poking holes in patriarchy

Although the ideological basis for *Ssenga* is primarily cultural, this is coloured by age, religion, class, and so forth. Many *Ssengas* do not conform to the script of normative gender and sexuality models; and there are *Ssengas* who carry emancipatory messages of women's economic independence and autonomy, women's ejaculation and orgasm, sexual foreplay, masturbation and sexual self-discovery.

> Live with a man for some time before committing yourself to him in marriage.[7]

> Why can't men stomach their wives' extramarital affairs when women endure it all the time? Men need to understand that their wives get similar feelings of betrayal, shame, hurt when they cheat on them.[8]

> It's extremely important for every woman to get some kind of in-come, however small.... Never depend on a man for all your financial needs. I myself learned the hard way raising two children on my own.[9]

> Home hygiene is the responsibility of everyone in the home, including the father. It should not be left exclusively to the wife/mother. Men must share in domestic chores.... Forget about old practices because culture evolves.[10]

The debate that ensued when *Ssenga* Najjemba made this last remark during her call-in FM programme is an indicator of *Ssengas'* potential to rock the cultural boat:

1st caller (male):	God placed the responsibility of home hygiene squarely on women; it's natural.
2nd caller (male):	Culture is not static and indeed we men should participate. In olden days women used to work exclusively in the home. Today, they work outside the home and we must share responsibilities at home.
Ssenga Najjemba:	Men should wash their own underwear, for example.
3rd caller (female):	Men should understand that we don't get married to become their slaves or maids.

4th caller (female):	No, no, no it's our role as women to take care of our homes, including washing our husband's underwear.
5th caller (male):	What is this rubbish, if my woman (*mukazi wange*)...
Ssenga Najjemba:	Correction, please refer to her as 'my wife' (*mukyala wange*).

The radical views expressed by *Ssenga* Najjemba are in fact fairly common among educated commercial *Ssengas*. Such *Ssengas* are by no means 'anti-culture'. In another programme, *Ssenga* Najjemba explains that she strongly supports those aspects of Kiganda tradition and custom that hold value. One commercial *Ssenga* shared the point that the most frequently asked question by women in her sessions is: *N'omukazi amala?* meaning, 'Do you mean even a woman can orgasm?' She revealed that she herself had been in a fifteen-year marriage with five children but had never experienced an orgasm. It was not until she got involved in an extramarital relationship that she discovered *entikko y'omukazi* (a woman's peak). That was reason enough for her to leave and now she lives in a happy sexual relationship. Hence, radical topics such as female ejaculation and clitoral orgasm are part of this particular *Ssenga's* repertoire of tutoring techniques. Of all the public *Ssenga* sessions that I attended, that of this particular *Ssenga* was the most striking for sheer presence, charisma and dynamism – not much different from the breed of modern charismatic Evangelical pastors who are so popular in today's Uganda. It would be interesting to investigate whether such lessons translate into liberatory politics for the women who benefit from them.

Similarly, there were many voices among *Ssenga* trainees that challenged hegemonic narratives embedded in the *Ssenga* institution, and questioned basic patriarchal assumptions embedded in the mainstream *Ssenga* discourse and in male/female sexual norms and practices. Some young women attending a private *Ssenga* session that I went to, for example, rejected the part of *Ssenga's* core lesson that implored them to prioritize their mothering role, taking their husbands as their 'first-born child'.

Below is a sample of some of their responses, which caused gasps and mutters:

> Do you mean we should remain docile even when he wrongs us? Should we remain quiet even where it is obvious that he's mistreating and abusing us?

> Wait a minute; all we've heard this evening is how to please a man? How we must wait on him and our children all the time, what we must do to please him in bed, blah, blah, blah…. Can you tell me what a man can do to please *me*?

Rejecting the ideological proposition that placed men on a pedestal, these women also defied the imposition of motherhood as the paradigmatic self-identity of Baganda women. Demands that men should also receive training in how to please their female partners sexually is a radical move on the part of young Baganda women. Most importantly, it points to the apparent fact that they regard sex not primarily for procreation but for leisure and pleasure, relocating sex from the medicalized/reproduction plane to the erotic zone. The erotic as a resource thus acts as an empowering tool for Baganda women.

Traditional sexuality has been complemented and enhanced with modern and foreign sexual practices. For instance, today, some *Ssengas'* instructions include lessons in oral sex, deep kissing, masturbation and other forms of self-discovery:

> Most of us are shy when it comes to kissing and oral sex…. Try it, you'll love it! I myself was truly ignorant about female ejaculation until I met my current lover…. It works best with the *Banyankore kachabali* (outer-course) technique. If your lover knows what he's doing, you'll pour rivers and experience multiple orgasms at the same time.[11]

Included in the curriculum of many *Ssengas* is the message of controlling and manipulating men through sex. In other words, they encourage women, through sex, to undermine patriarchal power from behind a façade of total subservience.

> Men are like children…. Let him believe that he's in control while you take charge. Spoil him, pamper him, treat him like a king and

you'll have him under your wing on a tether; he'll never leave you. He may get other women, but he'll always return to you.

The best time to ask your man for anything is during sex. Men's brains are weak when it comes to sex.... This is the time to manipulate them.

Such messages resonate with the old Chinese proverb: 'Man is the head of the family, woman the neck that turns the head!' The engagement in explicit and/or subversive sex talk, as well as the commentary that links men's sexual power to their economic and political dominance not only reveals women's embedded struggles, but also points to a legacy of cultural forms that marginalized groups appropriate in defining and pursuing their own needs and desires. Using sexuality as a manipulative tool can be empowering and, when stripped of any moral anchoring, can be subversive.

An analysis of commercial *Ssengas'* matchmaking services reveals that Baganda women are beginning to take the initiative in sexual relations. A popular segment of the weekly late-night Radio Simba programme, *Muyizi Tasubwa* – which translates as 'a must listen for learners' – is apportioned to reading out the basic resumés of those seeking partners. *Ssengas'* application forms require the applicant to provide a photograph plus such information as their age, tribe, clan, religion and marital status, as well as their preferences in a potential partner. Almost half of those that send in requests are women. It is worth noting that most female applicants indicate that interested partners must be ready to ascertain their sero status through an HIV/AIDS test. It is relatively new for Baganda women to take control of their sexuality and exercise power quite so emphatically and explicitly.

Of course, this sometimes sparks a backlash, as already seen in the government ban on staging *The Vagina Monologues*. Likewise, conservative forces denigrate the presence of *Ssengas* on university campuses and associate the practice with the promotion of promiscuity and immorality. During Makerere University's orientation week some years ago, the authorities roundly condemned commercial *Ssengas* who 'hawked their advice' to female students. The authorities were particularly concerned by the emphasis that campus *Ssenga* sessions placed on sexual intercourse techniques, how to attract men, and how to extract money from a lover. They felt that these were not matters on which honourable educated girls should be focusing (Ultimate Media 2004). It is clear, however, that much of their discomfort derived from the potential that such *Ssenga* sessions held for young women to take control of their sexuality.

Hence we see the significance of the *Ssenga* institution in redefining and reframing the ideology of urban domesticity in Kampala, through reinforcing and actualizing hierarchies of gender and sexuality. The sexual boundaries that the *Ssenga* tradition draws and redraws within the domestic arena speak to multiple issues of class, gender and religion, as well as to notions of conformity and transgression. The cultural connotations of sexuality as reflected in the evolving institution of *Ssenga* thus go beyond heterosexual intercourse and erotics.

The cultural labia

Women in diverse cultures have always fixed or otherwise transformed their bodies in order to fit their cultural norms. One of the ways that Baganda women fix their bodies is through an elaborate routine of packaging the vagina for men's maximum pleasure.

Between the age of nine and twelve, before experiencing menarche, a Muganda girl would be guided by her *Ssenga* to prepare her genitals for future sex. This was done by elongating the labia minora. Known as *okukyalira ensiko* (visiting the bush), this rite was traditionally performed in a clearing among bushes where the herbs (such as *mukasa, entengotengo, oluwoko*) used for the procedure were found. Pubescent girls would 'visit the bush' for a few hours every day over a period of about two weeks. The *Ssenga* would persuade them to comply by advising them that if they did not, no man would ever ask for their hand in marriage.[12]

Indeed, when a man discovered that his bride had not 'visited the bush' he would send her back to her parents for the *Ssenga* to fulfil her duty. Sengendo and Sekatawa (1999) explain:

> A [Muganda] woman who did not elongate the labia minora is traditionally despised and regarded as having a pit (*kiwowongole, kifufunkuli, funkuli muwompogoma*). If a bride was found not to have elongated her labia minora, she would be returned to her parents with disgrace. (1999: 45)

Over the years, how has this culturally specific practice been mediated and transfigured? When I began this study, I was under the impression that it was dying out. Findings revealed not only that it is alive and thriving in the urban and peri-urban areas around Kampala, but that it has also spread to many non-Baganda women (including some of European descent) who seek the services of commercial *Ssengas* to elongate their labia. Nevertheless, a great many younger women have chosen to opt out of this cultural practice, dismissing it as useless and primitive. It may no longer be obligatory, but it remains a well-entrenched tradition even among the Baganda elite. Many participants in this study were of the view that it was a practice worth preserving (*cf.* Sengendo and Sekatawa 1999).

The findings show that the practice of elongating the labia minora seems to serve three main purposes. The first one is functional in that the extended labia enhance the erotic experience of both the male and the female. When touched and manipulated in the correct manner during foreplay or mutual masturbation, they may be the source of immense pleasure to the couple. Secondly, elongated labia serve as a kind of self-identifier for Baganda women – the stamp of legitimacy for a true Muganda woman. The third function is a purely aesthetic one; several Baganda men interviewed said that they just love looking at and fondling the stretched labia of a woman. Some women also stated that they enjoy it when their elongated labia are touched as it transmits sensation to their clitoris.

These findings contrast sharply with the definition put forward by the World Health Organization (WHO). Classifying it and condemning it as type IV female genital mutilation, the WHO lumps this procedure together with FGM procedures that pose health hazards to women.[13] It completely disregards the ways in which this practice, encoded within the *Ssenga* institution, has enhanced sexual pleasure for women, and expanded their perceptions of themselves as active sexual beings. Interestingly, harmful cosmetic procedures (e.g. clitoral piercing) sometimes performed in Western countries are not listed under type IV FGM. Through such discourse, this global health body writes this African practice of sexual enhancement into the broad negative rubric of harmful cultural practices that violate the rights of women and children. Far from suffering feelings of 'incompleteness, anxiety and depression'[14] that the WHO associates with this practice, most of those interviewed in this study spoke positively of this cultural practice. This lived experience of Baganda women contradicts the negative blanket characterization of the cultural practice of labia elongation offered by the WHO.

Eroticism and sexual etiquette in the marital chamber

The basic *Ssenga* message to married women is: 'be a nice, humble wife but turn into a *malaya* (prostitute) in your bedroom'! As a sure recipe for healthy sexual relations women are constantly advised by *Ssengas* to throw shyness, coyness and embarrassment out the bedroom window. When *Ssengas* are talking about bedroom matters, their whole demeanour and comportment changes. They adopt a sensual, sexy voice to underscore their messages. In fact, a radio *Ssenga* will only be hired if she is endowed with a deep, soothing, romantic voice that will charm her listeners.

One of the primary sex paraphernalia associated with Kiganda sexuality are the stringed colourful waist beads called *obutiti*. Traditionally, the *obutiti* were made out of tiny, delicate clay beads that would make a sexy tinkling or rattling sound as they knocked against each other with any slight movement. The sight of a woman adorned with layers of rows of *obutiti* around her waist strutting around the bedroom chamber is a turn on for her male partner. The number of rows around a woman's waist is supposed to be uneven. This number signifies that she is one ahead of her rivals. When a man twirls the *obutiti* around or rubs them against the woman's body, they function as a stimulant or aphrodisiac. Special herbs are often injected or otherwise soaked into the beads to add to their potency.

Usually, during a private *Ssenga* session, observers will be taught how to enhance their lovemaking techniques through a guided performance. Two *Ssengas* may lie on a bed and take the couple or group through a blow-by-blow display of how it is supposed to be done. They come prepared with all the sex gear and gadgets (including dildos). Key among this sexual equipment is the *nkumbi*, a large, soft, absorbent white cloth used for hygienic purposes during and after sex. The practices and beliefs associated with *enkumbi* constitute a ritual enterprise that in itself is very important to the Baganda people. *Ssengas* even teach various lovemaking noises (*okukona ennyindo* – nasal; *okusiiya* – hiss; *okusika omukka* – breath/gasp). Watching two half-naked women in bed did not seem to suggest lesbianism to the absorbed tutees.

After the demonstration, the *Ssengas* display the different paraphernalia for sale, including *enkumbi*, *obutiti* and various sex herbs. A variety of herbs are prescribed for different effects. Among the aphrodisiacs recommended are *ekibwankulata* or the local viagra, *mulondo* or *olukindukindu*, both of which are said to be potent in bestowing 'power to the bull'. Several herbs are suggested for tightening the vagina and maintaining its warmth – the smoke of *ekkokozi* smouldering in a porcelain clay bowl directly into the vagina is recommended for this purpose. The Baganda prefer wet sex to dry sex. To this end, the leaves of *ekibwankulata* and the bark of *kiffabakazi* are either smoked into the vagina or boiled and taken orally to enhance vaginal lubrication for women. The crushed and rolled leaves of *kajjampuni* will tighten the vaginal walls if inserted a few hours before sex. Many women routinely grow these herbs in their backyards and gardens. Love potions recommended by *Ssenga* are numerous, such as the leaves of *kawulira* plant. When these are mixed into vegetables during cooking and fed to a man, they are supposed to win his favour.

Concluding remarks

This chapter has demonstrated the fundamental link between sexual politics and gender oppression, sexuality and power. It shows that body politics for African women possesses an empowering sub-text, reflected through resistance, negotiation, identity, self-desire, pleasure and silence. Whereas colonial and post-colonial forces attempted to exercise hegemony over learning processes around sexuality via the state and its modern public health and welfare institutions (now in the doldrums), the institution of *Ssenga* among the Baganda continues to dominate in this arena. Not only has it endured and survived but it has also expanded to correspond to the changes in the political economy of the country and the entire African region.

This study pushes further the limits of academic research on and theorizations of sexuality in Uganda specifically and the African continent generally. One important lesson that I learned from this research experience was that when we go beyond the traditional studies on African sexuality – which primarily focus on reproduction, violence and disease – to explore the area of desire and pleasure, we gain deeper insights into this complex subject. Broadening the scope of our research on sexuality in this way offers a fresh perspective on strategic interventions for critical areas such as sexual rights, HIV/AIDS and development. Specifically, we can envisage how practitioners in these fields can work inventively and collaboratively with communities that possess long and complex knowledge traditions of sexuality.

The evolution of *Ssenga* practices has allowed Baganda women to negotiate agency, autonomy and self-knowledge about their sexuality. This illuminates the liberatory value of indigenous institutions, and represents a very different perspective to their idyllic or nostalgic portrayals as repositories of tradition often seen in mainstream patriarchal Africanist thinking. Indeed, commercialization, professionalization, commodification and modernity have invested the institution of *Ssenga* with new scope for challenging subordination and sexual control. While the patriarchal agendas and discourses embedded within *Ssenga* are unmistakable, women's subversive and counter-hegemonic 'silent struggles' allow them to negotiate agency, providing a neat example of how African women can inherit and shape traditions of their own that go beyond the discourse of rights imposed from above.

Acknowledgements

I wish to register my gratitude to the following people who read drafts of this chapter and made very useful suggestions: Amina Mama, Charmaine Pereira, Takyiwaa Manuh and the entire team of the feminist research group on Mapping Sexualities in Africa. An earlier and longer version of this article appears in *Feminist Africa*, Vol. 5, 2005. Grateful thanks are due to *Feminist Africa* for permission to republish this adapted version.

Notes

1 Baganda (the singular form is Muganda) is the name of the largest ethnic group in Uganda. Their culture is referred to as Kiganda, and their language is Luganda.

2 Compare, for example, the sexual initiation roles played by the following *Ssenga* equivalents that have not developed into institutionalized forms: the *Shwenkazi* among the Banyankore of Uganda; the *Tete* among the Shona of Zimbabwe; the *Alangizi* among the Yao of Malawi and the Chew of Zambia; and the *Mayosenge* among the Bemba of Zambia.

3 The Luganda word *kojja* means maternal uncle. This mirror image of the *Ssenga* (paternal aunt) portrayed in the male version is interesting. Use of the term for paternal uncle was probably not appealing, given that it means the same thing as father (*taata*); it is taboo for a father to discuss sexual matters with his daughter.

4 For example, see *Bukedde Ssenga*, 'Weetegereze w'asuza emikono', 14 September 2004.

5 See Media Council ruling, 'In the Matter of the Press and Journalists Act and In the Matter of the Media Council and In the Matter

of a Play, "The Vagina Monologues'" (unpublished), 16 February 2005. See also Ahimbisibwe 2005; Wasike and Wafula 2005.

6 By the time the play was banned, pre-sale tickets worth Ushs20 million (US$11,500) had been collected. After the ban, only 20 people collected their ticket refunds. This was an important ·endorsement of people's solidarity with the cause and a protest to government (see *Daily Monitor* 2005; *New Vision* 2005).

7 *Ssenga* Hajjat Mariam Kayoga, *Muyizi Tasubwa*, Radio Simba, 18 September 2004, 12.40 am.

8 *Ssenga* Katana, public talk, Pride Theatre, 24 November 2004, 6.00–9.00 pm.

9 *Ssenga* Nakibuule Mukasa, *Abayita Ababiri*, Radio Simba, 5 December 2004, 5.00–7.00 pm.

10 *Ssenga* Eseza Najjemba, *Guno Mulembe ki?*, Akaboozi ku Bbiri FM, 23 November 2004, 5.35 pm.

11 Private session with *Ssenga* Katana at Wandegeya, 11 November 2004.

12 The cultural aesthetic practice of elongating the inner folds of the labia minora is quite common among several (mainly Bantu-speaking) communities of Eastern and Southern Africa, including the Tutsi (Rwanda), the Basotho (Lesotho), the Shona (Zimbabwe), the Nyakyusa and Karewe (Tanzania), the Khoisan (Southern Africa) and the Tsonga (Mozambique).

13 See the WHO definition of Type IV female genital mutilation at http://www.who.int/mediacentre/factsheets/fs241/en/.

14 *Ibid.*

References

Abdoulaye, L. (1999) 'Brief Notes on Eroticism among the Lawbe, Senegal', *CODESRIA Bulletin*, Nos 3 and 4, pp. 46–8.

Ahimbisibwe, F. (2005) 'Vagina Play Dropped', *New Vision*, 18 February.

Butler, J. (1990) *Gender Trouble: Feminism and the Subversion of Identity*, Routledge, London.

Daily Monitor (2005) 'Women Activists Blame Government for Violence', 28 June, p. 4.

Foucault, M. (1977) *Discipline and Punish: the Birth of the Prison*, Pantheon Books, New York.

—— (1990) *The History of Sexuality: the Use of Pleasure*, Knopf Doubleday, New York.

Kisekka, M. N. (1973) 'Heterosexual Relationships in Uganda', unpublished PhD thesis, University of Missouri.

Lorber, J. (1994) *Paradoxes of Gender*, Yale University Press, New Haven CT.

Lorde, A. (1984) 'Uses of the Erotic: the Erotic as Power', in A. Lorde (ed.), *Sister Outsider: Essays and Speeches*, The Crossing Press, New York.

Mama, A. (1996) 'Women's Studies and Studies of Women in Africa During the 1990s', *CODESRIA Working Paper*, No. 5/96, CODESRIA, Dakar.

McFadden, P. (2003) 'Sexual Pleasure as Feminist Choice', *Feminist Africa*, No. 2, pp. 50–60.

Musisi, N. (2002) 'The Politics of Perception or Perception as Politics? Colonial and Missionary Representations of Baganda Women, 1900–1945', in J. Allman, S. Geiger and N. Musisi (eds), *Women in African Colonial Histories*, Indiana University Press, Bloomington IN.

New Vision (2005) 'Women Activists Fetch Sh20m', 28 June, p. 4.

Pereira, C. (2003) 'Where Angels Fear to Tread? Some Thoughts on Patricia McFadden's "Sexual Pleasure as Feminism"', *Feminist Africa*, No. 2, pp. 61–5.

Schmidt, E. (1991) 'Patriarchy, Capitalism, and the Colonial State in Zimbabwe', *Signs: Journal of Women in Culture and Society*, Vol. 16, No. 4, pp. 732–56.

Sengendo J. and E. Sekatawa (1999) *A Cultural Approach to HIV/AIDS Prevention and Care,* Special Series on Cultural Policies for Development Unit, No. 1, UNESCO, Paris.

Tamale, S. (2001) 'Between a Rock and a Hard Place: Women's Self-Mobilization to Overcome Poverty in Uganda', in S. Rowbotham and S. Linkogle (eds), *Women Resist Globalization: Mobilizing for Livelihood and Rights*, Zed Books, London.

Tshikala, B. (1999) 'Eroticism and Sexuality in Africa: Directions and Illusions', *CODESRIA Bulletin*, Nos 3 and 4, pp. 41–6.

Ultimate Media (2004) 'Ssengas Invade Makerere', *Monitor,* 23 July.

UWONET (1998) *Structural Adjustment in Uganda*, Uganda Women's Network, Kampala.

Vaughan, M. (1991) *Curing Their Ills: Colonial Power and African Illness*, Stanford University Press, Stanford CA.

Wasike, A. and E. Wafula (2005) 'Government Opposes "Vagina Monologues"', *New Vision*, 11 February.

14

Laughter, the Subversive Body Organ

●●

Ana Francis Mor

Up against the soap operas

A few years ago, my cabaret-theatre company, Las Reinas Chulas, was invited by the Instituto Mexicano del Seguro Social (the Mexican Institute of Social Security) to take part in a programme bringing better health to the most vulnerable and poor communities in the country. The project was an initiative that had the visionary mission of mixing arts with health promotion to accomplish better results in changing people's attitudes towards health in every sense. For me, the experience was amazing.

The project consisted of running four-day workshops in several parts of the country, each with 100 women, 100 men and 100 young leaders from smaller surrounding towns. In total, we ran around 100 workshops. Part of the workshop process involved spending the morning in reflection groups of 25 people each, analysing the most significant problems of their communities regarding their personal situation in the context of improving health. In the afternoon, in larger groups, cabaret-theatre was used to work with all the topics covered during the morning. The main issues raised were self-esteem, clear and direct communication, gender equity, poverty and health. Every night, stories were performed, inspired by the experiences collected from these groups of people from all over the country.

Within the fields of activism and human rights promotion, socio-dramas are often used to tell people's stories. This is a technique that uses drama to reproduce real circumstances, including the problems portrayed. But when producing socio-dramas in Mexico there is an unbeatable enemy: television. During the last 50 years, Mexican television has become the communication instrument of the government, through which reality is reinvented. Mexican television – and more specifically Mexican soap opera – has turned into an instrument for the emotional education of the people. In the farthest and most hidden corners of the country, where only misery visits, it arrives accompanied by soap operas and their Cinderella stories: where the female hero has a terrible life during a hundred chapters or so and then, when she gets to the final chapter, finds happiness by getting married.

Beyond the triviality of the stories waits the true badland: the conventional and reactionary values they exalt. Gender roles are defined by victim and virginity narratives for women and violent chauvinism for men. The opportunities for diversity are very few and Catholicism remains the underlying ideology. It is with such stories, told in this way, that the Mexican population has grown up. In the last 30 years, the population has suffered a systematic impoverishment of education. So, for the 98 per cent of the population without access to internet, the world is just as soap operas tell it. In this specific context, the emotional and cultural struggle becomes titanic: real life stories do not match television and 'good girls' do not have 'good lives'. But people have no other cultural referents, so these are the stories they repeat.

What socio-dramas accomplish is the flawless repetition of melodramatic television models. People already know their scripts: woman = virtue = no pleasure = victim = tears = virginity = blackmail = guilt; men = macho or male chauvinist = never cries = alcohol = money = violence = sexual power = success or death.

Through socio-drama in Mexico we do not face reality; we just reproduce its squat and incomplete vision.

Discovering laughter

Facing these problems, we started to think that maybe stories could have alternative treatments. And then came the discovery of laughter. To tell stories in a funny way, there are two genres to draw on: farce and comedy. With a mixture of both, we decided to build characters with the absurd as a main farce feature, and then place those characters into more realistic situations, more in keeping with comedy. The purpose was to recount the daily tragedies derived from gender inequality, from the lack of pleasure, from established gender roles. How could we shatter monoliths as huge as male chauvinism? How could we look directly at the indignity of Catholic sexual un-education? By showing them in their entire splendour, showing how ridiculous they are, so that their unfairness is clearly brought to light. The logic is to ridicule tyranny, to knock it down; to laugh about our own disgrace to diminish its power.

So we started to work with laughter, to talk loud about our pain, but with the possibility of transforming our identities and our own personal classifications. We wanted to shift from being the ones who moan about pain to being the ones who laugh about it. This is how we built our characters' stories from laughter, from the Mexican tradition of laughing about every solemnity, of laughing even about death – because at the end of the day, death is the one that has the last laugh.

Learning with the body

When people get information, this doesn't necessarily imply or entail a change of attitudes leading to better healthcare, better protection, safe practices, et cetera. Let's take the example of cervical cancer. For the state, to prevent cervical cancer is cheaper than to cure it. To prevent it, women should be reviewed periodically so any signs or symptoms can be detected, treatment can be applied in good time, and women do not have to die from something that can be cured. So, according to the conventional logical dictates of public policy, it is necessary to inform women about the importance of screening through countless brochures, lectures, posters and medical advice. But with only this kind of action, little changes: women do not attend regular medical appointments, so they are still dying of cervical cancer. What is happening? Why is it not enough to know that your life is at risk to persuade you to go to the doctor and get checked? No, knowledge is not enough. At least, knowledge 'by the head' is not enough; one must also know in the body and the heart. It is here where laughter becomes a great free guide to recognizing pain and transforming it into pleasure.

In our project, people were represented by characters who looked at the absurdity of their situations and laughed about them. Through farce, characters suffered their own machismo, their violence, their guilt, their resignation to remain victims. The audience laughed and laughed as they watched their own stories represented. The next morning, the level of reflection was much deeper and pleasure slowly crept in everywhere – because laughter generates well-being. Laughter generates pleasure; it is felt through the body and leaves traces of the possibility of happiness.

Among the plays we presented in those workshops, there was one in which an indigenous woman asked the audience if they should come across her husband, to please tell him not to come back because she had already formed a relationship with the godmother of her child. She took the opportunity to tell the audience, with a string of funny anecdotes, how she discovered that she liked the godmother of her child, and how to follow that desire until 'the tree of her dignity' flourished within her. This fond and funny story didn't allow discrimination to become the central character, but rather the discovery of pleasure that transformed this person into a shiny and happy being. In focus groups following this play, young people mentioned that this was the first time they had asked themselves if they might like a person of their own sex, or what they would do if a member of their family were lesbian or gay. This implies that participants not only clearly understood the information that discrimination against lesbians and gays is against human rights, but they entered into a process of emotional reflection about it.

Reflecting lives in stories

As people, we are not equal, but we all need tools to nurture our happiness projects. Laughter gives us the sensation of looking closer at these happiness projects, and if we look even closer, maybe we can get close enough to make them happen.

I recall a woman from a Rarámuri community in the state of Chihuahua. Marta was amongst the first in her family to speak Spanish besides her mother tongue. In this community, women did not undergo any kind of gynaecological examination, and the resulting complications related to the lack of gynaecological attention were a significant mortality risk. These women simply couldn't open their legs because their beliefs wouldn't allow such a thing. There was a character in our show named 'La Vecina' (the neighbour), who embodied every possible and imaginable health issue related to or derived from disinformation and embarrassment. Her circumstances were so hilariously ridiculous that no one wanted to be like her. In one scene, this character mentioned that her decency had never allowed her to open her legs to check herself, and she began a detailed, disgusting description of the great variety of fauna and flora living in her genitals. The scene was gross – and very funny. Months after that, in one of the health centres, we came across Marta, the woman from the Rarámuri community; she was translating the consultation to an older woman from her community. She had become a very important link, since the doctors of the health centre communicated through her to reach other women in her community, even in cases that might require surgery. She told us, laughing, 'I brought my aunt so she doesn't have to go through the same stuff as the neighbour.'

Most of the time, people identified with the characters in the plays almost immediately. They were touched by their stories and used them to analyse their own. Six months after our workshops, evaluations of the process were performed. These found that, in quantitative terms, people did get information efficiently; but, in qualitative terms, they also went through very important reflection processes to do with their own attitudes and emotions. They also found that in all cases, community relationships with health services, as well as attendance at the health centres, had improved significantly after the workshops.

A missing link to empowerment

Besides these effects on communities, the three years of this programme not only radically transformed my own perspective about art as an instrument of change and reflection, but also transformed my vision of laughter as a means for empowerment. By making laughter a main character of our stories, we placed the pleasant choice above and before the painful one.

How can I transform my own self from feeling sorry to laughing about myself? Laughter gives us a route to this transformation, which is why it is so empowering. By laughing, the body feels able to transform pain into pleasure – and that is such a great power, like turning lead into gold. If we imagine the body as a whole that has the power to feel immense amounts of pleasure, laughter is an instant reminder, plausible and palpable, of these capacities.

Laughter gives us the opportunity to tell our stories not from the accumulation of our tragedies, but through our ability to reach a deeper understanding of these tragedies and transform them. Laughter allows us to place ourselves in positions far from solemnity and rigidity. It leads us to laugh at our fanaticism and question our structures, over and over again. With laughter we can complete the map of the body, the human anatomy, because if we try to understand people or communities without studying their ability to laugh, to feel pleasure, then our analysis remains incomplete. Because, as people, we are not only the sum of the situations that make us live in misery, violence, hunger and indignity. As people, it is necessary to add our laughter, our orgasms, what we dream of, what we love, what makes us explode with pleasure. We are also whatever we can imagine we are.

Through laughter, it is easier to imagine pleasant strategies than to talk about pleasure. Solemnity is, no doubt about it, a lead weight that falls heavily on our bodies. Our stories are not complete if our laughter is not accounted for – along with our misfortunes. If we only tell the story about how our bodies hurt, then our bodies are only pain. If we tell the story about how our bodies can feel pleasure, then our bodies will be able to feel pleasure. If we tell stories about how our bodies get happy, until our bodies feel happy, maybe they will acquire the habit of feeling this way.

If we fail to consider the anatomy of our bodies as also the sum of our emotions – not only flesh, bones and ideas – then we are doomed to live disconnected from ourselves.

The anatomy of pleasure: part of the human story

Where do we learn this anatomy? Physicians learn anatomy on corpses in the morgue, where the heart is a piece of flesh that is no longer animated. But if you look for imagination among all that flesh and grey matter, you will not find it. That is logical, since grey matter is just grey, and imagination is full of the colour of life. And dreams – which in life circulate through the veins and beyond – are no longer there, since they were inherited by a close relative or by a hidden surviving lover. So we cannot investigate the complete anatomy on the surgical table.

With women from indigenous and rural communities, we discovered that the real difficulty of treating or detecting cervical cancer was that women had to overcome the shame of opening their legs, a shame that had been systematically inculcated by 2000 years of Judaeo-Christian culture. That embarrassment, shared throughout Latin America, is in certain bodies, anatomically speaking, like a huge tumour extending from the breast to the fallopian tubes and going up to the buttocks. In other cases it is more like a shell that expands inside the chest or near the buttocks and cuts the impulse of moving the hips each time we hear horny music. In other cases, it is like a second skin; in others it is only located in the genital area; and in still others it is totally unknown.

This represents another difficulty: emotional anatomy is different in each person. The respiratory system is located at the same place in everyone, but the sighing system, well ... this varies from one person to another, because each one of us sighs for different reasons. Is it possible that at last the anatomy could be completed by an ever-changing map of emotions?

What makes a person with enough information decide not to use a condom? What makes a woman in a violent situation assume or appropriate the nomenclature of 'raped' for the rest of her life? The answers lie in many reasons that have little to do with the doctor, but above all depend on countless emotions that can barely be understood without the right tools.

When carrying out an analysis of a given culture, common customs, shared behaviours, similar identities and generalized beliefs can be 'measured' and studied, but the complex circulatory system of emotions and feelings is much harder to measure. In which body part is passion located? Where can we pin down the passion that makes us feel our head is exploding? At times, passion seems to be in the chest, at times in the genitals, and there are occasions when it is on the face. I also know of some Brazilians who feel passion in their feet.

At the same time, there are emotionally self-destructive habits that are so entrenched that only an artistic shock treatment can unclog them, such as the Catholic habit of feeling guilt from dawn till dusk. And the problem with guilt is that it is very hard to remove. It is pure dead, necrotic tissue – but, despite that, it is so enmeshed in various parts of the body, that to remove it we have to use very specific blades, such as humour and pleasure. Some say that humour is like a scalpel, which can not only take away bits of guilt, but can also transplant lots of pleasure.

When considering the full anatomy, measurements and descriptions change their expected format. The heart, for example, is not only located on the left side of the chest. Sometimes it is closer to the knees – who hasn't felt love expressing itself in the knees? And the heart doesn't only pump blood, sometimes it pumps tears, sometimes laughter, and sometimes those unique, intimate sounds.

One of the most complex systems of the anatomy – closely related to HIV and AIDS – is the female choosing system, which suffers from atrophy caused by the many years you've grown used to not making the decisions about your body. It is related to chronic knee pain, derived from consistently closing your legs to sit demurely every day of your life, and leads to the strong feeling that your body's major function is to give birth to another one, because then it is not even your own body you have to take care of. For some women, making choices about the body is as hard as speaking a language you haven't learned. If you are a woman, the usual situation is that someone else decides for you, and it is customary to abide by that decision. Changing this habit is like learning to walk again, with all the fear that comes from standing on your own feet (at least, that's what babies say).

And how about safe sex? How can sex be 'safe' if passion is an organ that grows so huge that it overflows and invades? At the same time, protected sex threatens morality because its practice involves premeditation, and premeditation is considered a felony. Sexual intent is indecent, immoral, sinful and a reason for excommunication. So then protected sex gets complicated, because latex has to be taboo and lie-resistant, and apparently condom-manufacturing companies are not willing to state on the packet that 'this product is resistant to attacks of disinformation, guilt, stigma and discrimination'.

Anatomy is complex, ever changing and different for each person; and to understand it requires looking at ourselves through the eyes of feelings and emotions. The correct instruments for this type of ophthalmology are art, laughter and pleasure.

Laughter reveals, but also heals

In revealing this complete anatomy, laughter is a kind of tomography – section by section imaging – that reveals the ability to enthuse; the capacity for innocence; the obstinate pain; the brightness of the eyes; the sighs, the oppression on the belly; the butterflies in one's stomach; the infinite sadness; the fear of suffering; the frustration from the lack of understanding; or the smoothness of a pleasant memory. Laughter is an x-ray that shows recent and future fractures.

Laughter provides a physical therapy that restores cut wings, and it looks like flying is good for health, like living by the sea. Laughter takes us to the possibility of being more alive; it is like a transfusion that transgresses static and mobilizes every cell in our body. How does it work? It works through the fibrillation of the muscles of hope, in combination with the acceleration and deceleration of respiration. Sometimes it steals your breath for a few seconds; sometimes it is so exciting that it connects you with the divine. The experience of laughter confronts us with the opportunity to feel godlike. And apparently God (the one which everyone wants or seeks, which everyone creates) wears a condom, practises safe sex, seeks dignity, has rights respected, doesn't live in a situation of violence, is not discriminated against, and it doesn't matter if it is HIV positive or has AIDS or not, nor if it is a he or a she or a ★. Its sexual orientation or colour or language doesn't matter, because dignity is its most important vital organ. And it is logical to think that God has all these advantages, because otherwise, what would be the point of being God?

Laughter is the home of the beauty of life. Laughter feeds the empty space between proteins and carbohydrates, including milk and vegetables, including seeds and fruits. If removed from our diet, it may cause soul anaemia. And the anaemic soul is far away from beauty.

Being a third-world lesbian, I am worn out by the patriarchal, economic and social conditions in which I live, immersing me in so much indignity that I have the right to feel like a victim. Laughter has given me the opportunity to shift my view to the landscape above my disgrace. This is my own revolution, my own crusade against solemnity and boredom, since these seem to me to be the twin locations of victimization. And victimization is another form of colonization.

About the Contributors

Dorothy Aken'Ova is the founder and executive director of the International Centre for Reproductive and Sexual Rights, which was founded in 2000. A human rights activist and feminist of repute, she is supportive of sexual minority issues in Nigeria and also was instrumental in the formation of the Coalition for the Defence of Sexual Minorities.

Bibi Bakare-Yusuf is a publisher based in Abuja, Nigeria. She started Cassava Republic Press in 2006. Her company is focused on publishing quality African writing at an affordable price. Cassava Republic is a social enterprise, driven by the dream to re-develop a reading (and writing) culture in Nigeria, as part of the bigger project of re-imagining Nigeria's future and being part of an African cultural and intellectual renaissance. Prior to setting up Cassava Republic, Bibi was an academic in the UK and Nigeria. She has a PhD in gender studies from the University of Warwick. Her thesis explored the relationship between embodiment and memory in the African diaspora, examining structures of retention found in New World cultures.

Anaïs Bertrand-Dansereau stumbled into the world of international development early on, living as an expat kid in China and Tunisia. She completed both her BA and her Masters at the Université du Québec à Montréal (UQAM), in Canada, before moving to Geneva to pursue her doctoral studies at the Graduate Institute of International and Development Studies. She believes sex should be a source of joy and well-being for everyone, and hopes her research can contribute to realizing that goal, however elusive it may seem at times.

Petra Boynton is a senior lecturer in International Health Services Research at University College London, where she teaches healthcare professionals to find, critique and apply evidence within their practices and communities. She specializes in researching sex and relationships health, particularly advice-giving within the mainstream media, and applies her research and teaching through blogging and working as an agony aunt.

Lorna Couldrick has been a researcher and campaigner in the area of disability and sexuality for over 15 years. Her interest arose from her experiences as an occupational therapist and as a counsellor working in physical disability, mental health and elder care services. This has been in a variety of contexts, including health and social care, voluntary organizations, and private practice. It inspired her to undertake further training in sexual issues and to research the subject. Her later career has focused on the education of health and social care professionals, particularly those working to support disabled people. She is a member of the Sexual Health and Disability Alliance.

Alex Cowan is a director of the disability consultancy ARC People, chairs the Disability Services Consultative Group of a large national health and social care organization, is active within the Sexual Health and Disability Alliance, carries out peer support for Outsiders, which promotes sex, relationships and friendships for disabled people, and co-trains on sex, disability and relationships at the Tavistock Centre for Couple Relationships for their masters degree students. In addition, Alex writes and gives talks for organizations such as the MS Society and has presented on television and radio. She is currently co-writing a toolkit for health professionals to help them tackle the issue of sex and sexuality with patients and clients. Alex has a BSc Hons in psychology and education, is a wheelchair user and has MS.

Jo Doezema has been a researcher and activist around sex worker rights for over 20 years. She holds a PhD from the Institute of Development Studies, University of Sussex. She is a member of the Paulo Longo Research Initiative. Her research interests include sexuality of sex worker clients, human rights, economic empowerment and participatory research methods. She is the author of several publications on sex workers, including *Global Sex Workers: Rights, Resistance and Redefinition* (co-edited with Kamala Kempadoo, 1998) and *Sex Slaves and Discourse Masters: The Construction of Trafficking in Women* (2010).

Krissy Ferris has worked with The Pleasure Project in various capacities since 2009, where she particularly enjoys teaching people about how safer sex practices can actually increase intimacy and pleasure within relationships. She holds a Master of Science degree in gender, sexuality and society from the University of Amsterdam, which was supported by a Fulbright Fellowship. She is currently the program director at Revati Wellness, a holistic concierge medical practice in Cleveland, Ohio, USA.

Xiaopei He: Hills trained me to be a professional shepherd and the Himalayas turned me into a full-time mountaineer. A government job made me an economist while the women's movement and gender studies converted me into a feminist. Participating in LGBTQ organizing in China helped me to realize there are many people, especially people with disabilities, HIV-positive women, bisexual women and sex workers, who are also oppressed due to their gender and sexualities. This is why I set up the Pink Space Sexuality Research Centre and promote sexual rights and sexual pleasure among people who are oppressed.

Ana Francis Mor is an artist and cabaret performer, part of Mexico's most prominent cabaret company Las Reinas Chulas. Her work is a creative mixture of political satire, humour, sexual rights and feminist perspective. She has participated in various conferences, including the International Association of Sexuality,

Society and Culture, the Latin American and the Caribbean Feminists meetings, and AIDS 2008. She has published *El Manual de la Buena Lesbiana* (The Manual of a Good Lesbian) (2009), a compilation of her columns in a political magazine.

Anne Philpott set up The Pleasure Project because she was frustrated that pleasure was rarely discussed when it came to sex education or condom promotion. This struck her more and more while she was working for the company that makes the female condom, and promoting it in Asia. Before that, she completed a Health Policy MSc while working for international sexual health charities in the UK. She has been a school sex educator and developed programmes in high teenage pregnancy areas of the UK, but first worked in a puppetry and AIDS awareness group in South Africa in the early 1990s.

Gulsah Seral Aksakal holds a BA in psychology and an MA in early childhood education and development from Boğaziçi University, Istanbul. She is currently undertaking an MA in clinical psychology. She was first programme assistant at, then national coordinator of, the Human Rights Education Programme for Women (HREP) at Women for Women's Human Rights – New Ways (WWHR) from 1997 to 2001. After returning to Istanbul in 2010 to continue her education, she became a WWHR board member and a member of the HREP Advisory Board, and worked on various publications until she became publications coordinator in 2011. She is one of the co-authors of the *Human Rights Education Program for Women: A Training Manual* (WWHR 2005).

Jaya Sharma is a founder member of Nirantar, a Centre for Gender and Education based in New Delhi, India. She has worked on issues of women's rights and education for over 20 years. For the past decade she has focused on issues of sexuality as they relate to empowerment and rights. She has founded queer activist forums based in Delhi and co-ordinated the Sexuality Education Initiative within Nirantar. This involved research and advocacy related to young people's right to sexuality education as well as sexuality-related perspective-building with grassroots programmes, working with rural women through workshops and educational material (see www.nirantar.net).

Sylvia Tamale is an associate professor and the immediate outgoing dean of law at Makerere University in Uganda. She holds a Bachelor of Laws from Makerere, a Masters in Law from Harvard Law School and a PhD in Sociology and Feminist Studies from the University of Minnesota. Sylvia founded and serves as coordinator of the Law, Gender and Sexuality Research Project at the School of Law. Her latest publication is *African Sexualities: A Reader* (2011).

Chi-Chi Undie was formerly a Ford Foundation post-doctoral fellow in sexuality at the African Population and Health Research Center, and later, an associate research scientist at the same institution. She is currently an associate in the Reproductive Health Services and Research Programme of the Population Council in Nairobi, Kenya, where she coordinates a multi-country study geared toward developing a comprehensive model of response to sexual and gender-based violence in the East and Southern Africa region.

Alice Welbourn has worked on international gender and health issues for nearly 30 years. After a PhD, she worked in rural parts of Africa for several years. Diagnosed HIV-positive in 1992, she wrote a training package on gender, HIV, communication and relationship skills called 'Stepping Stones' (www.stepping stonesfeedback.org), now widely used across Africa, Asia, the Pacific, Latin America and beyond. Alice is a former international chair of the International Community of Women Living with HIV/AIDS (www.icw.org) and the founding director of the Salamander Trust (www.salamandertrust.net). Alice works to uphold the rights of all people living with HIV globally.

Index